Another's Country

ANOTHER'S COUNTRY

Archaeological and Historical Perspectives on Cultural Interactions in the Southern Colonies

EDITED BY

J. W. Joseph and Martha Zierden

FOREWORD BY

Julia A. King

THE UNIVERSITY OF ALABAMA PRESS
Tuscaloosa and London

9 8 7 6 5 4 3 2 1
10 09 08 07 06 05 04 03 02

Typeface: Sabon

∞
The paper on which this book is printed meets the minimum requirements of
American National Standard for Information Science–Permanence of Paper for
Printed Library Materials, ANSI Z39.48-1984.

Library of Congress Cataloging-in-Publication Data

Another's country : archaeological and historical perspectives on cultural interactions
in the southern colonies / edited by J. W. Joseph and Martha Zierden.
    p.   cm.
Includes bibliographical references and index.
    ISBN 0-8173-1129-7 (alk. paper)
    1. Southern States—History—Colonial period, ca. 1600–1775. 2. Southern
States—Ethnic relations. 3. Acculturation—Southern States—History. 4. Intercultural
communication—Southern States—History. 5. Ethnology—Southern States—History.
6. Ethnicity—Southern States—History. 7. Group identity—Southern States—
History. 8. Southern States—Antiquities. I. Joseph, J. W., 1958– II. Zierden,
Martha A.
    F212 .A56 2002
    975'.02—dc21
                    2001004244

British Library Cataloguing-in-Publication Data available

Contents

Figures

Tables

Foreword

JULIA A. KING

The southern colonies occupy a special place in the modern American imagination. For much of the twentieth century, the dominant public memory of the colonial South spoke of gracious hospitality, genteel behavior, and selfless dedication to public service. The primary actors in this memory were white, usually of English descent, often Virginian by birth. By the end of the twentieth century, the historical reality of that memory had been challenged by a growing concern that a major part of the colonial South's population—Africans and African Americans—was given almost no voice in these histories. This was especially disturbing given the South's role in the rise of race-based slavery, with its enduring, often painful legacy for twentieth- and twenty-first–century America. Most Americans, regardless of their political views, now recognize that southern colonial history should be understood in black and in white.

But is this new memory and narrative really accurate, and if so, how did southern history come to be drawn along racial rather than cultural lines? The essays in this book challenge us to consider whether history "in black and white" captures the true diversity and complexity of the colonial experience in the southern British colonies and ask us to look at the ways a number of cultures joined in creating a new, southern, culture. Perhaps the antebellum South can be understood as a place occupied by blacks and by whites but, as these essays reveal, the colonial South was not simply an earlier mirror reflection of antebellum culture. Indeed, J. W. Joseph and Martha Zierden claim that the colonial South was one of the melting pots of the nation, a "multicultural region from its initial settlement." The essays they have included in this book support this statement in a powerful way: large numbers of French, German, and Scotch settlers joined the English and Africans in the southern colonies, and Native Americans, though reduced in population, remained an important presence through the colonial period. Many of these people had spent time in the Caribbean or in New England before coming to the South. The fluidity of their spatial experiences and their social and cultural encounters in this new world presented all sorts of situations and opportunities for change. *Another's Country* offers a fresh and important encounter with this colonial cultural diversity.

Earlier efforts to examine the colonial South from an archaeological perspective came from two directions. In the first, life in colonial Virginia came to stand for life in the colonial South. This is perhaps not surprising, given the development of the archaeological research program at the Colonial Williamsburg Foundation and the Foundation's effort to interpret eighteenth-century life in Virginia for the public. Certainly, Virginia was an important southern colony, but it would be a mistake to project colonial Virginia's experience throughout the South. Yet, this is precisely what researchers have done. For example, in a seminal article on earthfast architecture published in 1981, Cary Carson and a blue ribbon panel of co-authors declared their focus to be the "southern American colonies" (Carson et al. 1981), although nearly all their evidence came from Maryland or Virginia. Later research, including some on which several of the essays presented in this book are based, has demonstrated that considerable architectural variability existed in the Carolinas and Georgia, with forms unknown in the colonial Chesapeake colonies of Maryland and Virginia.

Alternatively, archaeological research in the states below Virginia was taking a decidedly different direction from that charted by Ivor Noel Hume, Carson, and other Chesapeake scholars. Stanley South's work at eighteenth-century Brunswick Town in North Carolina and elsewhere in the Carolinas was used to develop South's famous "Carolina Artifact Pattern" and its derivatives (South 1977). South strongly urged other historical archaeologists to quantify their artifact assemblages and identify patterning in their data. South's work put the archaeology of the colonial South on the map, although most archaeologists were more interested in South's methodology than in Brunswick Town's past. South's methodology, his artifact patterns, and the assumptions underpinning them have been criticized because they often fail to reflect categories of culture of interest to archaeologists and historians. Once widely used throughout the Southeast, South's artifact patterns are only used minimally by the authors of these essays.

Instead, the essays in this book use historical and archaeological evidence to illustrate the diversity and complexity of the colonial South. For example, Thomas Wheaton, Ellen Shlasko, and Carl Steen consider the implications and meaning of trench-set post and clay architecture, once considered solid evidence of "Africanism" in South Carolina. Now, it appears that French settlers in South Carolina also built trench-set post buildings (trench-set post architecture is also known from a large number of sites throughout the French colonies) and that its appearance in South Carolina may reflect cultural interaction between the French and Africans. In each of their essays, these authors present different interpretations to explain the presence of this style of architecture, interpretations that are not necessarily mutually exclusive. This group of essays serves as a reminder of the pitfalls of identifying ethnic markers in material culture.

On the other hand, many of the authors consider how colonial southerners attempted to deal with social and geographical fluidity. To counteract the destabilizing forces of colonialism, nearly all of the various groups attempted to establish some kind of boundary or boundaries, material, social, and ideological. Katherine Saunders draws our attention to the defensive boundary early Charlestonians erected around their town. This massive brick and earthen structure would not only protect the town's commercial activity, it would also establish the boundaries for the urban center that the Lords Proprietors hoped would anchor their vision of religious toleration and hereditary nobility. William Green, Chester B. De-Pratter, and Bobby Southerlin describe the struggle many southern Native Americans experienced as they established and reestablished group and territory boundaries. In the case of the Yamasee, staunch allies of the English in South Carolina, war became their remedy when their loyalty was continuously abused and their resources threatened.

More subtle ways were used to establish boundaries. Michael O. Hartley describes how, in response to the threat of Indian warfare, the Moravians who settled Bethania in North Carolina gathered into a nucleated town for protection. Yet, the plan used to lay out the town of Bethania had its roots in an ancient European form and suggests the corporate nature of Moravian tradition. In using this form, the North Carolina Moravians expressly sought political and religious control in their settlement to allow themselves greater autonomy. But this effort was not consistent: nearby Bethabara, also a Moravian town, was unplanned, although it provided important defensive capabilities. In New Windsor, a German-Swiss settlement on the Savannah River across from Augusta, Georgia, David Colin Crass, Bruce Penner, and Tammy Forehand find that the settlers there were surprisingly integrated into the English mercantile system and used artifacts in ways that would have been understood by the Charleston English.

Spiritual boundaries were used to foster group identity, particularly among the German-speaking groups that came to the South. Rita Folse Elliott and Daniel T. Elliott suggest that these groups, often lumped together in English eyes, defined themselves on the basis of their religious beliefs. These beliefs could be divisive, but German-speaking groups also adapted innovations in food and shelter when their survival depended on it. In another example of spiritual identity, Monica L. Beck considers the Dissenters of English descent who relocated from New England to Dorchester, South Carolina, in search of farmland to support their community. Despite initial economic and religious successes in their new location, the Dissenters soon found themselves in competition with the Anglican church. Anglicans established their church in the center of the town, while the Dissenters purposely located their meeting house outside the town's boundaries.

Despite attempts by the settlers to fix social and cultural boundaries, these boundaries were usually temporary, being negotiated and renegotiated as environmental and social conditions of the colonial situation changed. The artifacts we recover are as much a reflection of this fluidity as they are so-called ethnic markers. Ronald W. Anthony's consideration of colonoware from a Lowcountry plantation site suggests the problems that develop when one-to-one correspondences between artifacts and social categories are sought. Anthony describes how the paste analysis of the colonowares indicates that Native Americans were responsible for the production of a significant percentage of the colonoware vessels recovered from the site. On the other hand, precisely who these Native Americans were remains unsorted since, in the eyes of the English, they were usually lumped together, and the ongoing reallicances among these people are poorly understood. Further, Anthony argues, Native Americans interacted with enslaved blacks in the Lowcountry.

Natalie Adams's essay, a consideration of slave life in the pine forests of the Lower Cape Fear in North Carolina, suggests the dangers of using colonoware as an ethnic marker. Clay deposits in the Lower Cape Fear were unsuitable for the production of pottery, so the enslaved Africans and African Americans producing naval stores there had limited access to colonoware. Of course, the smaller number of slaves necessary for the operation of a pine plantation, the time demands of the extractive industries, and the nature of the local Native American population are also important variables to consider in the production of colonoware. Adams's work in the Lower Cape Fear suggests that the material conditions of slave life in the colonial South were variable, and archaeology has a great potential to advance this understanding.

Several of these studies consider a boundary that has not only been a focus of academic interest since the late nineteenth century, but also has been used to explain the American experience and support the idea of American exceptionalism: the frontier. While Crass, Penner, and Forehand consider the frontier that emerged in the mid-eighteenth-century South Carolina backcountry, Zierden considers the frontier that developed around Charleston in the late seventeenth century. Both essays also pose important questions for future research: why did some settlements in the colonial South fail, while others flourished and even survive as living communities today? Failed settlements are usually a source of delight and attraction for archaeologists because of the increased likelihood of archaeological preservation, while settlements still occupied, and presumably much more disturbed, generate less enthusiasm. Zierden suggests that Willtown, founded in the 1690s as a place of trade with and protection from the Lowcountry's native inhabitants, met its demise with the rise of plantation agriculture and the decline in the Indian trade. Her analysis of Willtown has important implications for the shape of colonial culture in this area in the eighteenth century.

J. W. Joseph's concluding essay poses an important question linking colonial culture in the South to antebellum culture. Joseph is concerned with the disappearance of much—although certainly not all—of the archaeological evidence of cultural diversity in Charleston by the end of the colonial period. While part of this change is linked to changes in industrial production in England and the economic success of Lowcountry agriculture, Joseph also argues that artifacts signifying ethnicity or cultural identity were forcibly eliminated by slaveholding white planters. Planters aimed to demonstrate social inferiority by forcing enslaved Africans and African Americans to use, wear, and occupy artifacts that signified their social position. The homogenization of the Charleston landscape and, by extension, the southern landscape began a process that has masked the extraordinary diversity of the South throughout its history.

Another's Country reminds us of the cultural diversity in the southern colonies, explores the theories and concepts that explain its loss, and provides an important new look at the formation of southern identity. The articles in this book are a valuable addition to the scholarship on southern colonial history, archaeology, and ethnicity.

Another's Country

I
Cultural Diversity in the Southern Colonies

J. W. JOSEPH AND MARTHA ZIERDEN

One of the most frequently cited observations on the cultural identity of the southern colonies (see both Wheaton and Steen, this volume) was offered by Samuel Dyselli, a Swiss immigrant arriving in Charleston in 1737, who remarked, "Carolina looks more like a negro country than like a country settled by white people" (Wood 1974:132). Dyselli's remarks indicated that to him the colony looked more African than European, a reflection of its population, which had achieved an African majority in the early 1700s, as well as of their material expressions including African-influenced landscapes, houses, pottery, and foodways. Had Dyselli been visiting the French Huguenot town of New Bordeaux or one of the outlying French plantations, he might have commented that Carolina looked more French than English. Had he traveled to one of the German settlements in the region, New Ebenezer, Amelia, Saxe-Gotha, Bethania, or Bethabara, he might have commented that the colony looked more German. Had he visited the Swiss communities of Purysburg or New Windsor, then he might have remarked that the colony looked like home. This diversity of origins and identities was noted by other colonists. Jacob Gallman, a Swiss settler in the town of Saxe-Gotha, wrote in a 1735 letter to family in Switzerland regarding his new home, "There are all sorts of nations and people here" (in Adams 2001:13).

During the colonial period the South was a melting pot, a place foreign to all arrivals, appearing to each to be another's country, not their own. The southern colonial experience engaged settlers from a number of cultures and countries in the processes of immigration, adaptation, acculturation, and creolization. Colonists from England, France, the Netherlands, Germany, Ireland, Scotland, Switzerland, and other locations and enslaved Africans all shared in the experience of adapting to the natural environment of the New World and in interaction with Native Americans. The result was an exceedingly rich and diverse historical mosaic whose complexities and meanings have yet to be fully grasped.

The eighteenth century is somewhat the underestimated century in southern history, an energetic period of cultural encounters that would ultimately define the meaning of life in the nineteenth-century South. The plantation society that coalesced from these interactions in the late eighteenth century and the Confederacy that sprang from the plantations have become the defining identities of the South, but southern history cannot fully be understood without first understanding the interaction and intermingling of the eighteenth-century settlers. This volume brings together a series of essays that looks at various aspects of different cultural experiences in the colonial South in an attempt to understand how cultural identity was expressed, why cultural diversity disappeared, and how these various cultures intermeshed.

The South was a multicultural region from its initial settlement onward (Joseph and Bense 1995). The first European settlers of the region were the French and Spaniards. The Spanish colonial empire would extend from Florida into the Carolinas and its capital was at Santa Elena, on present-day Parris Island, South Carolina, from 1576 to 1587 (South et al. 1988). The Spaniards would continue to dominate the history of Florida and much of the Gulf Coast throughout the colonial period. Florida would remain a Spanish colony until 1821, long after the American Revolution. Along the Gulf, in Mobile and New Orleans, and up the Mississippi, the French provided a vast and influential force that would direct the history of the regions under their claim. A variety of Native American groups provided the counterpoint to European settlement: first the small coastal tribes, then the more powerful nomadic groups such as the Yamasee and the Westo, and finally the larger interior tribes such as the Creek, Cherokee, Chickasaw, Seminoles, Catawba, and others. These would interact with European traders, trappers, and ultimately settlers, affecting the history of these settlements, and ultimately yielding to the effects of colonization among themselves. And Africans would become one of the unifying and defining cultures of the South, as southern cultural identity would arise in part from the defense of the "peculiar institution" of slavery and the definition and coalescence of all enslaved people as "African." While recognizing cultural diversity throughout the South, this volume examines one region in particular, the southern British colonies of the Carolinas and Georgia, to understand the ways in which a variety of cultures adapted to a new environment, intermeshed, intermarried, and established a common culture. These essays encourage us to disregard the eventual, and seemingly inevitable, outcome of these encounters—European domination, African bondage, and Native annihilation. In this regard, Karen Kupperman has urged us to recognize "the uncertainty and fear in which all sides lived, as well as the curiosity and sense of unimagined possibilities with which groups of people approached each other" (Kupperman 2000:x).

Charles Town and the Outer Townships

Our region is politically, culturally, and geographically centered on Charles Town (present-day Charleston), South Carolina (Figure 1.1). Established in 1670 as the first English outpost in this portion of the New World, and relocated to Oyster Point in 1681, Charles Town would evolve into a major cultural and mercantile entrepot, a place for the shipment and transfer of people, things, and ideas. The Oyster Point location at the confluence of the Ashley and Cooper rivers proved to be ideally suited for trade, as a network of rivers provided easy access to inland areas, while creeks behind the barrier islands up and down the coast led to larger rivers that drained the interior. Charles Town was heavily fortified, with a surrounding wall and later with additional fortifications: the threat of Spanish invasion plagued Carolina until the mid-eighteenth century, as did the threat of Native American attacks and later of African rebellion. Settlers immediately searched for a profitable staple crop, but it was deerskins, obtained from trade with Native Americans, that would become the colonists' first profitable export and the basis for Charles Town's early economy.

Younger sons of West Indian planters, lacking inherited wealth, found a familiar climate, cheap land, and familial connections in Carolina. This group transplanted money, experience, and slave-based agriculture to their new home. In accordance with British mercantilistic policies, the colonists immediately began experimenting with profitable staples not available in Britain. Rice would make these colonists wealthy, after many years of experimenting, and many shiploads of enslaved Africans were acquired from their home continent's rice-growing regions.

The accumulation of great wealth through trade in staples, supported by slave labor, led to the accumulation of material trappings. By the late eighteenth century, Charles Town was the wealthiest city (per capita) in the American colonies and the fourth-largest commercial center. The city's success as a commercial center was matched by its role as a center for the cultures of gentility and sociability, as the monied few enjoyed the trappings of European society at the expense of those forced to labor on their plantations (McInnis and Mack 1999). This prosperity, plus the vacant urban real estate created by the 1740 fire, allowed colonial leaders to create a city as visually impressive as it was economically and politically dominant.

Like Atlanta of the present, colonial Charles Town was an economically vibrant city that attracted settlers from around the globe. Many were Caribbean transplants, who were among the most successful of the Low-

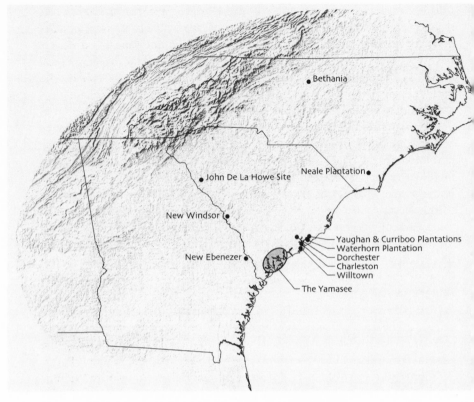

Figure 1.1. Locations of the sites discussed in this volume.

country planters. Although predominantly of British background, these families had begun the cultural transformation that was part of the adaptation to the tropical regions of the New World, and their experiences would have a lasting imprint on southern culture. They were met in town by a considerable number of French Huguenots, who would also demonstrate an ability for plantation agriculture and would rise to prominence in Charles Town society. Early commercial life in the town was influenced by Dutch immigrants, who migrated to Charles Town both from Holland directly as well as from New Amsterdam, present-day New York City. The number of Sephardic Jews who migrated to Charles Town from the Iberian Peninsula, as well as from northern locations in the American colonies, the Caribbean, and South America, was sufficient by 1750 to form a congregation (Hagy 1993). Following the unification of Scotland and England in 1707 a large number of Scots moved to Charles Town and they too would become major players in city commerce.

Upon arrival these immigrants joined a sizable number of English settlers, and yet for all their numbers, these European settlers were not the majority population in the colony. African immigrants, most brought as slaves from the west coast of Africa, were by 1708 the majority population in the Carolina colony (Wood 1974). While many found residence on the outlying plantations, others played crucial roles as craftsmen, builders, and artisans in the creation of the colonial city.

The presence of immigrants from various nations gave rise to a number of societies designed to aid and assist fellow immigrants in settling this part of the New World. French Protestants established the South Carolina Society in 1737, a German Friendly Society was formed in 1766, the Friendly Sons of St. Patrick was founded in 1774, and a Hebrew Orphanage was established in 1791 (Rogers 1989:6). These societies, as well as the presence and patronage of immigrants from different places who rose to prominence in Charles Town society, led to continued immigration to Charles Town and contributed to the formation of separate communities on the edge of the early frontier and culturally distinctive towns in the South Carolina backcountry a few decades later.

These towns were the product of a plan by the Lords Proprietors of the Carolina colony to lessen the threat of Native American and Spanish attacks on Charles Town. The result was a number of ethnic enclaves: the Swiss settlements of Purysburg and New Windsor on the Savannah River; the German settlements of Orangeburg on the Edisto, Amelia on the Santee, and Saxe-Gotha on the Congaree; the Scots-Irish settlement of Williamsburg on the Black River; and the French Huguenot settlement of New Bordeaux on Long Cane Creek (Rogers 1989:6–7). Similar policies in other colonies would result in the creation of the German settlement of New Ebenezer in Georgia and of the German Moravian settlements of Salem, Bethabara, and Bethania in North Carolina.

The result was a distinctively heterogeneous population by the middle of the eighteenth century. French, German, Swiss, Dutch, English, and Caribbean settlers, remnant Native Americans, and enslaved Africans and Native Americans all lived in this corner of the New World. How did they adjust to their new social and natural environments? What aspects of Old World life did the European and African colonists bring with them, and what did they leave behind? What aspects of European and African culture did Native Americans adopt, and what aspects did they change to suit their own cultural needs? Can we, as historians and archaeologists researching their settlements, recognize distinct cultural identities, and if so, by what markers and at what time? When did their identities change and why? These are questions of ethnicity, cultural adaptation, acculturation, and creolization—of the colonial cultural experience in the South.

Ethnicity and Culture Change

Historians and archaeologists have long grappled with the topic of ethnicity (see Ascher and Fairbanks 1971; Fairbanks 1974; Franklin and Fesler 1999; Schuyler 1980; Singleton 1999). Following Barth (1969), ethnicity is defined here as a form of cultural identity in which an individual identifies himself or herself on the basis of a shared cultural background or tradition. Ethnicity serves to identify and associate individuals with a common history as a separate entity within a larger social setting. In the New World, ethnicity was defined primarily on the basis of national origin, cultural history, and religion. One of the hallmarks of ethnicity is its distinctiveness—since ethnicity expressed shared cultural and social heritage and values, it thus follows that ethnicity should be expressed, to some degree, in material remains. Historical archaeologists have thus looked at the ways in which ethnicity was indicated through material culture.

All of the cultures that were introduced to this part of the New World would change. That change has been referred to by a number of terms and concepts: adaptation, acculturation, syncretism, and creolization primary among them. Cultural adaptation is the way in which a culture adjusts to changes in place, or time, while still maintaining cultural identity. Adaptation is a two-way street, referring both to the use of traditional materials, systems, and practices in New World settings as well as to the replacement of traditional items with materials from the New World.

Acculturation is the loss of cultural identity, or more specifically, the replacement of one cultural identity with the practices, beliefs, and materials of another culture. Acculturation always involves an element of force, as one culture dominates the other (Haviland 1999:764). Because the southern colonies were British colonies, because they were governed under British law, because the goods shipped to the colonies were largely British goods, and because the language of the land was English, it is often assumed that the various cultures whose members settled in the South eventually were assimilated into an Anglo-American cultural system. On the one hand this is true. The culture that developed within the North American colonies was predominantly a British culture and evidence of the British cultural system could be seen from Plymouth to Charles Town. On the other hand, the South in particular shows that this Anglo-colonial culture was not unified. Southerners would develop a distinctive identity, one sufficiently strong to cause the South to separate from the rest of the United States. The creation of a distinctive southern culture can be explained in part using the concepts of creolization and syncretism.

As the people of different cultural backgrounds interacted in the colonial South, they created a new culture. A recently developed term (although one that is still controversial) used by several authors in this volume to refer to the creation of a new culture through the combination of different cultural elements is *creolization*. Creolization has been defined by Leland Ferguson as "a process involving multicultural interaction and exchange that produces new cultural forms" (Ferguson 1992:xlii). Theresa Singleton suggests that in African American archaeology it "allows for the study of social action, wherein African Americans are seen as active agents engaged in production and reproduction of their world" (Singleton 1999:5). Most recently, Shannon Dawdy (2000) has focused discussion on the creolization concept through discussion of the creolization vocabulary. She organizes the myriad definitions and uses of the terms into three categories, involving linguistics, studies of self-identified creole peoples, and racial terminology. The third group involves hybridity and syncretism, the blending of genetic and cultural traits within a plural population, particularly in regard to the transplantation of Old World culture to the New World. While summarizing the development of the creolization concept, Dawdy and her colleagues are quick to point out that there is no single agreed-upon definition of the term. Anthropologist Grey Gundaker further argues for a diachronic element in the definition of creolization; in her words, this "involves continually managing and distributing resources, not just 'mixing' them once and for all to make 'culture'" (Gundaker 2000:132).

Some authors in this volume prefer to use another traditional anthropological term, *syncretism*, to describe the cultural blending that may result from culture contact. In this context, syncretism is the blending of indigenous and foreign elements into a new system (Haviland 1999:771). Still other authors discussing historical archaeology in the American South have used the term *cultural transformation* (Armstrong 1999) to describe the process that resulted from the movement of Old World peoples to the New World. Whatever their choice of descriptive term, all authors in this volume share the view that no one culture completely dominated another on the colonial scene, that in situations in which power and persuasion were inequitable, the dominant group did not completely erase the cultural signature of the subordinate. Further, all of the authors search for evidence of syncretism and cultural transformation, not mere cultural survival, a trend that marked early archaeological studies of ethnicity (cf. Singleton 1999:4).

In their search for material indicators of ethnicity, the authors in this volume find that its evidence is subtle. As Carl Steen notes, many of the settlers arriving in the New World were impoverished and brought with them very few artifacts from home. The material culture to which they had access in the New World was primarily of British origin. Thus French settlements are not distinguished by French pottery and German settlements by Rhenish stonewares. What these settlers did bring with them was a knowledge of construction and a sense of how things should be arranged, and in these two areas, architecture and landscape, archaeologists have had their greatest successes in recognizing ethnicity.

The built environment shows both evidence of ethnic architecture and the interactions between members of different cultural and ethnic groups. As Ellen Shlasko and Carl Steen both note, the wall trench architecture identified by Thomas Wheaton and J. W. Joseph in their studies as African also had French counterparts (there were also English and Native American counterparts and corollaries; see Ferguson [1992:77] and Kelso [1979:58–59]). Wheaton and Steen present conflicting interpretations of the cultural origin of this architectural style, while Shlasko's analysis of the presence of African-style dwellings on French Huguenot plantations suggests the ways in which cultural interaction in the adaptation to the New World created creole landscapes. Shlasko suggests that these plantations may have been both French and African in appearance and that African wall trench architecture may have been less acceptable to English planters than to French planters who were more accustomed to this style of construction (note also that Wheaton suggests the French may have been more liberal in their attitudes about race than the British, and hence more accepting of the appearance of African architecture on their plantations). Natalie Adams's chapter looks at expressions of African ethnicity on the pine plantations of North Carolina and, along with Shlasko's work, highlights the fact that the southern colonial landscape was more a mosaic than a tapestry, composed of a varied set of landscapes, each reflecting the interactions of the cultures involved, as well as the interactions of those cultures with the natural environment. Joseph, Martha Zierden, Rita and Daniel Elliott, David Crass, Bruce Penner, and Tammy Forehand, and to some extent Shlasko and Steen all also discuss the architectural components of sites occupied by people from a variety of backgrounds, occupying different class niches.

Several of the contributors discuss alterations to the North American landscape to suit the cultural patterns of new settlers. Landscape has been defined as the natural world altered by the people who occupy it to suit their particular cultural needs. People shape, and are in turn shaped by, the land within a dynamic cultural and natural context (Jackson 1984; Zierden and Stine 1997:xi). These discussions include the type of natural environment chosen by various groups, the changes made to the landscape, and the resulting influence of the landscape on the settlers. Zierden, Michael Hartley, and Katherine Saunders review the choices made by newly arrived Europeans for new communities, as well as the difficulties encountered in adapting Old World plans to New World environments. Defense, commerce, and communication were all factors influencing their choice of settlement. Crass, Penner, and Forehand, Steen, and the Elliotts focus particularly on the governmental township plan for providing protective communities of specific ethnic and religious groups. Adams, Wheaton, Zierden, and Shlasko discuss landscape choices and alterations influenced by the plantation system and slave-based labor. Saunders and Joseph consider the role of economic growth in creating and altering the landscape of Charleston as the urban hub. Monica Beck comments on the changes to a village landscape as the mainstream Anglicans gradually replaced a community of Dissenters. Finally, William Green, Chester DePratter, and Bobby Southerlin discuss the effect of the much-altered colonial landscape on the Native Americans who survived the colonial period and remained in Carolina.

Ethnicity is also found in the material possessions created, purchased, and curated by the various colonial groups. The most often discussed artifact of colonial Carolina is colonoware, a locally made pottery showing African, Native American, and to a lesser extent European characteristics. Ron Anthony describes a significant collection of this pottery in detail and ascribes its creation to a mixing of both people and influence. Joseph reports on an assemblage from an urban neighborhood of the same period reflecting similar interactions. Green, DePratter, and Southerlin discuss Native American material culture of the eighteenth century. Zierden, Adams, and Joseph also review the manufactured goods of European origin and their meanings for various colonial residents. The Elliotts note that locally manufactured pottery was also identified with German ethnicity in the communities of New Ebenezer, Georgia, and in Salem, Bethania, and Bethabara, North Carolina. As an artifact, the production and use of colonoware is also adaptive, providing a locally manufactured ceramic that could augment more costly wares imported from Europe.

Cultural adaptations are seen in a number of places. As Leland Ferguson has noted (1992:72), the wall trench structures found in the colonial South and discussed by Wheaton, Steen, Shlasko, and Joseph were well suited to the tropical climate of Georgia and the Carolinas, their walls providing an insulated and cooler interior. As Hartley notes, the German plan of Bethania helped the residents adapt to the backcountry, as the compact settlement discouraged Native American attacks while its location on the frontier highway, the Great Wagon Road, provided access to resident craftsmen and merchants. Beck notes similar attributes for Dorchester.

It is interesting to note that the essays in this volume suggest that adaptation and creolization may have occurred hand-in-hand. Anthony's discussion of colonoware from the Stobo plantation in particular highlights the ways in which Native Americans and Africans may have merged their knowledge and styles of pottery to create a new form that, while familiar, was also novel to both. The chapters dealing with wall trench architecture also suggest that both French and African colonial immigrants adapted architectural styles from their homelands to the New World, and that this adaptation also implied interaction among members of different cultures who were familiar with similar types of construction. These points of familiarity may be some of the key points of interaction at which immigrants from different cultures worked together to create new cultural forms that were still familiar to each and, in the process, perhaps began to establish new, creole, cultures.

Why did this cultural diversity fade? The articles in this volume suggest that ethnic identity lessened in part because the South was a predominantly rural culture, and the lack of urban centers limited the growth of cultural communities in the cities. Because the South was predominantly agrarian, the early ethnic towns gave way to dispersed settlement, a situation noted by the Elliotts, Steen, Crass, Penner, and Forehand, Hartley, Beck, and Zierden. This dispersal may have lessened the social forces of ethnicity, as well as the need to maintain separate ethnic identity. Where urban centers existed, however, the impetus to form cultural and ethnic communities was far less than it was in the north. In part, cultural identity faded from the landscape because subsequent waves of immigration had much less influence on the South. As the plantation economy took root and enslaved labor became the dominant work force, the attraction of the Old South to impoverished European immigrants was substantially reduced, and immigrants instead focused on northern industrialized cities whose economies offered better opportunities. Thus the early waves of settlers lacked sustained reinforcements and perhaps abandoned their cultural traditions merely as a result of time's dissolution of their past.

But, as the Elliotts note, our perception of ethnicity may be too simplistic, and ethnic identity may not have been shared to the extent we would like to think. The Elliotts point out that the many people defined as "German" in the colonial South were actually from a variety of locations, spoke a variety of dialects, and practiced a variety of religions. Thus other "Germans" may have been no more familiar to them than the English. The same is true of the many Africans in the colonial South, who represented an even greater diversity of cultures, languages, and beliefs (see Gomez 1998). The studies in this volume suggest that the colonial immigrants may have been seeking new identities almost from the time they set foot in the New World. To a large extent, the loss of cultural diversity and ethnicity would be a product of the American Revolution, which created a new nation, a new identity, and a new ethnicity, the American.

Another factor in the loss of ethnic identity was that the cultural history of the South was written in the interaction and definition of relationships between races, more than cultures. Race would be the most influential cultural construct in the South, and its focus would in turn diminish the attention given to cultural differences (see Montagu 1964). Michael Gomez, in his insightful study *Exchanging Our Country Marks*, writes that African ethnic identity was lost in a social and cultural setting that emphasized race over culture and that placed Africans in a common setting where collective cooperation was necessary for survival:

> The creation of the African American collective involved a movement in emphasis away from ethnicity and toward race as the primary criterion of inclusion. . . . [A]n identity based upon ethnicity was often a practice both very African and very ancient; race, a social construction intimately informed by political context, was relatively new and without significant meaning in much of Africa at the dawn of the transatlantic slave trade. (Gomez 1998:11)

A corollary argument can be made for the loss of European ethnic identities during the colonial period. The creation of a collective southern identity was the product of a society that united whites in a political and economic system that oppressed blacks and in which identity was based on racial, rather than cultural, terms. Thus southern colonial immigrants became members of one of two new ethnicities: white southern or African American. In reading the articles in this volume, it is interesting to note the degree to which as well as the times and settings in which ethnic identity was lost. Zierden, Anthony, and Joseph all pinpoint 1740 as a breakwater in the ethnic sea, and as Zierden discusses in detail, the African American Stono Rebellion would dramatically alter relationships between European and African immigrants and result in the Negro codes with their legal codification of race as a defining social construct. It is also interesting to note that ethnicity appears to have been lost more rapidly and more extensively as colonists became more involved in the plantation economy and as the plantation economy matured (see Wheaton, Anthony, Crass, Steen, Shlasko, Zierden, and Joseph on this topic). Finally, Joseph notes that the emergent southern social system of caste and class, itself a product of a culture based on racial identity, served to de-emphasize the material images of ethnic status in favor of a material culture that displayed social status, and Beck suggests that southern Anglicanism may have gained religious favor after the 1740s because it emphasized social place and social order.

The chapters in this volume offer a taste of the cultures that combined into southern gumbo. They provide a series of discussions of various cultures in the South, their adaptations, interactions, and transformations. And they propose a range of interpretations of the material remains of those cultures. It is our hope that these discussions will encourage further study of the colonial South's diversity and help us to understand the ways in which different cultures dealt with their arrival in the South, as well as the ways in which they merged and emerged as a common culture or cultures.

Acknowledgments

We are very appreciative of the comments and suggestions offered by the reviewers of this volume, James Gibb and Greg Waselkov. Their reviews have helped focus the volume and improve its contents, and we thank them for their superlative effort. We have been shepherded through the publication process by Judith Knight of the University of Alabama Press, and we thank Judith for all of her work in seeing this book to publication.

2

The Yamasee in South Carolina: Native American Adaptation and Interaction along the Carolina Frontier

WILLIAM GREEN, CHESTER B. DePRATTER, AND
BOBBY SOUTHERLIN

The Yamasee were a multiethnic confederation that began arriving in the Port Royal area of South Carolina in 1683. Composed mainly of groups from the former Georgia chiefdoms of Tama and Guale, the Yamasee lived for over thirty years with the Carolina colonists as their trading partners, as mercenaries, and as slave raiders. For most of their tenure in Carolina, the Yamasee were the colonists' closest native allies; however, trader abuses, encroachment upon their land, mounting debt, and a fear of enslavement eventually turned these trusted allies into the colonists' most bitter enemies.

In 1989, Chester DePratter, William Green, and David McKivergan began the Yamasee Archaeological Project (DePratter and Green 1990; Green 1992; McKivergan 1991). The goals of the project were to (1) trace the origins of the Yamasee; (2) locate Yamasee villages in South Carolina; and (3) provide an inventory of Yamasee material culture. During the course of this work, over a dozen archaeological sites containing Yamasee components were found, with two of these sites, Altamaha (38BU1206) and Pocosabo (38BU1279), eventually being listed in the National Register of Historic Places. Perhaps most important, though, we identified a basis for an archaeological signature of the Yamasee in South Carolina.

More than a decade has passed since the Yamasee Archaeological Project began, and with the staggering amount of residential and commercial development along the lower South Carolina coast, there has been a proliferation of Cultural Resource Management (CRM) studies that have identified additional Yamasee sites (e.g., Elliott and Cable 1994; Fletcher and Harvey 2000; Jordan et al. 1999; Rust et al. 1995; Southerlin 2000). Today, there are over twenty-five recorded Yamasee sites in South Carolina alone (Green and DePratter 2000). Similarly, during the past ten years there has been a vast increase in the amount of information available for the

Yamasee's occupations in the Georgia and Florida missions (e.g., Bushnell 1994; Hann 1988, 1990, 1991, 1996; Saunders 2000; Worth 1995, 1998). This new information allows us to provide an updated synthesis of the history and archaeology of the Yamasee Indians and provides insights into their complex interaction with and adaptation to the changing sociopolitical environment of the colonial Southeast.

Origin of the Yamasee

A 1715 census compiled by John Barnwell lists 1,220 Yamasee living in ten villages near the Port Royal area of South Carolina (Sainsbury 1928–1947, vol. 7:238). Based on a 1712 entry in the *Journals of the Commissioners of Indian Trade*, these towns were divided into the Upper and Lower Yamasee (McDowell 1955:31). The upper towns were headed by the town of Pocotaligo, whereas the lower towns were led by Altamaha (Figure 2.1). Because late seventeenth-century documents tell us that these groups were not indigenous to the area, the question remains, where did the Yamasee come from?

The earliest reference to groups that eventually formed part of the Yamasee confederacy comes to us from accounts of the de Soto expedition (Bourne 1904; Varner and Varner 1988). After spending the winter in Apalachee, de Soto departed in early March of 1540 in search of the province of Cofitachequi, where he was told he would find great riches such as gold, silver, and pearls (Elvas in Bourne 1904:51; Garcilaso in Varner and Varner 1988:254). After passing through the province of Capachequi, the Spaniards arrived in the province of Toa, where they "found a town rather larger than any [they] had seen to that time" (Biedma in Bourne 1904:11). According to Worth (1988) this province was located in the Middle Flint River area of southwest Georgia and may have included the Neisler (9TR1) and/or Hartley-Posey (9TR12) sites.

After leaving Toa and traveling for two days, de Soto arrived at the first settlement in the province of Ichisi. Ichisi was a very large chiefdom, as we are told that de Soto spent "five or six days going through this province" (Biedma in Bourne 1904:10). The main town of Ichisi is most likely the Lamar site (9BI2) located on the Ocmulgee River near Macon, Georgia (Hudson et al. 1984). Before departing Ichisi, de Soto learned of "a great lord, whose territory was called Ocute" (Elvas in Bourne 1904:55). Heading northeast in search of this province, the Spaniards traveled for two days until they reached "a river that had a course not southwardly, like the rest we had passed, but eastward to the sea" (Biedma in Bourne 1904:10). Here the Spaniards were greeted by messengers from Altamaha who supplied them with food and took them to the principal town. Hudson et al. (1984:70) and Williams (1990) suggest that the main town of Altamaha

YAMASEE SETTLEMENT PATTERNS

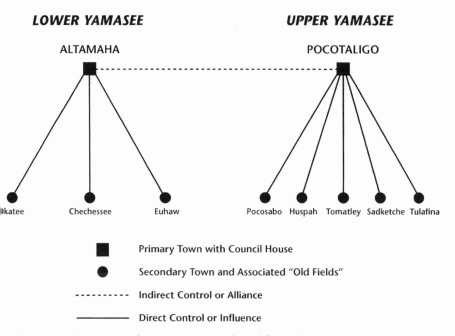

Figure 2.1. Yamasee settlement patterns (adapted from Blitz 1999, table 1).

was probably located at the Shinholser site (9BL1) on the Oconee River near Milledgeville, Georgia.

While in the town of Altamaha, the cacique Camumo informed de Soto that he was subject to the chief of Ocute, and that Ocute was currently at war with another chief named Cofitachequi (Ranjel in Bourne 1904:89–90). De Soto told Camumo of his interest in reaching Cofitachequi, but was informed "it was not possible to go thither, there being no road, and on the journey [they would] famish, there being no food" (Biedma in Bourne 1904:11). Camumo sent messengers to Ocute to notify him of de Soto's arrival. Ocute then traveled to Altamaha where he was greeted with a "cap of yellow satin and shirt and a plume" as token of the Spaniard's friendship (Ranjel in Bourne 1904:90).

After leaving Altamaha, de Soto traveled for one day until he reached the main town of Ocute, possibly the Dyar site (9GE5) located along the Oconee River near Greensboro, Georgia. Upon de Soto's arrival at Ocute, "the Cacique sent him a present, by two thousand Indians, of many conies [rabbits] and partridges, maize bread, many dogs, and two turkeys" (Elvas in Bourne 1904:56). These gifts were offered as redress, for Ocute had made de Soto angry as the result of some unspecified offense (Ranjel in Bourne 1904:90). Before leaving Ocute, de Soto obtained provisions and procured the assistance of four hundred Indians to help carry the Spaniards' supplies for their long trek to Cofitachequi, located in the Wateree River Valley near Camden, South Carolina (Cable et al. 2000; DePratter 1989). As will be seen, it is these four interior Georgia chiefdoms, Toa, Ichisi, Altamaha, and Ocute, that later formed the Lower Yamasee.

During the late sixteenth and early seventeenth centuries, a number of important changes were happening in interior and coastal Georgia. First, it appears that power was shifting away from Ocute and toward Altamaha. During the mid-sixteenth century, as the de Soto accounts clearly indicate, Ocute was the paramount chiefdom, yet during the next one hundred fifty years Ocute is barely mentioned in the documents. It is also during this time that the region became known to the Spanish as La Tama, a term clearly derived from Altamaha.

At the end of the sixteenth century we also begin seeing evidence that links the people of Tama with the Guale and Salchiches (Satuache/Sadketche) of the Georgia coast. In 1597, there was an uprising by the Guale known as the Juanillo Rebellion. In addition to the Guale, this widespread revolt involved groups ranging from the Timucua in Florida, to the Tama in central Georgia, and as far north as the coastal tribes in South Carolina. It was reported that the Salchiches of Tulafina were the instigators of this uprising, and it was at Tulafina that Father de Avila was taken prisoner (Lanning 1935). After the uprising had been quelled, the leaders of the rebellion fled from Guale to live among the Salchiches (Thomas 1990:375).

In 1661, Spanish officials received word that some "cannibalistic Chichumecos" (Westo/Erie; see Green 1995, 1998) from Virginia had attacked the Guale and taken many of them prisoner (Crane 1928:5–6; Lanning 1935:209; Worth 1995:15–16). Other Guale escaped and took refuge among the Tama; however, respite from these attacks was not to last as Tama was attacked shortly afterward in 1662. Hann (1988:35) speculates that the raids by the Westo may have forced the Tama southward into Apalachee. It is also possible that the Westo occupied the province of Tama for a brief time after its abandonment by the Yamasee (Worth 1995:16–17).

By 1665, some Yamasee were living in Guale and voluntarily sending laborers to work in the *repartimiento*. In fact, draft orders from between 1665 and 1669 state that pagans, mostly Yamasee, formed the majority of the labor force at St. Augustine (Worth 1995:20–21). Subsequent mission lists and descriptions from 1675 (Pedro de Arcos; Fernandez de Florencia), 1681 (Fernandez de Florencia; Francisco de Fuentes; Manuel Rico), and 1682 (the Friars of Anacape and Mayaca) show that there were approximately four hundred Yamasee living in Guale and Mocamo, three hundred in Apalachee, and another one hundred living in the Timucuan missions of Anacape and Mayaca (Hann 1988:35, 1990:505, 507; Worth 1995:101-2, 200, 1998:134, 137). All told, between seven and eight hundred Yamasee were living in Spanish Florida during this period. It is likely that an equal or greater number were also living in interior Georgia, possibly reinhabiting the old Tama province after the Westo had moved to the Savannah River sometime prior to 1674. Some, as shown below, may also have been living among the Lower Creek.

Although it is relatively straightforward connecting the eighteenth-century Yamasee towns of Chechessee, Altamaha, and Okatee to the sixteenth-century provinces of Ichisi, Altamaha, and Ocute, it is more difficult to establish a link between the Yamasee and the Toa. Green (1992:9) speculates that sometime during the second half of the sixteenth century, the Toa deserted their homeland on the Flint River and moved to Guale territory on the Georgia coast, where they became known as the Yoa, and later, the Euhaw band of the Yamasee. The abandonment of the Toa chiefdom is supported archaeologically, as late Lockett phase sites (A.D. 1450–1550) of the middle Flint River area were abandoned shortly after the time of de Soto's expedition (Worth 1988:179).

While the four interior Georgia chiefdoms, Toa, Ichisi, Altamaha, and Ocute, later formed what became known as the Lower Yamasee, the origins of groups that formed the Upper Yamasee remain problematic (Table 2.1). Certainly, part of the Upper Yamasee were formed by Guale groups that had abandoned the Georgia coast during the last two decades of the seventeenth century. This includes the towns of Ospo, Zapala, Asao, Satuache, and Tulafina. However, other groups such as the Pocotaligo, Pocosabo, and Tomatley are of less certain origin.

There are two other groups, the Tuscagy and Chehawes, whose origins can be traced back to the province of Coosa, that seem to have some relationship to the Yamasee. A March 25, 1713, entry in the *Journals of Commissioners of the Indian Trade* states that "the Cheehawes who ware formerly belonging to the Yamassees and now settled att the Creek might return" (McDowell 1955:42). Documentary evidence for the Tuscagy's occupation in Carolina comes from a January 1693 entry in the *Journals of the Commons House of Assembly.* This entry states the Assembly was informed that "some Northern Indians were come to settle amongst *Taskegus*" (Salley 1907a:10, emphasis added). During this period, the Tuscagy village (38CN140) was situated along the Ashepoo River where a plat shows them living near the Chechessee (McKivergan 1991:64). In 1716, we learn from Diego Pena that the Tasquiqui, then living with the Lower Creek, spoke the Yamasee language (Hann 1988:363).

Table 2.1. Yamasee Towns in South Carolina

Site No.	Town Name (variants)	Probable Origin
LOWER TOWNS		
38BU1206	Altamaha (Altamaca, Altapaha, Arrotamahaw)	Altamaha
38BU1231	Okatee (Oketee, Ocute, Ocatoses, Ocotoque)	Ocute
38BU48	Chechessee (Ichisi, Chasee, Chachise)	Ichisi
	Euhaw (Toa, Toalli, Yoa)	Toa/Guale
UPPER TOWNS		
38CN47*	Pocotaligo (Pocotalaca)	Unknown
38BU1279	Pocosabo (Pocosapa, Pocolabo, Pockasauba)	Unknown
38BU1428	Huspah (Huspaw, Ospo)	Guale
	Sadketche (Satuache, Chatuache, Salchiche)	Guale
	Tulafina (Tulfinny)	Guale
	Tomatley (Tamathli, Tamasle, Tomotlee)	Uncertain (Tama, Cherokee, or Lower Creek)
ADDITIONAL TOWNS ASSOCIATED WITH THE YAMASEE		
38CN140	Tuscagy (Tuskegee, Tasquiqui)	Coosa
	Chehawes (Chiaha)	Coosa
	Saupalau (Sapella, Zapala)	Guale
	Soho (Asao)	Guale
	Sapicbay	Guale
	Aspalaga	Apalachee

*This is the site of Pocotaligo on the Ashepoo River. The location of the town after this group left the Ashepoo is unknown, although it is probably somewhere on Mackay Point in Jasper County.

There is one final group that may be associated with the Yamasee, those from the Apalachee village of Aspalaga. A 1710 reference states, "the Apalachia Indians desire that their People may be restrained from leaving their own Town and goeing to reside at the Assapallago Town" (McDowell 1955:4). A second reference the following year involves a letter sent by John Cockett "from the Archpellauga Town informing the Agent of the Kings wayting there for his Assistance in removing their people to their respective Towns" (McDowell 1955:7). Although the location of Aspalaga is not specified, Pinckney Island, located just north of Hilton Head, was known as "Espalamga" (Ivers 1972:121n), a likely derivation of Aspalaga. If their village was located on Pinckney Island, this would place them just a little over nine miles south of the Lower Yamasee settlements.

The Yamasee in South Carolina

In a letter to the Lords Proprietors dated January 10, 1685, Lord Cardross (Henry Erskine), a Scottish settler at Stuarts Town, proclaimed the arrival of the Yamasee in South Carolina: "Wee thought fitt to acquaint you that yesterday some moe of the nation of the Yamasees arrived at St. Helena to settle with those of their nation formerly settled there having come from about St. Augustine" (Sainsbury 1928–1947, vol. 2:1). A little over a month later, Caleb Westbrooke, an Indian trader, announced that over a thousand more Yamasee had just come from the Lower Creek and were accompanied by "3 nations of the Spanish Indians that are Christians, Sapella, Soho, and Sapicbay" (Sainsbury 1928–1947, vol. 2:8–9). Based on Westbrooke's account, it appears that the town of Altamaha was initially located on an unnamed island, but that their island was becoming full and they were conferring with the Scots about expanding to Hilton Head. Later, in a 1698 land grant to John Stewart, we learn that the town of Pocotaligo had been situated on St. Helena Island (Salley 1973:582).

Although none of these early towns has been located, archaeological evidence from later Yamasee sites in northern Beaufort County indicates that the Yamasee lived in non-nucleated or "dispersed town" settlements. Households were spaced between 50 and 120 meters apart and each covered an area of between 30 and 60 meters in diameter (DePratter 1994; Fletcher and Harvey 2000; Green 1992; Southerlin 2000). This pattern is similar to that observed by Robert Sandford for the Edisto in 1666 (Salley 1911:91) and for late seventeenth-century Guale villages on St. Catherines Island in Georgia and San Juan Island near St. Augustine (Jones 1978:192). It is also likely that both of these principal towns had large, circular council houses similar to those described by Sandford for the Edisto and St. Helena Indians (Salley 1911:91, 100).

In terms of subsistence, historical accounts indicate that while in South Carolina the Yamasee hunted white-tailed deer and wild boar, raised "hoggs" and "fowles," and grew corn, peas, and watermelons (Dunlop 1929:130–31; Sainsbury 1928–1947, vol. 6:110; Salley 1932:21, 1934:48). Archaeological evidence from site 38BU1605 (Figure 2.2) has confirmed the presence of Old World animals including chickens (*Gallus gallus*), pigs (*Sus scrofa*), and cows (*Bos taurus*), but the site's occupants mainly relied on native species such as bear (*Ursus americana*), deer (*Odocoileus virginianus*), raccoon (*Procyon lotor*), squirrel (*Sciurus* sp.), turtle *(Testudines)*, and assorted fish and shellfish species. Botanical remains from features at the site have also yielded an Old World domesticate, the peach (*Prunus persica*); however, native species and tropical cultigens such as maize (*Zea mays*), common bean (*Phaseolus vulgaris*), sour cherry (*Prunus*

Figure 2.2. Archaeologists at work at the Yamasee site of Chechessee Old Field I (38BU1605).

cerasus), chokeberry (*Aronia arbutifolia*), lambsquarter (*Chenopodium album*), knotweed (*Polygonum* sp.), hickory (*Carya* sp.), walnut (*Juglans* sp.), acorn (*Quercus* sp.), tarweed (*Hemizonia congesta*), dayflower (*Commelina virginica*), blackhaw (*Virburnum prunifolium*), bedstraw (*Galium* sp.), and pepperweed (*Lepidium campestre*) still formed the core of the Yamasee diet (Southerlin et al. 2000).

The documents by Cardross and Westbrooke cited above make clear the majority of Yamasee settled in the Port Royal area during the early part of 1685; however, when they first arrived in South Carolina remains uncertain. The most likely possibility is that some of the Yamasee arrived during the late spring or early summer of 1683, shortly after the French pirate Grammont raided St. Augustine. After his attack, Grammont proceeded northward and attacked the Yamasee living in the towns of San Juan and San Phelipe on Cumberland Island, and possibly Santa Maria and San Pedro on Amelia Island as well (Worth 1995:36). Forced from these islands, the Yamasee moved to Port Royal to live with or near approximately one hundred sixty St. Helena Indians already occupying the area (John Crafford 1683 cited in Waddell 1974:10; see also the 1683 Alonso Solana map in Worth 1995:fig. 3). Worth (1995:19–20), citing a pair of seventeenth-century Spanish documents, thinks that the Yamasee may have been living in South Carolina on the mainland in the former province of Escamacu as early as the 1660s. However, it seems unlikely that the Yamasee were in South Carolina at the time as neither Sandford, who traveled thirty miles inland from Port Royal in 1666, nor the English trader Henry Woodward, who traveled across the mainland from Charleston to the Savannah River in 1674, mentioned any Indians living in the area.

Although the Scots initially had reservations about the Yamasee, they soon were sending them on slave-catching forays to the Spanish missions. In February 1685, approximately fifty Yamasee from St. Helena and "Cosapue" raided the Timucuan mission of Santa Catalina de Afuica, killing eighteen men and women and capturing twenty-five slaves who were taken back to Carolina (Hann 1990:472; Lanning 1935:220-22; Sainsbury 1928-1947, vol. 2:8-9). In addition, they ransacked the mission and carried away many of the church ornaments, some of which were later recovered by the Spanish from Governor Joseph Morton's plantation on Edisto Island (Worth 1995:148-49). On the way back from Santa Catalina, the Yamasee stopped at their former village of Tama on Amelia Island to celebrate their victory.

With the Scots convinced that the Yamasee no longer had any ties to the Spanish, they quickly formed a profitable trading alliance that hinged on the deerskin trade. In fact, by March 1685, Cardross was warning the English traders at Charles Town "that noe Englishman should trade from Sta. Helena to the Westoe [Savannah] River for all the Indians was his" (Crane 1928:29). This confidence expressed by Cardross was not to last. On August 17, 1686, the Spanish attacked and destroyed Stuarts Town and the nearby Yamasee villages. This attack was partly in retaliation for the Yamasee's attack on Santa Catalina and partly because Henry Woodward was beginning to trade with the Lower Creek. The Spanish strongly opposed this English intrusion into the Creek Indian trade (Hann 1988:188; Lanning 1935:178, 221).

After the destruction of Stuarts Town, the Yamasee fled northward to the Ashepoo and Combahee rivers (McKivergan 1991), a move clearly designed to put them in a remote location safe from Spanish attacks. In his 1687 journal, Captain William Dunlop wrote, "on April 19 . . . I went up the Ahepow river to speak with the Yamassies and at night came up to Matamaha's [Altamaha's] house" (Dunlop 1929:129). Dunlop was trying to persuade the Yamasee to accompany him on a retaliatory raid against the Spanish, which initially the Yamasee agreed to do. Accompanied by thirty-seven Englishmen, sixty Yamasee, and three Wimbee, Dunlop proceeded down the coast toward St. Augustine, stopping at a deserted town on Sapelo Island (possibly their former village on the southern tip of the island; see the 1681 Fuentes Census in Worth 1995:200). According to Dunlop, as they were planning to attack the lookout on Amelia Island, the cacique Altamaha suddenly balked and refused to go any farther, declaring "he wold not goe kill Spaniards for they had never killed any of his people" (Dunlop 1929:133). Even though some of the Yamasee wanted to continue the raid, Altamaha prevailed and the Yamasee returned to Carolina.

Although Altamaha is the only Yamasee town mentioned in the Carolina documents as being located in the vicinity of the Ashepoo River, a number of plats and land records also place the Chechessee, Pocotaligo, Pocosabo, Okatee, Tuscagy, and Chehawes in the area (McKivergan 1991:114). Sometime between 1687 and 1695, the Yamasee moved away from the Ashepoo and closer to Port Royal (Figure 2.3). A 1695 letter from Governor Archdale places the Yamasee about eighty miles from Charles Town (Carroll 1836:106). Because the Ashepoo and Combahee rivers are only about forty miles from Charles Town, the Yamasee must have moved closer to Port Royal by this date. The reason for their departure from the Ashepoo was probably the expansion of English settlements to areas outside of Charles Town. In 1697, for example, land "on the east side of the Ashepoo River at a place commonly known by the Poketaligoes Settlement" was granted to Robert Seabrook (Secretary of State, Royal Grants, in McKivergan 1991:130). Similarly, in 1700, 1,590 acres on the Ashepoo River, including the former towns of Tuscagy and Chechessee, were granted to John Stanyarne (McKivergan 1991:fig. 3.1).

Throughout their tenure in South Carolina, the Yamasee remained staunch allies of the English, becoming their virtual mercenaries during Queen Anne's War (1702–1713). The Yamasee also acted as a buffer protecting the English from Spanish attacks originating at St. Augustine. The location of their villages near Port Royal made them well suited for this task, and lookouts were established on Daufuskie Island in 1701, on Pinckney Island in 1703 and 1707, and at Seabrook Point in 1715, directly across the Whale Branch from the town of Pocosabo (Ivers 1972). To further their efforts, in 1701 the Carolina government even sent the Yamasee "a present . . . [of] one hundred weight of powder and one hundred and fifty weight of shott with one great gun, five hundred of flints and two gross of knives . . . for their use, only in emergent necessity" (Salley 1924:24).

Although a large number of armaments were given to the Yamasee, surprisingly few of these artifacts have been recovered from archaeological contexts. On the other hand, numerous other trade items such as kaolin pipes, glass and metal beads, brass rings and buttons, nails and spikes, iron kettle fragments, lead-glazed slipwares, tin-enameled wares, and other types of late seventeenth-century and early eighteenth-century European ceramics have been found at Yamasee sites in South Carolina (Green 1992; McKivergan 1991; Southerlin 2000) (Figure 2.2). Other goods that are known to have been traded to the Indians during this period include hatch-

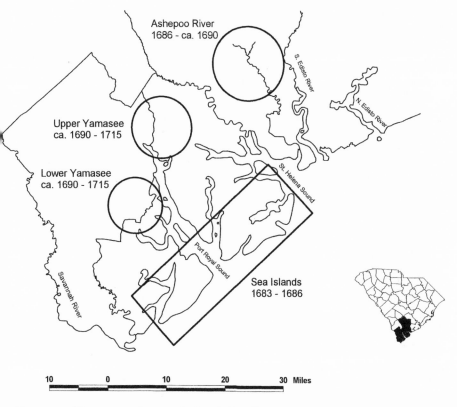

Figure 2.3. Yamasee settlements in South Carolina.

ets, hoes, adzes, scissors, mirrors, bells, Jew's harps, blankets, cloth, and rum (Crane 1928:332; Gregorie 1926:24; Wilder n.d.:15–16).

In 1702, Carolina Governor James Moore and Colonel Robert Daniel led a force composed of colonists, Yamasee, and Creek on a raid of St. Augustine (Arnade 1959; Crane 1928; Deagan 1983). Encouraged by reports of the War of Spanish Succession in Europe, Moore planned his attack to clear the way for a conquest of the French living on the Gulf Coast (Crane 1928:75; Salley 1924:32). In October 1702, Moore's forces succeeded in capturing Cumberland and Amelia islands, but could not break down the defenses of the Castillo de San Marcos (Covington 1968:11). The taking of the islands north of St. Augustine, however, did force the desertion of some of the remaining Spanish allies, including the Yoa (Euhaw) who fled to Carolina in February of 1703 and requested a place "to the northward of some of ye Yamassee settlements" (Salley 1934:48). Nonetheless, many Carolinians felt the expedition was a failure and regarded it "as a miserable plundering and slave-catching adventure" (Crane 1928:75).

As was typical of the Carolina traders, it did not take them long to forget that the Yamasee were their allies. On their return from St. Augustine, some of Moore's soldiers stole hogs belonging to a Yamasee Indian (Salley 1934:48). In addition, on February 5, 1703, the Commons House of Assembly recorded a complaint that John Cochran, later killed by the Yamasee at Pocotaligo, "hath by pretended authority from the Governor, taken away from severall Yamasee Indians, the plunder which they had taken at St. Augustine" (Salley 1934:38). Trying to make amends, the Assembly "being sensible of ye service the Yamasees did this collony . . . ordered that the publick powder receiver do deliver to Alatamaha, and ye rest of the Yamasees Kings now in towne one Barrel of Powder and 250 weight of shott" (Salley 1934:48). This trend of abuses by the traders, followed by some token compensation from the government, remained a typical pattern in colonial South Carolina, a pattern that almost cost the Carolinians their colony in 1715.

James Moore, despite his prior failure at St. Augustine in 1702, began a similar campaign in Apalachee in 1704. This time he had different results. Between January and August, Moore ravaged the province of Apalachee, destroying approximately fourteen mission villages and enslaving much of the surviving population (Hann 1988:264). He also brought back to Carolina three hundred free Apalachee from five villages to settle along the middle Savannah River Valley (Hann 1988:265–79). Among these émigrés were a number of Yamasee from the villages of Ocatoses and Tama. Although these Yamasee initially settled on the Savannah River with the rest of the Apalachee, Carolina officials were soon inquiring "whether the Yamasee Indians, now brought from the Spaniards are more inclined to continue where they now live or to come down and settle here with their nation, and they willing to entertain them" (Hann 1988:295–96). Whether these Yamasee ultimately moved to be with their kinsmen is not known.

When the Yamasee moved away from the Ashepoo River around 1690, they were trying to escape encroachment by English settlers. By 1707, with expansion continuing, they began to encounter the same problem in Port Royal. To protect the Yamasee's land, the government, on July 19, 1707, ratified an act "To Limit the Bounds of the Yamasee Settlement, to Prevent Persons from Disturbing them with the Stocks, and to Remove such as are Settled within the Limitation hereafter Mentioned." The boundaries of the so-called "Indian Land" were as follows:

All that tract of land on the main bounded to the north-east by Combohee river, to the south-east by the marshes and islands on Coosaw and Port Royal rivers, to the north-west by a line drawn from the head of the Combohee river to the head of the Savana river, and also one island [Halls Island] lying between the Pocosabo town and the north branch of Port Royal river, commonly called Coosawhachee, now inhabited by the said Yamasee Indians, to and for their use only. (Cooper and McCord 1836:317)

In addition to protecting their land, this act essentially restricted the Yamasee settlements to the mainland and precluded their resettlement of the sea islands.

In spite of the government's apparently good intentions this act proved ineffective. In 1711, a complaint was recorded in the *Journals of the Commissioners of the Indian Trade* that Thomas Jones, John Whitehead, Joseph Bryan, Robert Steale, John Palmer, and Barnaby Bull were settled within the Yamasee's territory (McDowell 1955:11). Later that same year, the Commissioners declared "The Island against Aratamau Town [Callawassie Island], we will endevour, shall be secured for the Indians and Saunders prevented from taking itt from them" (McDowell 1955:18). In 1713, John Wright, former Indian Agent to the Yamasee, attempted to force the Yamasee of Pocotaligo to build a house for him next to their council house (McDowell 1955:42).

Despite these abuses, the Yamasee remained loyal to the English. In 1711, John Barnwell led eighty-seven Yamasee, fifty-five Apalachee, ten Yuchi, and five Cusabo to North Carolina to fight against the Tuscarora (Milling 1940:118). Barnwell, extolling the virtues of the Yamasee, wrote, "the greatest part of our Indians are unwilling to proceed into unknown country where they may be hem'd in by a numerous Enemy and not know how to extricate themselves; but my brave Yamasees told me they would go wherever I led them. They will live and die with me, and indeed I have that dependence on them that I would not refuse to give battle to the whole Nation of Tuscaruros with them" (Milling 1940:119). For their bravery, along with their desire for slaves, the Yamasee paid a heavy toll. In 1713, Dr. Francis Le Jau, an English clergyman, noted "that nation was formerly very numerous but by degrees they are come to very little. They could muster 800 fighting men and now they are hardly 400. . . . The reason of it is the continual Warr they make against their Indian Neighbours" (Klingberg 1956:134).

From 1710 to 1715, tensions between the Yamasee and English became more acute as the list of abuses continued to mount. An entry in the *Journals of the Commissioners of the Indian Trade* dated April 12, 1715, warns of an impending attack on the Carolina colonists by the Yamasee and Creek (McDowell 1955:65). The Commissioners immediately dispatched agent Thomas Nairne along with William Bray, Samuel Warner, John Wright, and John Cochran to Pocotaligo to assuage the anger of the

Yamasee, but it was too little too late. The Yamasee killed Nairne, Bray, Warner, and Wright, while Cochran and his wife were kept as captives and then subsequently killed (Rowland et al. 1996:96).

Most historians agree that the Yamasee War was one of the most significant and far-reaching events in southern colonial history. As Richard Hann (1982:342) points out, the Yamasee War "disrupted the Indian trade and forced a reform of that institution, delayed the expansion of South Carolina's frontier . . . hastened the near extinction of several coastal tribes . . . and catalyzed the emergence of the Creek Confederacy." The effects of this little-known war were felt for many years throughout the South.

Because the Yamasee War was such an important event, there has been a great deal of speculation, both by contemporaries and historians, regarding the causes of the war. Governor Craven speculated that it was the Spanish at St. Augustine who encouraged the Yamasee to attack (Headlam 1928:228). On the other hand, one Virginia Council member placed the burden on "the Carolinians themselves, for their traders have so abused and so imposed upon the Indians in selling them goods at exorbitant prices, and receiving their peltry at very low rates" (Great Britain Public Record Office 1924:54). David Crawley, a contemporary observer, also placed the blame on the traders, stating they often went into the Yamasee's fields and took what they wanted without compensation. He also said the traders forced the Indians to carry heavy burdens for "3 or 4 and sumtimes 500 miles and pay very little for it, and when they had sent the men away . . . they brag to each other of debauching their wives" (Sainsbury 1928–1947, vol. 6:110–12). An additional explanation, given by William Tredwell Bull, states, "the vast debts, which I'm inform'd they have contracted, which with all their diligence tis impossible for them to pay in many years, have put them upon this war, which at once blotts out all their debts" (Klingberg 1962:26).

Modern historians have generally discounted the theory that the cause of the Yamasee War was a Spanish-inspired conspiracy, and instead cite the long list of abuses as the primary motivation for the war (Milling 1940:135–40). Recently, some historians have begun to build upon Bull's suggestion that the war was caused by the Yamasee's mounting debt. For example, Richard Hann (1982:343), adding an ecological theme to this interpretation, argues that "the hunting of white-tail deer, the expansion of cattle and pig raising, the rapid development of rice cultivation, and the elimination of the Spanish mission Indians of Florida and Georgia combined to exhaust the Yamasee's trade resources." The depletion of their resources, especially of white-tailed deer, combined with a rapidly diminishing pool of Indian slaves and an increasing debt, led the Yamasee to fear that they were going to be the next ones enslaved. In fact, by that time many of the traders were already taking slaves from the Yamasee, or enslaving the Yamasee themselves, in payment for real or imaginary debts (McDowell 1955:11–12, 28, 48). Their enumeration in the 1715 census (Sainsbury 1928–1947, vol. 7:238) also may have been an indication to the Yamasee that they were being counted for possible enslavement or elimination. By 1715, there were an estimated 1,850 Indian slaves in South Carolina alone (Snell 1973:table 1), with many more being exported out of the colony.

Although Hann's argument is valid, one cannot overlook the abuses done to the Yamasee during their stay in Carolina. When one examines the history of the cacique Altamaha, we see that his son was abducted in 1692 (Salley 1907b:38) and his sister beaten in 1712 (McDowell 1955:37), and another son may have been abducted by John Cochran in January 1715 just prior to the outbreak of the Yamasee War (Klingberg 1960:10). If the leader of the Yamasee was treated in this manner, then we can only assume that atrocities against other Yamasee must have been horrendous.

The reasons behind the Yamasee War were many: trader abuse, fear of enslavement, encroachment upon their land, and a depletion of resources each contributed to its commencement. It is also likely that the Spanish did play some role, although the nature of their involvement is not clear. By 1715, the factors cited above combined to create an atmosphere that was like a powder keg ready to explode. When it did, the entire South felt its consequences. (For a good synopsis of the Yamasee War, see Rowland et al. 1996:95–110.)

After the War

After the war the majority of the Yamasee moved near St. Augustine to be under the protection of the Spanish. The diary of Colonel George Chicken states that "all the Yeamoesees are gone to Saint Augusten exceapt the Tomatleys which is att ye Cricke among them" (Cheves 1894:336). In 1716, the governor of St. Augustine declared the Yamasee to be "subjects of Spain who a long time ago revolted from that Crown but were now return'd, and would be under Spanish protection" (Headlam 1930:219). This angered the English who declared it to be a breach of the first article of the Treaty of Utrecht, the treaty that ended the War of Spanish Succession (Headlam 1930:218).

By 1717, the Yamasee had established three main settlements near St. Augustine. These included Nuestra Señora de Candelaria de la Tamaja, with residents from the South Carolina towns of Altamaha and Ocute; Pocotalaca, with residents from Pocotaligo and Euhaw; and a settlement at Pocosapa. Additional Yamasee were scattered among non-Yamasee settlements, including nineteen Chachise (Chechessee) living at the Timucuan settlement of San Buena Bentura de Palica (Hann 1989:184–86). From these settlements, armed and provisioned by the Spanish, the Yamasee continued their attacks on South Carolina. In return, they were repeatedly attacked by native groups allied to the English, especially the Yuchi (Sainsbury 1928–1947, vol. 13:145). The peak of these retaliatory raids against the Yamasee occurred in the early 1720s and there was additional stimulus in 1724 when the Yamasee killed Ouletta, the pro-English son of the Lower Creek headman Brims (Hann 1988:289).

The most devastating blow to the Yamasee occurred in 1728, when a force of two hundred English and their Indian allies, led by Colonel John Palmer, attacked and burned the Yamasee town of Nombre de Dios near St. Augustine (Hann 1989:197; Sainsbury 1928–1947, vol. 8:187–89). In a separate raid, the Yuchi attacked the Yamasee town of Tamasle killing all of the women and children in addition to a number of warriors (Hann 1988:327). These attacks inspired Fray Bullones to note that the Yamasee of Tamaja were "hated by the rest of the Nations. And they made war on them so much that they were being exterminated little by little" (Bullones to the King, October 5, 1728, cited in Hann 1989:193). Despite these attacks, the Yamasee persisted even though their numbers continued to dwindle. By the mid-eighteenth century, the Yamasee were scattered about the Southeast living among the Lower Creek, Cherokee, Yamacraw, and Catawba. In addition, there were some Yamasee still living with the Spanish near St. Augustine and Pensacola. When the Spanish surrendered Florida to the English in 1763, the Yamasee at St. Augustine went with Spaniards to Cuba (Gold 1965), while those living in Pensacola relocated to the village of San Carlos de Chachalacas in New Spain (Palerm 1952).

Conclusion

This chapter has examined over two hundred years of Yamasee history, tracing their origins in powerful Mississippian chiefdoms in interior and coastal Georgia, their complex history in Carolina, and their return to the Florida missions where they were decimated by their former allies, both Native and European. Although the Yamasee were once feared throughout most of the region, and were a major force in helping to shape the history and geography of the colonial Southeast, their name has fallen into relative obscurity. Only a few river names (e.g., Tulfinny River and Euhaw Creek) and small towns (e.g., Pocotaligo and Salkehatchie) that dot the landscape of the Lowcountry remain as a testimony to their tenure in South Carolina.

Nevertheless, the Yamasee have left to us a rich archaeological record, although unprecedented development along South Carolina's coast is rapidly destroying this legacy. As we are writing this chapter, the towns of Altamaha and Huspah and the "old fields" associated with the towns of Okatee and Chechessee are threatened by development. If we do not help protect some of these sites, we will soon be left with nothing but a few place names to remind us of this once formidable group known as the Yamasee.

Acknowledgments

This chapter is dedicated to the memory of our friend and colleague David A. McKivergan, Jr. We would also like to thank Tim Belshaw, Joe Joseph, Erin Shaw, and Martha Zierden for their help and encouragement. Their input and assistance added tremendously to the quality of this essay.

3
Colonial African American Plantation Villages

Thomas R. Wheaton

A central problem for archaeologists is the extreme difficulty of address-ing issues of power and resistance, change and continuity, emic and etic perspectives, from archaeological data. Simply trying to determine the function of an artifact within a presumably unambiguous context is often difficult; as Brown and Cooper (1990:18–19) show, meaning is the product of the social context within which an artifact is used, which is not neces-sarily always the context for which it was originally intended. We can only approximate how people thought about what they made, purchased, used, and discarded. How people thought about these things in the complex con-text of daily life on a colonial southern plantation under slavery is even more tenuous.

The current trend to address individual artifacts within very specific as-sociational contexts is good. A few buttons, crystals, or bones in a particu-lar, very well controlled context and viewed from a broader perspective of research into African cultures, power, and cultural continuity can, and have, produced insights not otherwise available. Broader patterns and con-texts on the plantation can also indicate culture change and "provide new insights into the cultural evolution of Africans into African Americans" (Brown and Cooper 1990:19). Yaughan and Curriboo, two Lowcountry colonial plantations along the Santee River in St. Stephens, South Carolina, are examples of where broader patterns can be seen and interpreted.

Work at these two plantations in 1979 identified what turned out to be three slave quarters of two adjacent Huguenot plantations settled in the eighteenth to early nineteenth centuries (Wheaton 1999; Wheaton et al. 1983). Yaughan plantation had two workers' quarters (Figure 3.1), and Curriboo had one (Figure 3.2), along with various other plantation depen-dencies. The first quarter at Yaughan (site 38BK75) dated from the 1780s to the 1820s, while the second (38BK76) was occupied from the 1740s to

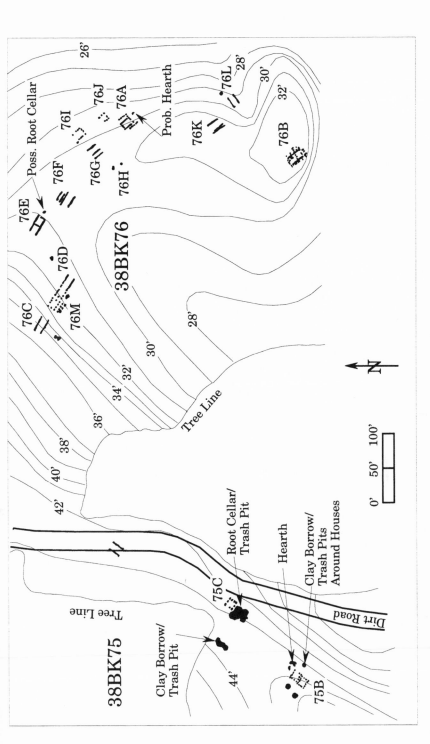

Figure 3.1. Yaughan structures and major features (based on Wheaton et al. 1983).

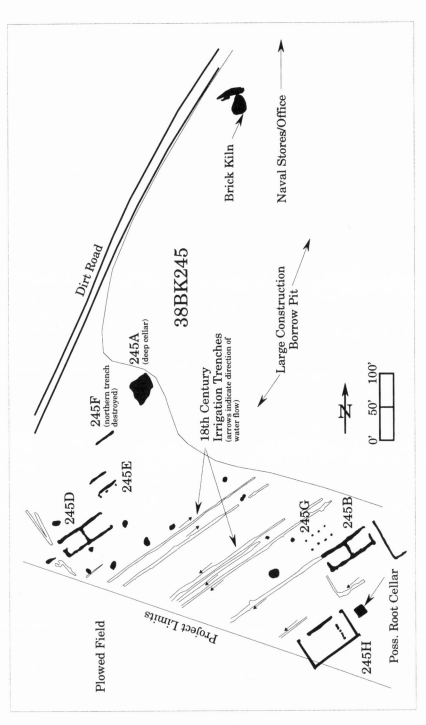

Figure 3.2. Curriboo structures and major features (based on Wheaton et al. 1983).

Dirt Road

38BK245

Brick Kiln

Naval Stores/Office

Large Construction
Borrow Pit

245F
(northern trench
destroyed)

245A
(deep cellar)

18th Century
Irrigation Trenches
(arrows indicate direction of
water flow)

N

0'   50'   100'

245D

245E

Plowed Field

Project Limits

245G

245B

245H

Poss. Root Cellar

the 1790s. The quarter at Curriboo (38BK245) dated from the 1740s to around 1800, although other parts of Curriboo continued to be occupied until the 1840s. This study, unlike many previous archaeological and historical studies, provided insights into the pre-Revolutionary rather than the antebellum character of life on a southern plantation.

A total of twenty-six clearly defined buildings or parts of buildings were exposed along with several hundred other features, and over 35,000 artifacts were recovered. All of the five structures at the later quarter at Yaughan (38BK75) and twelve at the earlier quarter (38BK76) were either dwellings or small outbuildings associated with the two slave quarters. The nine structures found at Curriboo (38BK245) were mostly domestic structures used by the enslaved population, with three other structures serving other functions: a barn, an "office" or other nondomestic building, and a naval stores warehouse. Curriboo also had a brick clamp. A summary of the data upon which much of the argument presented here rests is included in Wheaton et al. (1983) and Wheaton (2000).

In 1983 (Wheaton et al. 1983) and in 1985 (Wheaton and Garrow 1985), I and my colleagues argued that the African population of the plantations was rapidly becoming African American so that by sometime in the nineteenth century it would be impossible to distinguish archaeologically an African American settlement from a Euro-American settlement. It was assumed that this change from African to African American was steady and applied evenly to the material culture and by extension to the nonmaterial culture. Because of subsequent work I conducted at the freedmen's town of James City, North Carolina, in 1989 (Wheaton et al. 1990) and the work of others (e.g., Brown and Cooper 1990; Westmacott 1992), I have modified this position to one that allows for differential rates of change in aspects of African American culture and for the retention to the present day of Africanisms that can be identified archaeologically.

Culture Change and Continuity at Yaughan and Curriboo

The historical research conducted for Yaughan and Curriboo (Friedlander 1985; Wheaton et al. 1983) concluded that the initial populations of the workers' settlements almost certainly had a significant number of Africans, as well as African Americans from South Carolina or the Caribbean. Only one, or possibly two, of the enslaved were Native Americans. The makeup of this population remained fairly stable during the eighteenth and the beginning of the nineteenth centuries. Black society in the parish was characterized by a network of family and friends who may have changed residence as the result of inheritance and sale, but who generally remained in the vicinity. Family groups on these plantations were often recognized by the owners and often guided inheritance decisions. The majority of the population of the parish was black from early in the eighteenth century, before Yaughan and Curriboo were settled, and the ratio of blacks to whites increased throughout most of the century, particularly on the larger plantations such as those studied here. This makeup of the parish is reinforced by the impression of a 1737 visitor to the Lowcountry who noted, "Carolina looks more like a negro country than like a country settled by white people" (Wood 1974:132). The black to white ratio became more balanced toward the end of the eighteenth century.

Partly as a result of this majority black population, the relation between blacks and whites was not one of clear dominance by white plantation owners over their black slaves in all situations. On the isolated plantations and on the oftentimes isolated quarters within the plantations, contact between blacks and whites was less frequent than in urban centers. The African majority, coupled with the value of their skills and knowledge of rice production, gave enslaved Africans a certain negotiating power, albeit limited, with slaveholders. Whites were outnumbered, and they often did not have the agricultural and engineering skills to run an efficient rice plantation. It was therefore in the planter's interest to give a little to get a lot.

In this negotiation (see Berlin 1999), the enslaved population succeeded in obtaining considerable freedom of movement ("autonomy," according to Terry [1981]) and in establishing a work pattern that was known as the task labor system. Task labor required that a certain unit of work or a task be completed each day, and once it was finished the enslaved workers' time was their own. This allowed them more time to produce food and goods on their own, and many kept gardens, hunted or trapped, or worked at craft production. There are numerous accounts of slaveholders purchasing or bartering for food and manufactured items produced by their slaves. Another illustration of autonomous African American production is the colonoware found at Yaughan and Curriboo, but only rarely mentioned in the historic documents (Crane 1993). Here, colonoware refers to the ceramics made by the enslaved Africans on the plantations, not that made by Native Americans (see Anthony this volume).

This is not to imply that the enslaved were like serfs or peasants. One cannot forget the terms under which they ultimately lived and their legal status as property. But the history and archaeology of eighteenth-century Lowcountry plantations do indicate that the slaveholders did not have all of the power, and that the enslaved were willing to use what power they had to modify certain aspects of the plantation system.

The historical resources on issues dealing with enslaved African Americans are virtually all from a Euro-American or outsider's viewpoint. Even when the historical resources are used critically, read between the lines, so to speak, the writer only wrote about what he or she felt was important. Obviously, the most biased historic documents are those that present the writer's conclusions about the enslaved population's view on slavery. But even when the writer's biases are known (as when they try to influence an abolitionist, another slaveholder, or a family member, for example) or when dealing only with account books and probate inventories, it is impossible to know what was left out. A good case in point is that most slaveholders never mentioned the most ubiquitous artifact produced and used by their slaves in the Lowcountry in the eighteenth century, colonoware. This is perhaps because it was an important commodity only within the slave community. So even a critical reading of the documents only presents a partial picture in the best of circumstances. Virtually no African American documents have survived on life in the quarter, and I know of no oral accounts of eighteenth-century slavery in the Lowcountry.

Any examination of culture change within the slave community must include archaeology to be at all complete, although the archaeological record, like the archival record, has its own set of biases. Just as historians only have part of the documentary record, archaeologists, because of differential retention, preservation, and recovery techniques, only have part of the entire potential archaeological record and even less of the original material culture. Items such as iron pots would have been curated and removed when houses were abandoned. Soil conditions may favor the preservation of one type of artifact but not another. And limited field recovery techniques may make it impossible to talk about settlement layout and other issues. Similar to the historian, the archaeologist, with his or her outsider's viewpoint, can also bias the results by misinterpreting context and function or by emphasizing one aspect of culture and history over another.

The changes evident in the archaeological record at Yaughan and Curriboo suffer from all of these problems. There is the problem of assigning function. Should nails be included with architectural items or were they used as hooks to hang clothing or personal items? Were glass bottles used to contain liquids for cooking and consumption, so that they therefore belong with kitchen items, or did they serve a storage or medicinal function?

More to the point, does the high number of ball clay pipe stem and bowl fragments found around the house designated 76A at the earlier slave village at Yaughan indicate the dwelling of a heavy smoker, a high-status individual who could afford some conspicuous consumption, or a healer who used tobacco in a medicinal way, or was this house the location for communal gathering at the end of the day when people sat around smoking and telling stories under a nearby oak tree that did not come down until the spring of 1979? If it was the house of a high-status individual, were tobacco and pipes an attempt by the owner or overseer to establish a hierarchy in the quarter that the owner thought he could control?

Also at the same house a gold button was found in the general excavation levels. How did this button end up there? Could it have been stolen from the mainhouse (one probate inventory mentioned a set of gold buttons) and later lost, and was it therefore a sign of resistance? Was it given to a "favorite" slave and therefore a sign of preference, and possibly an attempt by the owner to show favoritism and perhaps control? Could it have been lost by the owner during a visit, perhaps surreptitious, to the slave village? Or could it have been introduced as a result of postdepositional site formation processes and have nothing to do with the lives of African Americans on the plantation?

Even with better context and the proper interpretation of that context, one could not answer these questions, although the answers would have been very easy for the one who lost the button or smoked the tobacco to have explained. Instead, what the data at Yaughan and Curriboo can tell us, from a more general context, is something about the broad changes and continuities going on at the plantations during the eighteenth century.

The combination of extensive hand excavation and large-scale mechanical stripping at the plantations provided more information and a greater breadth of information than if the sites had been examined with more traditional, small-scale excavations. Virtually all of the large trash deposits were mapped and excavated, and all of the houses at the earlier settlement at Yaughan and many at the other two settlements were exposed and mapped. The data from these plantations therefore allowed more confidence in the trends in the data than would normally be the case. The following are the main conclusions of the project concerning changes in the material culture in the three workers' settlements at two Huguenot plantations in the Carolina Lowcountry.

Change in Settlement

The excavations at the older of the slave villages at Yaughan and at Curriboo revealed evidence of post-in-trench earth-walled architecture, considered to be African in origin. The wall trenches were relatively long and narrow features, varying from 0.8 to 1.5 feet in width and 1.5 to 2.5 feet in depth. They were straight walled and flat bottomed. Posts were placed at 2.2-foot intervals on average, and the walls themselves were constructed of clay built up within the trench, with the posts providing vertical support. These structures were rectangular and ranged from 9.5 by 13 feet to 14 by 20.5 feet.

At the later Yaughan village were structures built with post-in-ground construction. These were also present at the older village superimposed over some of the earlier wall trench structures. These posthole structures presumably had frame siding and the posts were spaced at 3.75-foot intervals. While still rectangular, these structures were not as elongated as the wall trench structures, and houses ranged in dimension from 10.25 by

12.75 feet to 12 by 13 feet. These dimensions as well as construction style are in keeping with Anglo-American architecture of the same period (1740s–1790s).

The wall trench structures with their clay wall superstructure appear to be of African origin, comparable to clay and cobb wall–constructed buildings reported in West Africa (Agorsah 1983; Posnansky 1999). While Europeans had clay-walled architecture (see Steen and Shlasko this volume), neither the use of trenches nor clay walls have been reported on early Euro-American sites in the Carolina Lowcountry, although Carl Steen (1999, this volume) has reported a late eighteenth-century mainhouse site with significant amounts of daub that may represent clay walls in the Carolina backcountry along the Savannah River. The presence of this type of architecture in the Lowcountry probably indicates the influx of newly arrived Africans in the 1730s.

Otto (1975) and others have noted that during the antebellum period slave owners were careful not to allow such obvious Africanisms to be built, presumably because planters regarded them as challenges to their authority. Given the economic and political nature of the times and the northern criticism of slavery, slaveholders probably did not feel they could allow such challenges to go unanswered. Why then did so many "African style" houses go unchallenged in the eighteenth century in the Lowcountry? One possible answer could be that the early landowner was absentee and did not care what was built as long as the land was cleared and the rice dikes built. This might explain part of the reason for such houses at Yaughan, but not at Curriboo where the owner lived within a few hundred feet of such houses. Therefore the practice was not only due to the absence of a landowner or the isolation of the quarter on the plantation. Shlasko, in this volume, suggests that French Huguenot planters may have accepted earth-walled construction because they were familiar with similar constructions in France; however, even at the Huguenot-owned Yaughan plantation this architectural style disappeared by the turn of the century. One is left with the conclusion that the eighteenth-century owner did not feel threatened by such houses in the same way that the nineteenth-century owner did. On the other hand, the enslaved Africans who built these houses may not have seen such construction as a challenge to authority but simply as a logical way to build a house that gave them a sense of home and comfort. It is also possible that the African builders did see this as a challenge and the owner either did not recognize it as such or did not feel particularly threatened. All of these possibilities seem to agree with the conclusion of the historical research that slaves in the parish had a certain autonomy and were negotiating work and perhaps living conditions with the landowner. In any case, such houses appear on a number of Lowcountry plantations up to the fourth quarter of the eighteenth century, when they began to be replaced by post-in-ground frame structures (Drucker and Anthony 1979; Joseph this volume; Wheaton et al. 1983; Zierden et al. 1986).

As the style of architecture changed, the settlement pattern of the workers' quarter also changed from an organic layout following the natural contours of the land at the early quarter on Yaughan to a more regular layout at the later quarter. As many other researchers have pointed out, on later antebellum plantations regularity of spacing, size, and shape and the use of a grid system of regular streets were seen as a clear exercise of control by the landowner, whatever other motives he may have had with respect to health and economics (Lewis and Haskell 1980; Orser et al. 1982; Otto 1975). The early quarter at Yaughan did not show this kind of control.

If the enslaved and the slaveholder had accepted trench, clay-walled houses loosely arranged within certain prescribed parameters on the plantation for most of the eighteenth century, what changed in the culture that resulted in a new style of architecture and layout? Were these changes imposed by the owner, and if they were, why at that time? Coincidentally, Glassie (1975), studying folk housing in Virginia, notes a similar trend toward regularity in the landscape of white owned and occupied settlement in the nineteenth century.

If the decision to make these changes were made within a creolized enslaved population does this indicate a change in how they viewed the function of a house? How would they have seen the change from what was basically an enclosed bedroom with an exterior living space to a building that incorporated more of those functions on the interior? It is of course difficult to say, and equally difficult to know whether the material change of building style and layout reflects a real cultural change or only the external acceptance of a material item, with little or no change in cultural outlook.

However, these changes do seem to have profound implications for the world view of the inhabitants. Moving from a house where most activities were conducted out-of-doors to one where some of those activities were moved indoors must have had an influence on the people of the settlement. The change would have meant less social interaction with neighbors and more privacy for things that had previously been public, changes that were occurring within other segments of the late eighteenth- and nineteenth-century population. Even if these changes had been imposed by the owner, they are too profound not to have either resulted in a changed outlook or been the result of a changed outlook on the part of the inhabitants.

The changes in the workers' settlements at Yaughan and Curriboo may not be the result of the enslaved becoming or trying to become like the dominant white society. However, it is impossible to deny that some kind of change was taking place that was more than just an outward material change. After nearly a century of continuity in an "African" house style, a new style of house and new ways of living and interacting with the community were emerging, perhaps in response to the owner's new "industrial" outlook on plantation production (Joseph 1989, 1993b). Recent studies (Westmacott 1992) of the usage of African American yards in the rural South show that the change from houses used primarily as bedrooms and storage areas, with most activities occurring out-of-doors, to ones where virtually all activities are conducted indoors is still not complete, and may never be so. They also show that the roots of this relationship of house to yard (and ultimately to the road in front of the house and to the rest of the community) may go back to West Africa (Agorsah 1983).

Change in Domestic Production

One of the most intriguing things about Yaughan and Curriboo is the colonoware ceramics and our ability to show that most of this material was made on the plantation by enslaved Africans and/or African Americans. We initially hypothesized that colonoware was made to supplement supplies from the owner and, therefore, indicated poverty and low status. The owner may have found colonoware production to his economic advantage, especially during the early years of settlement. Although this may have been true in part, because the production of colonoware continued into the nineteenth century, when nonlocal ceramics became more readily available, the users may have regarded colonoware as more than an expedient replacement for European goods. Recent work by Ferguson (1992), Crane (1993), and Kennedy and Espenshade (2001) shows not only that there were other functions for colonoware, but also that by antebellum times even white people were emotionally attached to colonoware cooking jars. Certain foods just tasted better cooked in colonoware pots. Colonoware was more than an economic response to low supplies from the owner. Given the power negotiations evident in the documents and perhaps in the architecture and settlement patterns, colonoware may have been as much a conscious continuity of generalized African ceramic traditions as it was an economic response.

Colonoware production decreased relative to the use of nonlocal ceramics and iron cooking pots until by the Civil War very little was made. During the last twenty or thirty years of that period it may have been used almost exclusively for medicinal and ritual purposes (Ferguson 1992; Kennedy and Espenshade 2001). What caused this change? In 1983, we hypothesized that the change may have been due to easier access to nonlocal ceramics. We assumed that such ceramics would have been preferred and therefore used when they became more readily available. Subsequent research shows that nonlocal ceramics may not have been preferred for practical reasons, such as how they fit into the overall foodways or the better heat retention of cooking jars, and for cultural reasons, such as colonoware's association with the African roots of an increasingly creolized culture. If ready availability of nonlocal ceramics were the main reason colonoware was replaced, then the shift to nonlocal ceramics should have been more complete and earlier than it appears to have been. The industrial revolution made British ceramics much more affordable by the 1780s and 1790s, while colonoware was still the overwhelming majority ceramic type in the quarters into the nineteenth century. Rather than acculturation, this slow shift toward the use of nonlocal ceramics may show a strong cultural continuity.

Change in Foodways

The change in the production and use of colonoware cannot be completely divorced from changes in the activity it is most closely associated with, food preparation and consumption. These changes included a decrease in the use of cooking jars, an increase in iron cooking pots and flatwares, and a possible change from outdoor to indoor hearths. However, research also has shown little change in the makeup of the diet, mostly vegetal, or in the high number of bowls in relation to other forms, at least at the later quarter at Yaughan. DeCorse (1999) notes that bowl forms still predominated over other forms at Elmina in Ghana even after the introduction of European ceramics. While iron cooking pots seem to have been replacing colonoware jars, the basic set of foodways appears to have been changing very little, comprising a mostly boiled, vegetal diet cooked in pots and served in bowls. Because so few tableware items were found, perhaps because of differential curation and preservation, it is impossible to know whether the number of spoons decreased relative to forks, which might have indicated a change in the types of foods and the way they were prepared. The only change in these patterns that might indicate a change in foodways is the small increase in flatware forms.

Most of the foodways appear to have been slow to change, which argues for the change being internal to the enslaved community rather than being imposed by the owner. If the change had been imposed from the outside one might expect more kinds of changes and more rapid change, not change in just one of the ceramic forms such as increasing amounts of flatware.

Taken together, the changes apparent in the material world in the workers' settlement were slow and support the idea of an internal change or the slow development of a creole culture for most of the century, rather than an abrupt change imposed from the outside either by the owner or by newly arrived slaves or as the result of some other cause. If this is so, then the changes in the material culture may be more justifiably thought of as reflecting changes within that culture. This view of change in the slave community is somewhat at odds with the picture put forth by us in 1983 and 1985 of a slave culture inexorably becoming more and more like the dominant culture (Wheaton and Garrow 1985; Wheaton et al. 1983). This view suggests that there was more continuity and perhaps resistance to the dominant culture than our earlier simplified acculturation model suggested.

Reflections

The archaeological tools used for this analysis (house type, shape, size, and orientation; and changes in the relative amounts of a few ceramic types and foodways) seemed to show that if the trends evident at Yaughan and Curriboo continued, it would eventually become very difficult to differentiate ethnicity or black from white, so to speak, in the archaeological record. Comparing house types or relative percentages of ceramics and ceramic forms today would probably show little difference between black and white Americans of the same income level. Of course, cultural differences would still be present, they would just be difficult to determine using the archaeological tools we used at Yaughan and Curriboo plantations. Indeed, this was one of the main points of the original report; that is, other tools would be needed on later sites to examine culture change and ethnicity. Such tools would have to be more finely tuned or would have to address different aspects of the material culture.

In 1989, at James City, North Carolina, a community established during the Civil War to settle African American families who had escaped from nearby plantations, I was able to test some of these ideas of culture change in the archaeological record (Wheaton et al. 1990). That project involved the hand excavation of four house sites and the machine stripping and mapping of over 2,000 features from thirteen lots on one-half of an entire block of the town that was occupied into the early twentieth century (Figure 3.3). In 1893, James City was also the site of perhaps the first case of civil disobedience to military authority in North Carolina by African Americans (Mobley 1981).

Following the conclusions from Yaughan and Curriboo about the ability to recognize ethnicity in the material culture, it was initially assumed that the archaeology at James City would not show significant differences between African American communities and white communities, at least using the same tools we used at Yaughan and Curriboo. And at the level of

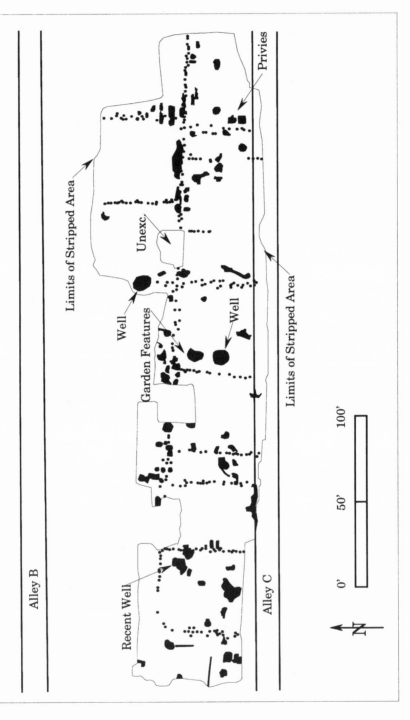

Figure 3.3. James City major features and selected postholes (based on Wheaton et al. 1990).

house types and locations, colonoware and artifact patterns, this was true. But to have concluded that the nonmaterial culture of James City was the same as the white culture of nearby New Bern would have been wrong.

Two things, besides the historic documents, kept us from reaching that mistaken conclusion. One of these things was the general similarity of artifact and feature patterns and socioeconomic scaling among the lots examined, despite the fact that the historic documents indicated what would normally be considered major status differences in occupation and between those living on the main street and those living on the alleys or the interior of the block. There was an egalitarian nature to the deposits that one would not expect to find on a similar white urban block with such occupational and status differences.

The second was the absence of wells on the individual lots. Stewart-Abernathy's (1986) urban farmstead model would have dictated a well on every lot in the absence of city water, reflecting privacy and the desire to be separate from one's neighbors. At James City, there were only two wells on the entire block, both located in the center of the block, and both undoubtedly used by various families on the block on a daily basis.

Combining this with the egalitarian nature of the rest of the deposits led to a view of this society as decidedly communal, a society that downplayed economic and social differences. The people of James City had gone through the dark tunnel of slavery, and particularly antebellum slavery, and emerged out the other end seemingly changed to the point of being indistinguishable from white society in their material culture. But at another level, they had maintained significant nonmaterial elements of their Africaness. James City represents a triumph of adaptation, resistance, and cultural continuity. It also points out the inadequacies and difficulties of developing archaeological research tools to illuminate the nonmaterial culture in the material record.

Conclusion

The archaeology of Lowcountry plantations shows us a gradual shift from a society clearly descended from African roots in the early colonial period with a significant amount of cultural continuity in the eighteenth century. By the end of the colonial period changes in this culture were becoming apparent as a generalized African culture was slowly becoming an African American culture. The regimentation and the "industrialization" on the antebellum plantation as owners and white society in general tried to exert more control over the black majority ultimately proved to be less overwhelming than a reading of historical records and a cursory view of plantation layouts might indicate. By the end of the Civil War, an underlying African American culture emerged, changed, but in many important respects intact despite the best efforts of the dominant white society to make it otherwise.

Acknowledgments

I would like to thank J. W. Joseph and Martha Zierden, editors of this volume, for the opportunity and encouragement to prepare this chapter. I would also like to thank Patrick H. Garrow for the opportunity to direct the original project and Amy Friedlander for her close and well-informed collaboration on the historical research. I would like to make clear, however, that the revised conclusions in this article are my own and do not necessarily reflect those of either of the two co-authors of the original report.

4
Tangible Interaction: Evidence from Stobo Plantation

RONALD W. ANTHONY

I always enjoy the beginning of each semester, specifically the beginning of my Introduction to Anthropology class because this is when we discuss the nature, goals, and value of the discipline. During discussions of the various subfields of anthropology, often quite a few students are surprised to learn that most North American archaeologists have been trained in anthropology and that they are interested in, and excited about, more than merely reconstructing or documenting the past. I try to impart to them that the research goals of many archaeologists are basically concerned with addressing anthropological questions like researchers in the other branches of the field and that, in a sense, the major differences in the subfields of anthropology are, to a large degree, simply the nature or types of data gathered and the methods of acquiring the information. Because of my training, the class usually hears more about archaeology than the other subfields and this gives me the opportunity to talk about, for example, how archaeology is in a unique position to address issues concerning the past such as culture change. This enables me to launch into discussions about general mechanisms of culture change: diffusion, innovation, cultural loss, and acculturation (Haviland 1999). Another concept, increasingly used in the literature relating to culture change, is creolization.

Ferguson (1992:150) notes that "creolization is similar to the familiar anthropological concept of acculturation," but lacks the "Eurocentric" baggage that some currently associate with the term *acculturation*. In an effort to be objective, several scholars use the term *creolization* to describe "the building of a new culture from diverse elements" (Ferguson 1992: 150). Its use emphasizes creativity and expresses mutual exchange and contribution by all cultures in contact. Often acculturation—"major cultural changes people are forced to make due to intensive firsthand contact" (Haviland 1999:764)—as one example of how cultures change, captures my class's attention, particularly when outcomes of acculturation such as genocide and revitalization movements are discussed. Conversation about another reaction to acculturation, syncretism, "the blending of indigenous and foreign traits to form a new system" (Haviland 1999:771), also usually generates positive responses from the students, especially when connections or examples are provided, at times literally, from their own backyards. One such example that reflects syncretism, or creolization, as some social scientists would say, that I inevitably talk about and that I am able to physically show to the class, is colonoware.

Colonoware is an unglazed, low-fired earthenware of local manufacture. Distributed within mid- and south-Atlantic states, the majority of these ceramics likely were produced and used during the eighteenth century by enslaved African Americans and historic period Native Americans. Some of these ceramics may have been manufactured specifically as a result of African American and Native American interaction (Ferguson 1980, 1992; Noel Hume 1962; Zierden et al. 1999). Colonoware expresses the dynamics, complexities, diversity, and energy of cultural encounters in the colonial South and helps to demonstrate that the eighteenth-century South was "more a mosaic than a tapestry" (Joseph and Zierden this volume). Much of the anthropological value ascribed to these ceramics centers on the belief that they represent one of the best-surviving examples of tangible evidence regarding culture contact in the South and thus offer an opportunity to examine and understand cultural interaction among African American, Native American, and European American populations during the colonial period. Building upon data published about colonoware from extensively and intensively investigated South Carolina plantations such as Fountainhead (Spiers Landing) (Anthony 1979), Yaughan and Curriboo (Wheaton et al. 1983), Lesesne and Fairbanks (Anthony 1986), and Broom Hall (Trinkley et al. 1995), the recent study of colonoware from Stobo plantation revealed subtle, yet provocative, physical evidence of such cultural interaction (Zierden et al. 1999). This chapter presents this evidence via a discussion of published colonoware varieties observed at Stobo and other South Carolina plantations.

Colonoware

In South Carolina the accelerated study of and interest in colonoware has generally tracked with the increasing pace of plantation archaeology and, more recently, the investigation of colonial and antebellum urban contexts. Within the past twenty-five years or so major archaeological investigations of South Carolina plantations have moved away from particularistic approaches toward more anthropologically oriented research (Drucker and Anthony 1979; Lees 1980; Orser et al. 1982; Steen 1999; Trinkley et al.

1995; Wheaton et al. 1983; Zierden et al. 1986; Zierden et al. 1999). Accompanying this redirection in research focus has been an increasing use of interdisciplinary techniques and search for pattern, often integrated into a general systems theory framework (e.g., Drucker and Anthony 1979; Trinkley et al. 1995; Wheaton et al. 1983; Zierden et al. 1986; Zierden et al. 1999).

Within this realm of inquiry and linked to the increased attention given to colonoware, African American archaeological research has been a popular and much-needed avenue of pursuit. By the late 1970s and 1980s, interest in this topic had increased dramatically, particularly within South Carolina and Georgia, incorporating both rural and urban archaeological sites (Drucker and Anthony 1979; Ferguson 1980; Singleton 1980; Wheaton et al. 1983; Zierden and Calhoun 1983; Zierden et al. 1986). The first intensive archaeological investigation of an African American slave site in a rural South Carolina context was the salvage of the Spiers Landing site (Drucker and Anthony 1979). Other major South Carolina investigations providing data on African American life-style and settlement pattern include work at Limerick and Hampton plantations (Lees 1980; Lewis and Haskell 1980), Yaughan and Curriboo plantations (Wheaton et al. 1983; Wheaton this volume), Campfield plantation (Zierden and Calhoun 1983); Lesesne and Fairbanks plantations (Zierden et al. 1986); and Broom Hall plantation (Trinkley et al. 1995), among others.

Singleton (1999:1) states that "the archaeological study of African-American life has become a well established research interest within American historical archaeology." While African American cultural patterns during the early historic period can be elusive, significant groundwork regarding material culture has been provided by Ferguson (1980), who suggested that much of what had been traditionally called "Colono-Indian" ware (Noel Hume 1962), a low-fired earthenware thought to have been produced by historic period Native Americans for sale to European Americans, was likely produced and used by African Americans during the colonial and early antebellum periods. This view reflected the growing recognition of certain formal, decorative, and manufacturing characteristics of low-fired, unglazed earthenware from the South Carolina Lowcountry thought to have been somewhat atypical of the market wares produced by Native Americans during this period. Ferguson (1980) proposed the term *Colonoware* to generically encompass these wares, a broad classification analogous to the term *British ceramics*. Thus, both African American and Native American earthenware of the early historic period are meant to fall under the umbrella of colonoware, although several researchers have used the term in reference only to ceramics believed to have been manufactured and used by African Americans. This practice likely reflected early simplistic perspectives by some who, caught up in the excitement of a new avenue of research, consciously or unconsciously viewed cultural interaction on colonial and early antebellum plantations as essentially "black and white." Cooper and Steen (1998:5) note that in the zeal for "empowering African-Americans, Native Americans were disenfranchised."

In South Carolina, early support for Ferguson's hypothesis was provided by archaeological investigations of the slave site at Spiers Landing (Anthony 1979; Drucker and Anthony 1979) and at Yaughan and Curriboo plantations (Wheaton et al. 1983). Colonowares at these sites comprise more than half of the total ceramic assemblages recovered. Additionally, the Yaughan and Curriboo investigations revealed colonoware sherds with spalling marks, produced during firing, along with possible examples of unfired colonoware sherds (Wheaton et al. 1983). Since these studies, other plantation sites, such as Lesesne, have also yielded colonowares with spalling marks (Anthony 1986).

Ferguson's (1985) early work on the distribution of colonoware as it relates to social structure and foodways was oriented toward a delineation of cultural differences between high and lower socioeconomic status in colonial South Carolina populations, and to illustrating how aspects of African American slave material culture functioned as "resistance" to a dominant planter society. More recently, Ferguson has studied colonowares (bowl forms) marked with an X on their exterior or interior bases (Ferguson 1992). He suggests that the marks are associated with Central African-rooted belief systems and ritual (Ferguson 1992, 1999). Other investigations have recovered X marks on gaming pieces such as colonoware marbles (Zierden et al. 1999) and pewter spoon bowls (Anthony 1995). While these marks may ultimately be linked to African belief systems, DeCorse (1999) believes that in New World contexts they likely retained different cultural meaning than they had in Africa because of the existence of different social systems.

Colonoware research in South Carolina has traditionally focused on (1) spatial and temporal distribution; (2) variation, including ceramic vessel and non-vessel items; (3) changes in function; and (4) the ethnic affiliation of the producers and users of colonoware.

Early studies of colonoware were primarily based on comparison between colonoware vessel forms and West African forms; these results inferred the possibility of similar foodways between enslaved Africans and their West African ancestors and contemporaries during the eighteenth century (Ferguson 1985). Along similar lines, several researchers have noted similarities between vessel forms from British colonial plantations in the West Indies and the southeastern United States (Crane 1993; Ebanks 1974; Gartley 1979; Henry 1980; Mathewson 1973; Wheaton et al. 1983). Numerically, in South Carolina the two most common colonoware vessel forms are simple unrestricted hemispherical bowls and both large and small globular jars with everted rims. Several researchers have noted that some vessels clearly reflect a blend of Native American, African American, and European traditions (Anthony 1986; Cooper and Steen 1998; Ferguson 1992; Wheaton et al. 1983). Containers that readily evidence this mix include foot-ringed bowls, various multipodal vessels, vessels with strap and loop handles, chamber pots, teapots, pitchers, Dutch oven–like vessels, shallow pans with crenellated (pie crust) rims, and various bottles and cups (Figure 4.1). Late nineteenth- and early twentieth-century collections of Pamunkey and Catawba aboriginal pottery evidence some of these forms, such as pipkin-like vessels, cups, shallow pans, and straight-sided flat-bottomed bowls (Fewkes 1944; Harrington 1908; Holmes 1903). Several colonoware vessels from both rural and urban contexts exhibit painted surfaces depicting floral or geometric motifs normally in red or black pigments. Interestingly, nineteenth-century documents discuss the pigmentation of "Catawba" vessels (Fewkes 1944; Gregorie 1925; Simms 1841). Several colors were reportedly used, including green, red, blue, and yellow (Simms 1841). Moreover, non-container colonoware items recovered archaeologically, such as pipe fragments, gaming pieces (marbles), a doll leg, lids, and spindle whorls also likely reflect the blending of different cultural traditions (Anthony 1986; Garrow and Wheaton 1989). Scholars think that continued progress on determining the origins and cultural affiliation of colonoware and its manufacture will require sustained, intercontinental effort of archaeological and ethnological research, minimally involving West Africa, the West Indies, and the Americas, focusing on both African American and historic Native American sites. Both Posnansky (1999) and DeCorse (1999) have recently expressed the need for those working in African American archaeology to expand and intensify their familiarity with West African cultural systems. This appears to be a necessary step for accomplishing goals such as the assignment of cultural affiliation and for helping to realize the larger objectives of delineating and understanding some of the syncretic processes operative in colonial America.

Since the late 1970s, colonoware investigation in Lowcountry South Carolina has been carried out at varying scales of analysis. Some researchers have studied collections of essentially "whole" vessels and have attempted interregional comparative studies in order to glean behavioral data regarding lower socioeconomic groups, while others, principally using data recovered from Cultural Resource Management (CRM) investigations, have delved into intraregional analyses of these wares (e.g., Anthony 1979, 1986; Crane 1993; Espenshade 1996; Ferguson 1992; Huddleston 1998; Trinkley et al. 1995; Wheaton et al. 1983). Those who have studied colonoware intraregionally have noticed for some time considerable morphological variability in Lowcountry colonowares.

Cooper and Steen (1998), in advocating the primacy of intraregional

Figure 4.1. Colonoware and creamware bowls with foot rings (courtesy The Charleston Museum and South Carolina Department of Archives and History).

colonoware research, have cogently presented pitfalls associated with excessively broad-scaled studies. This stance recognizes colonoware variability and diversity and should be applied when investigating all forms of material culture encountered from plantation contexts (Anthony 1989). Cooper and Steen (1998:1) warn that many of the "macro scale" or interregional studies have "removed Colonoware from its context of manufacture and use." In other words, empirical data gleaned from large-scale studies of colonoware have been used to investigate local assemblages, an exercise that often does not appreciate notable intraregional variability. A method such as this, decontextualizing colonoware, will obscure sought-after cultural meaning available primarily through the study of more localized operative cultural processes reflected in this low-fired earthenware.

In South Carolina much of the investigation of colonoware has focused on integrating its functional and expressive social elements with socioeconomic status and spatial distribution within rural contexts (Drucker and Anthony 1979; Ferguson 1985, 1992; Wheaton et al. 1983). Several of these investigations have been concerned with a search for ethnicity, an effort to correlate particular named working categories of colonoware with particular socioeconomic groups. Often the initial impetus for these lines of inquiry was simply the need to determine basic site function at many undocumented historic sites.

Colonoware variation from site to site as well as within the confines of a single site can be pronounced, and challenging to study. As noted by several researchers, descriptive analyses have demonstrated that this variability can be readily observed morphologically in surface treatment, vessel form, method of manufacture, and paste characteristics (Anthony 1979, 1986; Trinkley et al. 1995; Wheaton et al. 1983). Colonoware pastes and tempers particularly vary considerably in these spatial constructs. To facilitate the study of South Carolina colonoware, while recognizing variation, several type-variety descriptions have been offered (Anthony 1986; Ferguson 1985, 1989; Garrow and Wheaton 1989; Wheaton et al. 1983). Information derived from descriptive analysis, producing, for example, constructs such as ceramic classifications, continues to furnish baseline data useful for formulating hypotheses regarding models of colonial period lifeways; a case in point is provided by the recent archaeological study of Stobo plantation (Zierden et al. 1999; Zierden this volume).

Colonoware at Stobo Plantation

The archaeological investigation of James Stobo's plantation was part of an extensive multiphased project centering on an archaeological and historical study of the 1690s town of Willtown, located on the South Edisto River, about thirty miles south of Charleston, South Carolina (Zierden et al. 1999; Zierden this volume). Stobo plantation (38CH1659), located approximately a mile east of Willtown proper, is situated atop a well-drained knoll overlooking abandoned inland rice fields (Figure 4.2). This exceptionally well-preserved plantation site was contemporaneous with Willtown, demonstrating historic period occupation from the early eighteenth to the early nineteenth century. Historical and archaeological evidence indicates that Stobo plantation was most intensively used during the middle eighteenth century (Zierden et al. 1999). Cultural materials from the site were recovered through systematic shovel testing followed by extensive test unit and block excavations (Zierden et al. 1999). The primary block excavation revealed a relatively large (40 by 40 feet) multiroomed dwelling surrounding a central courtyard (Zierden et al. 1999). Dating of the site's proveniences was accomplished by standard concepts of stratigraphic point of initiation in combination with determination of a given deposit's Terminus Post Quem (TPQ) (Zierden et al. 1999). Because the site was relatively intact, dating of the strata was fairly straightforward, particularly for deeper deposits associated with the site's main residence. Several building, abandonment, and demolition episodes are represented by the stratigraphic and artifact record of this structure. Because of the depth and stratigraphic integrity of the archaeological deposits within the main house complex, proveniences encountered offered some of the best temporal controls at the

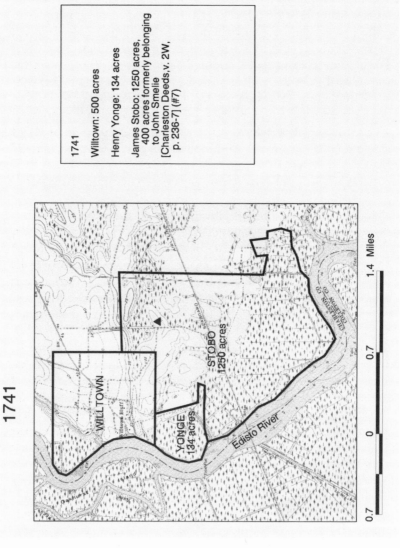

1741

Willtown: 500 acres

Henry Yonge: 134 acres

James Stobo: 1250 acres,
400 acres formerly belonging
to John Smelie
[Charleston Deeds, v. 2W,
p. 236-7] (#7)

1741

WILLTOWN

YONGE
134 acres

STOBO
1250 acres

Edisto River

0.7   0   0.7   1.4 Miles

Figure 4.2. Location of Stobo plantation in Charleston County, South Carolina (illustration by Suzanne Linder and Marta Thacker, courtesy The Charleston Museum and South Carolina Department of Arsite. For artifact analysis, these proveniences were grouped into three sets that spanned a period from before to after James Stobo's ownership.

One of the most common artifacts recovered from Stobo plantation was colonoware, which was recovered from both within and outside of the main residential structural complex. Colonoware from the site was classified according to currently published varieties: River Burnished, Yaughan, and Lesesne Lustered, as well as a fourth unnamed grouping, likely associated with historic period Native Americans (Anthony 1986; Ferguson 1989; Garrow 1985; Garrow and Wheaton 1989; Wheaton et al. 1983; Wheaton and Garrow 1985). This fourth category may help explain the notable physical variability within many South Carolina Lowcountry colonoware assemblages. An additional classification, Lesesne Smoothed, initially used during the study of Lesesne and Fairbanks plantations (Anthony 1986; Zierden et al. 1986), appears not to be useful, based on subsequent observations. Colonoware previously classified as Lesesne Smoothed should be categorized as Yaughan colonoware.

River Burnished is a well-fired, well-burnished colonoware, usually with a micaceous paste. Characterized by thin vessel walls, three to seven millimeters thick (average thickness 5 millimeters), River Burnished dates from the late eighteenth century to the early nineteenth century (Ferguson 1985, 1989). Although generally sharing some of the morphological attributes of other varieties of colonoware, this variety is most easily distinguished by its relatively hard, well-fired, nonlaminar paste, often micaceous with fine sand, and relatively thin vessel walls. Some vessels exhibit painted designs most frequently in black or a luminescent red. Designs observed include dots, lines, and floral motifs. Vessel shapes include straight-sided, flat-bottomed, unrestricted bowls, and relatively straight/vertical necked jars (Anthony 1986; Ferguson 1985). Jar forms may be characterized by lug or strap handles attached via plugs that were inserted into holes in vessel walls and smoothed on the inside (Ferguson 1985, 1989; Trinkley et al. 1995). Several River Burnished vessels have been observed whose vessel forms mimic those of European-made vessels. Additionally, some of the vessels appear to have an intentionally reduced (fired in an oxygen-poor atmosphere) black finish (Ferguson 1985). No River Burnished colonoware was observed at Stobo plantation, possibly indicating that this variety was primarily a nineteenth-century phenomenon. Several researchers attribute their manufacture to Native American populations collectively known as the Catawba (Baker 1972; Wheaton et al. 1983). This amalgam of populations, whose original members may have been descendants of the chiefdom of Cofitacheque, underwent substantial cultural change during the colonial period (Ferguson 1989). John Lawson, during his travels in the Catawba-Wateree Valley in 1701, observed several Native American towns, the northernmost of which was "Kadapau" or Catawba (Ferguson 1989;

Lefler 1967). Apparently, this name eventually was used to refer to all of the Native Americans in the valley. As other displaced aboriginal groups, such as the Congarees, Santees, Saponis, Cussoes, Yamasees, Enos, Chowans, and Nachees, aggregated with the core Catawba-Wateree Valley population, they became the Catawba Nation in the eyes of the British colonists (Baker 1975; Ferguson 1989; Merrell 1984). Furthermore, Ferguson (1989:186) states that "some blacks lived within the Catawba Nation" and that "the Catawba interacted with slaves on the plantations in the Lowcountry." Clearly, during the colonial period, Catawba society was dynamic and emerged from a rather complex set of cultural interactions and encounters.

Yaughan ceramics are found most frequently in association with African American slave villages and are thought by many to have been made and used by enslaved African Americans. Vessel forms dominating Yaughan assemblages include convex-sided, rounded to slightly flat-bottomed bowls and both large and small globular jars with everted rims and gently rounded bottoms. Some jars are characterized by strap or lug handles, which do not appear to have been attached by plug insertion. Bowls generally far outnumber jars in archaeologically recovered collections. Other Yaughan vessel forms include chamber pots, bottles, cups, plates, and lidded vessels, possibly serving a function similar to a Dutch oven. Yaughan smoking pipe fragments and gaming pieces, such as marbles, have also been recovered from eighteenth- and early nineteenth-century contexts. Unlike River Burnished and to a degree Lesesne Lustered, Yaughan pottery generally exhibits a readily observable low-fired laminar paste. The laminar paste and the lack of coil breaks indicate that most Yaughan vessels were manufactured by hand modeling rather than coiling (Anthony 1979; Wheaton et al. 1983). Yaughan colonoware, characterized by a medium-coarse paste with fine (1/8 to 1/4 millimeter) to medium (1/4 to 1/2 millimeter) subrounded to sub-angular sand, is generally thicker walled than the other colonoware varieties. Vessel wall thickness is often not uniform, unlike other colonoware varieties. Yaughan vessel surfaces are often crudely smoothed, although burnished or rubbed surfaces do occur. Other forms of surface treatment include punctation, incision, and possibly, in a minority of specimens, cord marking and rouletting. At times characterized by firing clouds, Yaughan ceramics are normally incompletely reduced or oxidized. Yaughan pottery seems to have been produced from at least the early eighteenth century into the mid-nineteenth century in South Carolina, although the frequency of these ceramics appears to decrease dramatically after the first decade of the nineteenth century.

Lesesne Lustered colonoware lies morphologically between River Burnished and Yaughan varieties of colonoware (Anthony 1986). It apparently was produced from the early eighteenth century into the early nineteenth

Table 4.1. Colonware from Stobo Plantation

Classification	No.
Yaughan	974
Lesesne Lustered	570
Historic aboriginal	579
Residuals	693
TOTAL	2,816

century in South Carolina. Examples of this pottery have been recovered from sealed contexts at Stono plantation, in Charleston County, dating to no later than 1725 to 1730 (Anthony 1995). The producers of this pottery are presently unknown; however, Lesesne Lustered is more frequently found than other varieties in association with planter occupations and may represent a locally manufactured market ware (Anthony 1986, 1995). This variety of colonoware and possibly others were likely used routinely in planter households (Anthony 1986; Zierden et al. 1986). Like other varieties of colonoware, most Lesesne Lustered vessels are bowls, both straight and convex sided with slightly rounded to almost flat bottoms. Unlike Yaughan bowls, a relatively high proportion of these examples are large with vessel orifices up to fourteen inches in diameter. Frequently these bowls are characterized by a distinctive bulbous lip. Other Lesesne Lustered forms include both necked and neckless jars, bottles, cups, and multipodal vessels reminiscent of some early European vessel forms (Anthony 1986). Vessel lid fragments have been recovered as well as vessels with loop and strap handles. Lesesne Lustered ceramics are characterized by burnished or rubbed surfaces that are often not as completely or evenly rubbed as River Burnished vessels, although they often retain a smooth, almost waxy feel. Usually exhibiting a fine to medium paste, and, at times, virtually temperless, Lesesne Lustered pottery is not as well-fired as River Burnished colonoware and is not characterized by a pronounced laminar paste like Yaughan ceramics. Additionally, Lesesne Lustered pottery is characterized by vessel walls that are generally thicker than most River Burnished vessels, although the wall thickness is more uniform than frequently observed on Yaughan colonoware. Lesesne Lustered sherds can be incompletely oxidized or incompletely reduced, and sometimes oxidized.

The fourth category of colonoware (n = 579) from Stobo plantation includes both rim and body sherds (Table 4.1). The pottery from this grouping is believed to have been produced by historic period aboriginals and/or produced and used by those interacting or having interacted with historic Native American populations. Ninety-seven sherds from this grouping are characterized by complicated stamped surface decorations, both curvi-

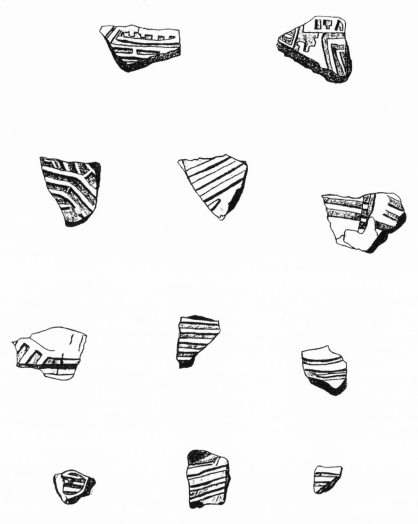

Figure 4.3. Examples of complicated stamped motifs from Stobo plantation (drawing by Robbie Ratcliff).

linear and rectilinear (Figure 4.3). Stamped motifs are generally large and bold and poorly applied. Several motifs are reminiscent of those present within the Altamaha and Ashley series (Chester DePratter, personal communication 1998; William Green, personal communication 1998; Green et al. this volume). These ceramics are relatively thin walled with an average thickness of 5.7 millimeters. Several body sherds exhibit soot on exterior surfaces. Interior vessel surfaces are extremely well smoothed and, at times, burnished.

Other than complicated stamped surfaces, the most striking physical characteristic of the vast majority of these ceramics is their paste, which is easily discernible from that of other colonoware varieties on site. The paste is nonlaminar and, at times, friable, and can appear somewhat contorted. Most examples are incompletely oxidized/reduced and are generally less well-fired than Lesesne Lustered or River Burnished colonoware. In notable contrast to other colonoware varieties, their paste contains substantial quantities of sub-angular to angular coarse sand (1/2 to 1.0 millimeter); however, five complicated stamped sherds exhibit pastes indistinguishable from the Lesesne Lustered pottery found on site. Ceramics very similar to these have been observed at Stono and Lesesne plantations a few miles south and north, respectively, of Charleston. On Stono plantation (James Island, South Carolina) these ceramics have been recovered from sealed contexts dating no later than 1730 (Anthony 1995).

The majority of this category of ceramics (n = 482) consists of sherds lacking complicated stamped decoration but characterized by the distinctive paste described above. These ceramics consist of both bowl and jar forms, whose vessel walls average 7.0 and 6.6 millimeters in thickness, respectively. Bowls occur more frequently than jars. Vessel orifice diameters average 11.5 inches. The majority (82 percent) of the bowls in this assemblage are straight sided, like most Lesesne Lustered and River Burnished bowls and examples of Catawba and Pamunkey pottery, while the remaining specimens are convex sided, like most Yaughan variety bowls. All jar forms exhibit everted rims. Additionally, most vessel lip forms are round and bulbous; a few are flat. A popular lip form characterizing these ceramics from Stobo plantation appears to be a readily observable bulbous lip similar to those observed on Lesesne Lustered bowls (Figures 4.4 and 4.5).

The study of the colonoware from Stobo plantation, according to the above-enumerated classifications, produced an assemblage that exhibits less morphological variation and diversity internally than seen at several other Lowcountry sites (Anthony 1986; Huddleston 1998; Trinkley et al. 1995). More specifically, colonoware from Stobo plantation exhibits less physical variation within a defined variety. These observations are particularly evident in terms of paste characteristics and vessel shape, and, secondarily, surface treatment. As mentioned above, one of the most variable morphological aspects of Lowcountry colonoware is paste (Anthony 1986; Trinkley et al. 1995). Examination of the colonoware from Stobo plantation suggests that much of the perceived paste/temper variability within some Lowcountry colonoware assemblages may be explained by the presence of previously unrecognized historic aboriginal inspired or made pottery.

Three sets of proveniences at Stobo plantation, located inside of the main house complex, provided the best temporal controls (Zierden et al. 1999). These sets consist of (1) proveniences predating James Stobo's own-

Figure 4.4. Colonoware bowls (depicted 50 percent of actual size). *Above,* Lesesne Lustered bowl with bulbous lip. *Below,* Historic period aboriginal bowl with bulbous lip (courtesy The Charleston Museum and South Carolina Department of Archives and History).

ership (ca. 1710–1740), (2) proveniences dating to Stobo's occupation, but prior to demolition (ca. 1741–1770), and (3) proveniences (TPQ ca. 1780) postdating Stobo's occupation associated with the demolition of the Stobo house and subsequent occupation (see Zierden this volume) (Table 4.2).

Yaughan, Lesesne Lustered, and historic aboriginal ceramics were recovered from all three sets of proveniences. Within the earliest set, frequencies of all colonoware groupings are about the same. Proveniences dating to about 1741 to 1770 exhibit substantially higher frequencies of Lesesne Lustered ceramics, almost double the number of Yaughan ceramics. In proveniences containing pearlware, Yaughan ceramics are twice as prevalent as both Lesesne Lustered and historic aboriginal pottery. These findings suggest that Yaughan ceramic popularity increased and may indicate a degree of aboriginal cultural loss through time.

Deagan (1999:5) states that "it was *only* in domestic settings that the actuality of lived and learned experiences was played out for *all* members of Atlantic World Societies." Several researchers have noted that over twenty-five percent of the early South Carolina slave population was Native American and that by about 1730 most Native Americans of the Lowcountry were no longer present in significant numbers (Cooper and Steen

Figure 4.5. Colonoware rimsherd profiles. *Above, left to right:* Lesesne Lustered bowl with bulbous lip; Lesesne Lustered bowl with bulbous lip; aboriginal bowl with bulbous lip; aboriginal bowl with bulbous lip. *Below, left to right,* Yaughan bowl with flattened lip; Yaughan bowl with flattened lip; Yaughan bowl with rounded/semibeveled lip (drawing by Robbie Ratcliff).

Table 4.2. Stobo House Complex Artifact Assemblage

	1710–1740	1741–1770	post–1779
CERAMICS			
Porcelain, overglaze	60	74	120
Porcelain, blue on white	3	321	915
Porcelain, burned	1	15	18
Brown salt-glazed stoneware	17	28	70
Bellarmine	—	—	1
Grey salt-glazed stoneware	2	7	32
Westerwald stoneware	2	19	83
Slip-dipped stoneware	—	—	14
White salt-glazed stoneware	2	42	199
Scratch blue stoneware	—	—	3
Nottingham stoneware	4	14	52
Nottingham earthenware	6	—	10
Langerwehe	—	—	22
"Blumenkubel"	—	14	18
Elers ware	—	—	8
Black basalte	—	—	2
Glazed red stoneware	—	1	—
Whieldon ware	3	17	41
Creamware	—	240	1,062
Pearlware, undecorated	—	26	441
Pearlware, hand painted	—	9	97
Pearlware, polychrome	—	3	12
Pearlware, brown transfer print	—	—	2
Pearlware, other transfer print	—	19	189
Pearlware, shell edged	—	9	133
Pearlware, annular	—	2	86
Agate ware	—	—	4
Astbury ware	—	3	4
Jackfield ware	1	4	66
Delft, undecorated	18	50	308
Delft, blue on white	8	20	59
Delft, polychrome	5	8	13
North Devon ware	16	1	24
Slipware, combed & trailed	25	64	295
Slipware, sgraffitto	—	—	1
Slipware, American	—	—	11
Buckley ware	—	1	3
Mid-Atlantic ware	—	—	1
Mottled ware	2	4	37
Slip-coated ware	—	1	2
Southern Euro. ware	—	2	14
Black lead-glazed ware	2	3	31

Table 4.2. *Continued*

	1710–1740	1741–1770	post–1779
Misc. lead-glazed earthen ware	5	8	41
Complicated stamped ware	10	6	10
Colonowares	78	214	305
OTHER KITCHEN			
Olive green bottle glass	130	1,071	3,349
Olive green wine bottle	2	14	17
Olive green case bottle	1	6	7
Clear bottle glass	8	251	659
Aqua container glass	3	42	146
Pharmaceutical glass	8	19	66
Table glass	22	166	622
Goblet	—	5	10
Tumbler	—	1	21
Other	1	1	6
Kettle fragment	—	3	7
Cutlery	—	2	1
ARCHITECTURE			
Window glass	144	1,051	5,425
Nail, wrought	182	517	5,115
Nail, cut	—	37	1,437
Unidentified nail	50	262	645
Nail fragment	38	133	949
Building hardware	—	1	10
Lock	—	—	6
Hinge	1	—	—
Key	—	1	5
Beam bolt	4	2	—
Spike, etc.	—	2	13
Dressed marble fragment	—	2	13
ARMS			
Lead shot	—	7	12
Sprue	—	—	2
Musket ball	1	1	3
Gunflint	1	5	20
Gun hardware	—	1	1
Sword	1	—	—
Pike	1	—	—
CLOTHING			
Pewter button	2	1	1
Copper alloy button	—	—	20
Bone button	—	—	7
Hook & eye	1	—	3

Table 4.2. *Continued*

	1710–1740	1741–1770	post–1779
Lacing tip	—	—	3
Bead	—	4	1
Pin	1	4	1
Scissors	—	1	4
Thimble	1	—	2
Copper-alloy buckle	1	—	5
Iron buckle	—	3	4
PERSONAL			
Parasol rib	—	2	2
Slate pencil/slate	—	2	3
Fan fragment	—	3	3
Ruler	—	—	1
Jewelry	—	1	5
Pocket knife	—	1	3
Cane tip	1	—	—
Bone comb	—	1	—
Crystal/religious	—	1	—
Pin/personal case	—	1	—
Watch key	—	—	1
Toothbrush	—	—	1
FURNITURE			
Upholstery tack	1	7	22
Curtain ring	2	1	6
Drawer pull	—	3	14
Lock	—	4	1
Fireplace finial	—	2	2
Misc. hardware	—	4	15
Leather book clasp	—	1	—
Wall sconce	—	1	—
PIPES			
Tobacco pipe fragments	41	94	401
ACTIVITIES			
Marble/toy	1	2	8
Iron wedge	—	—	2
Scale weight	—	—	2
Net weight	—	—	1
Equestrian item	1	7	3
Hoe	2	1	2
Tool	1	2	12
Barrel strap fragment	30	217	93
TOTAL	954	5,223	24,080

1998; Hudson 1971; Menard 1995). Perhaps this perceived absence is valid in terms of political viability; however, it is possible that during the eighteenth century there were still sufficient numbers of Native Americans residing on isolated farmsteads, possibly in extended family groups, or on plantations to help fuel dynamic syncretic processes. Researchers in the Chesapeake area of Virginia have observed that early documents indicate the disappearance of Native Americans in that area as well; however, the researchers think that this early documentation was essentially propaganda that helped relieve the tension felt by potential immigrants regarding aboriginal uprisings (Mouer et al. 1999). They stress the need for critical interpretation of primary documentation that discusses numbers of Native Americans present in the Mid-Atlantic area during the early settlement period.

Conclusions

At Stobo plantation, the physical similarities between historic aboriginal ceramics and other colonoware varieties is intriguing. These ceramics offer tangible evidence of historic Native American occupation and/or notable interaction between aborigines and other plantation workers (see Joseph this volume). Deagan (1999) notes that African American households incorporated Native American and European material elements. The physical characteristics of Stobo plantation colonoware support Deagan's contention by strongly suggesting notable interaction between enslaved African Americans and historic period Native Americans.

Stobo plantation and other similar sites offer invaluable opportunities to explore syncretism on the Carolina frontier. Colonoware, a product of culture contact among people of widely divergent cultural backgrounds, tangibly reflects the emergence of new cultural systems: new systems forged as these populations adapted to unfamiliar physical and social settings. Besides documenting the actual location of various interactions, colonoware will be useful as a means to monitor and measure the dates, rates, and dynamic nature of culture change and formation in the colonial South. Further intraregional study of colonoware assemblages will provide an avenue to reconstruct and understand some of the processes of culture change experienced by pioneering African American, Native American, and European American populations in contact during the American colonial and early antebellum periods.

Acknowledgments

I would like to express my gratitude to Mr. Hugh C. Lane, Sr., whose willingness and vision were responsible for the Willtown project. His appreciation of the past and its relevance to the present and future is commendable. Also, I am grateful to Martha Zierden and Joe Joseph for asking me to contribute to this volume and for their helpful comments and patience concerning this chapter. Last, I would like to acknowledge and thank Mr. Larry Cadigan for literally years of tireless volunteer work and camaraderie at Stono and Stobo plantations as well as for his help with numerous other Charleston Museum archaeological projects.

5

A Pattern of Living: A View of the African American Slave Experience in the Pine Forests of the Lower Cape Fear

Natalie P. Adams

The variables surrounding the lives of slaves and how slave culture developed depended heavily upon the requirements of the staple crops as well as upon the environment and the physical nature of the land. According to Ira Berlin and Philip Morgan (1996:3) the staple crops "shaped the nature of the work force, the organization of production, and the division of labor. These, in turn, rested upon the geography, the demographic balance of slave and free and black and white, the size of the slaveholding units, the character of technology, and the management techniques prevalent at different times and in different places." Not only did environment and natural resources affect slaves' working conditions, it affected their ability to carry on, without modification, traditions in food, architecture, and material culture. The totality of the slave experience in a particular area was affected by a web of variables that patterned their lives.

Naval stores—tar, pitch, and turpentine—brought a group of South Carolina settlers to the Lower Cape Fear (Figure 5.1) in the 1720s. The vast pine forests were a crop ready to be harvested and would bring enormous immediate financial returns. These planters, many of whom brought slaves with them from the rice-growing Goose Creek area in Berkeley County, near Charleston, knew that they could operate a pine plantation with little up-front capital. While it took at least thirty slaves and an overseer for the operation of a rice plantation, a pine plantation could operate with only a handful of slaves (Clifton 1973). One planter remarked that it could be "carried on with little capital, on lands too poor for cultivation and is, therefore, well suited to persons of small means" (Anonymous 1855).

Using archaeological data from different regions of North and South Carolina, this chapter illustrates how environmental and economic circumstances affected the lives of slaves. I discuss what is historically known

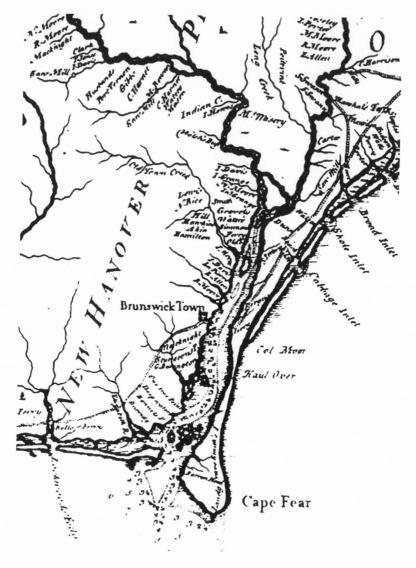

Figure 5.1. The 1733 Moseley map showing the Lower Cape Fear area (courtesy North Carolina Division of Archives and History).

about how the naval stores industry affected the slaves' work pattern and how that shaped their living conditions. Data from the Samuel Neale plantation are used to archaeologically verify these historical accounts. This information is also compared with data from elsewhere in the Carolinas to show how the environment and economy affected the slaves' material culture—specifically, how it could have prohibited them from manufacturing colonoware on a large scale and how it may have increased reliance on domestic redwares.

The Work Pattern for Naval Stores

Like the rice plantations of South Carolina, North Carolina pine plantations operated under the task labor system. Tasking allowed slaves to work intensively to complete their daily work in order to appropriate a portion of the day for themselves (Morgan 1988). This worked well since the work required that slaves spread out in all directions in the forest (Outland 1996:43–44). The task system, along with the nature of the work on pine plantations, made it impractical for planters to closely oversee the work. James Avirett (1901:70) of Onslow County noted that "the laborers, and notably the chippers, are employed in large, wooded tracts of country, out of the range of anything like close oversight and must be stimulated to their best work, as well by premiums for best crops as by so regulating their work that a portion of each week is their own to do as they please with."

The year-round scheduling of activities revolved around the needs of the crops. During the winter months when the pine sap did not run, trees could be boxed, which entailed cutting cavities into the pine trees about one foot above the base. Boxing did not require full-time attention and could be performed along with other plantation activities. Fredrick Law Olmsted noted that one slave could box seventy-five to one hundred trees a day (Olmsted 1968).

About mid-March, the sap would begin to flow into the boxes, from which it was then transferred to barrels. The flow peaked in July and August and then tapered off at the beginning of November (Outland 1996:34). In the late eighteenth century, German traveler Johann Schoepf noted that "one man can readily care for 3000 boxes, and that number is generally assigned to one negro, the negroes doing the most of this work. At the best and warmest season one negro can easily fill 15–20 barrels of turpentine a day. . . . It is reckoned that from 3000 boxes more than 100–120 barrels in the average should be obtained in a summer. For these 3000 boxes some 12–15 acres of forest should suffice, according as the trees stand close or far apart, and are strong or not" (Morrison 1911:141).

Slaves were employed as hackers (also known as chippers) once a week. This involved making cuts into the trees to encourage sap flow (Figure 5.2). Dippers were constantly busy emptying the boxes as they filled. Because of the constant care needed in hacking and dipping during the warmer months, slaves—typically males—were sent out to work the trees and lived in "workers' camps" set up in the woods (Outland 1996:46; Robinson 1997:55). According to Avirett (1901:69) it usually took no more than ten to twelve years to deplete a section of forest of sap. After that, the wood

Figure 5.2. Slaves collecting turpentine as depicted in *Frank Leslie's Illustrated Newspaper,* 1866 (courtesy North Carolina Division of Archives and History).

was cut for lumber or staves and the slaves moved on to a new area. Therefore, these camps were typically small isolated sites occupied seasonally for only a few years.

By the late eighteenth century, most trees contained the mark of the naval stores industry. Ebenezer Hazard, who traveled through the area in the late 1770s, noted that it was "very dangerous riding in No. Carolina when the Winds blow hard, for you ride all the Way through Pines, many of which have been 'boxed' to get Turpentine out & others have been so much burned by burning the Woods that a high Winds is very apt to overset them" (Johnston 1959:375–76). As late as 1858, Mary Harper Beall wrote, "You don't know the gloominess until you travel through that country. Even the pine trees look ghastly with their hearts scalped instead of their heads" (Beall 1858).

Living Conditions for Slaves in Naval Stores

Historians consider the living conditions of slaves working in these "ghastly" pine forests to have been far worse than conditions of those involved in agriculture (Outland 1996; Starobin 1970). Because they were assigned to several half-acre squares, they were fairly distant from one another and could not interact to break the monotony of their work. On many of the larger plantations, the workers' camps were so far away from the agricultural plantations that the male slaves who typically dominated the naval stores work force had no regular contact with their families or with any female companionship (Outland 1996).

In his book *Industrial Slavery in the Old South,* Robert Starobin provides many descriptions of the poor housing provided to industrial workers. For those working in naval stores and as lumbermen in the forests, an observer in 1809 described rude lean-tos "barely wide enough for five or six men to lie in, closely packed side by side—their heads to the back wall, and their feet stretched to the open front, close by a fire kept up through the night." He continued, "The roof is sloping, to shed the rain and where highest, not above four feet from the floor. . . . The [wood] shavings . . . make a bed for the laborers" (Lewis 1845:122–23). This description corresponds well with archaeological evidence from a mid-eighteenth-century workers' camp at the Neale plantation where a 15 by 13.5-foot earthfast structure was identified (Adams 1998a). The roof configuration was interpreted to be that of a shed, based on the size and depth of postholes. The sparsity of nails and the absence of window glass indicate that the structure was insubstantial, and the size of the nails suggests that they were used primarily for siding. The earthfast structure probably had pine-board siding and, perhaps, a thatched or shingled roof. In front of the structure was a hearth, and in the side yard were two storage pits (Figure 5.3).

Olmsted noted that although many pine farmers raised corn, they purchased most of their foods. Rations were brought to the workers' camps and kept at a subsistence level since food was the largest maintenance cost (Outland 1996; Starobin 1970). One advantage that pine slaves had over other slaves is that they had more freedom of movement and had more opportunities to catch wild animals and collect edible plants and herbs. Squirrels, opossums, raccoons, rabbits, and turtles supplemented their diet (Outland 1996:51). Subsistence data from the Neale plantation indicate evidence for peach and corn as the only vegetable, fruit, and grain edibles at the site. As for meats, a small amount of pork, beef, and poultry was found, which was probably the result of provisioning. The workers heavily relied on turtle and fish, which they could have easily caught within a short distance of the site, since the site is situated near the confluence of the Northwest Cape Fear River and Livingston Creek. Other wild game included opossum, squirrel, and rabbit, which could have been taken with traps or snares. The absence of deer and wild birds suggests that the occupants did not have firearms (Adams 1998a:110).

Berlin and Morgan (1993:23) note that in nonagricultural operations such as mining, provisions were in short supply. Therefore, mine owners gave slaves large blocks of time to provide for themselves in lieu of rations. One sugar planter instructed his overseer to grow more corn and added, "I am glad you have cut down the rations as pork will be $20 p bbl here be-

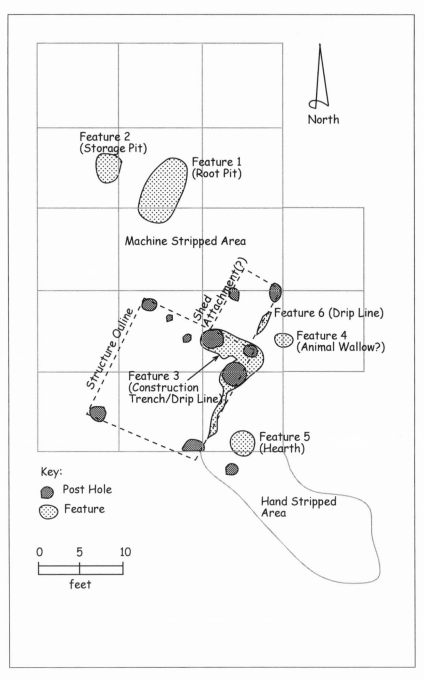

Figure 5.3. Workers' camp at 31Cb110, Samuel Neale plantation.

fore two weeks. tis now $17.12. You will do well to let them Fish" (White 1852). This would have allowed a substantial savings in slave maintenance costs (Starobin 1970:54).

Outland (1996:53) argues that because of the loneliness of the work, the poor housing and provisions, and its physical demands, work in the naval stores industry tended to be more strenuous than labor in agriculture. He (1996:54–55) states that slaves in naval stores operations tended to run away often, although it is unclear whether they ran away significantly more often than those in agriculture. One slave who ran away was found by a former neighbor of his master, and he wrote to his former neighbor that "the work and the manner of life in making turpentine he cannot stand, it is hard work and would kill him by piecemeal, and he had rather be killed at once" (quoted in Outland 1996:55).

Samuel Neale's Plantation, Demography, Colonoware, and Redware

Samuel Neale's plantation was relatively small—especially when compared to Benjamin Smith's nearby Blue Banks plantation, which comprised 3,480 acres. Neale inherited three hundred twenty acres from his father in 1735 and purchased an additional five hundred acres on the opposite side of the Northwest Cape Fear River a year later, across from his plantation. As his plantation was small, so was his work force. In the early 1770s just before his death, Neale owned only thirteen slaves. Six of his slaves were male, and as a general rule, every fifth male on a pine plantation was a cooper (Outland 1996:41). Although women and children were sometimes involved in dipping, men were solely responsible for boxing and hacking the trees (Outland 1996:43). Some authorities advised against using women. In 1846 the *Southern Cultivator* reported that "the same boxes will stand tending or chipping from eight to ten years, which labor is performed by males, both white and slave, women and children not being very serviceable" (Anonymous 1846). The seven females on Neale's plantation could have been involved in raising corn, livestock, and provisions for the plantation. Neale probably served as his own overseer.

Archaeological survey and testing on the Neale tract identified a plantation house, a possible overseer's house, several slave houses, and other occupations that were probably in use during the occupation of the workers' camp site (Lautzenheiser et al. 1995, 1997). The permanent slave settlement was located near the overseer and planter's house. These were approximately 3,600 feet away from the workers' camp site (Figure 5.4). Although this is not necessarily a prohibitive distance, workers may have been required to stay on site to monitor tar kilns or watch out for forest fires.

Of particular interest at the Neale plantation complex was the near ab-

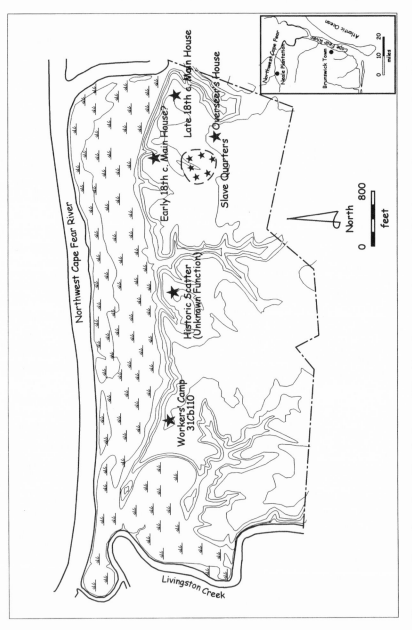

Figure 5.4. Location of pre–Revolutionary War historic occupations on the Neale tract (base map adapted from Lautzenheiser et al. 1997).

sence of slave-made colonoware and the relative abundance of redware—not only at the Neale plantation, but also farther down the river at Brunswick where the slave population was denser. This dense slave population, at one point, rivaled that of the South Carolina Lowcountry. Thomas Loftfield and Michael Stoner (1997) state that the presence of colonoware in Brunswick Town was due to an inaccessibility of cheap domestic or imported ceramics and the fact that in the Lower Cape Fear region many slaves were living on large plantations with large and dense populations of Africans and African Americans. However, they do not explain why colonoware does not occur in densities more similar to that of the Goose Creek area of South Carolina since, as they state, "during the time that Brunswick Town was occupied, the Lower Cape Fear region exhibited demographic characteristics more extreme than those typical of the South Carolina lowcountry" (Loftfield and Stoner 1997:10; see also Kay and Cary 1995:24).

It is unlikely that the area occupied by the Neale plantation ever saw the demographic extremes experienced by Brunswick Town. The plantation was located at the northern boundary of what historians such as James Clifton (1973) and Lawrence Lee (1965) have referred to as the "Lower Cape Fear Region." The plantation is situated in Columbus County, just south of the Bladen County line at the confluence of Livingston Creek and the Northwest Cape Fear River. In 1790 only four out of every ten inhabitants of Bladen County were African American slaves. These slaves may have lived among a great many white inhabitants, but there may have been little interaction. For instance, in nearby Onslow County, James Avirett hired white families to put out forest fires and feed his livestock "by placing here and there all over the orchards double log cabins for the families of some twenty or more white men" (Avirett 1901:70). Avirett (1901:71) adds, "They form a distinct element in the organism of this large landed estate. They never mingle with the more thrifty white people, while the negroes on the estate look down upon them, calling them, most disdainfully, 'poor white trash.'"

By the mid-eighteenth century, slaves constituted about half of the population in the Cape Fear Region, with the vast majority residing on large plantations along the Lower Cape Fear (Kay and Cary 1995). On the average, however, most plantations contained relatively few slaves—particularly farther up the Cape Fear and in surrounding areas. In Brunswick County only twenty-six households owned more than ten taxable slaves (Ekirch 1981). During a visit to Brunswick, New Bern, and surrounding areas, Josiah Quincy noted that the number of slaves was much less than in South Carolina. He stated that "their staple commodity is not so valuable, not being in so great a demand as the rice, indigo, etc. of the South. . . . You see husbandmen, yeomen, and white laborers scattered through the county, instead of herds of negroes and slaves" (State of North Carolina 1886–1890). In nearby Onslow County, where the naval stores industry also predominated, only one planter in five owned slaves. Those having slaves only owned an average of eleven (Cecelski 1997:10).

Even with these demographic differences between Brunswick Town and the Neale plantation, colonoware only accounts for no more than zero to ten percent of the ceramic collections at Brunswick Town (Gray 1989:appendix B; South 1959:85, 1977:132–37) and zero to two percent on the Neale tract (Adams 1998a; Lautzenheiser et al. 1997). At plantations in Berkeley County, South Carolina, colonowares often account for over seventy percent of the ceramics (see, for instance, Trinkley et al. 1995:198–224; Wheaton et al. 1983) while in Charleston they account for fifteen to thirty percent (Joseph this volume).

If the demography between the two areas was similar during the colonial period, it seems likely that the colonoware percentages would have been similar—but they are not. Unlike prehistoric pottery-making Native Americans, colonial slaves could not travel freely across the landscape. Therefore pottery production occurred and, perhaps, predominated only if slaves had easy access to clay, so that the effort to obtain clay did not outweigh the need for the pottery. In the Goose Creek area there is an abundance of easily accessible clay, known as Spring Grove clay, accessible at about one foot below ground surface (Robinson et al. 1961). Many plantation slave sites in this area have numerous clay extraction pits, indicating that slaves often did not even have to leave their settlements to find suitable potting clay (see Adams 1995; Wheaton et al. 1983). Berkeley and Georgetown counties have the highest proportion of colonowares in coastal South Carolina and also the highest percentages of their upland soils underlain by clay (Long 1980; Stuckey 1982) (Table 5.1).

Portions of Charleston County are also underlain by clay (Miller 1971), concentrated in the Wando River region where the brick-making industry flourished and also near Ravenel, southwest of Charleston. Colonoware percentages are known to be high in the Wando area (see, for example, Wayne and Dickinson 1990). Table 5.1 exhibits a quantifiable positive correlation between the presence of clay subsoils and the presence of colonoware. The relationship between colonoware and redware is negative, although rather weakly.

Places such as the Beaufort County, South Carolina, Sea Islands that have little clay also tend to have little colonoware. So far, mainland sites in Beaufort County, South Carolina, where clay sources are more common have shown to contain moderate amounts of colonoware (see, for example, Kennedy et al. 1994). Also, one site on Spring Island in Beaufort County produced respectable amounts of colonoware (Eubanks et al. 1994). This is possibly because of several patches of soils that are shallowly underlain by clay on the island. Also, this site is immediately adjacent to Callawassie Island, which has numerous patches of clay (Stuck 1980), although it is unknown how much of this is suitable for potting.

Unfortunately, there is far less data on early low-status historic sites in North Carolina. To date, the work at Neale plantation accounts for all the work on low-status sites in the lower portion of the Cape Fear. The data from Brunswick Town are not directly comparable since it is an urban context, and only one of the loci (Nath Moore's front) has been analyzed in any detail (Gray 1989). Other archaeological work has been undertaken in areas of the state dominated by other staple crops, and many of these are from planter contexts.

On the basis of the artifacts from the Neale plantation and Brunswick Town, as well as geological data, it appears that many slaves in the Lower Cape Fear region had little opportunity to make colonoware. Sources of potting clay were probably small exposures along creek and river banks. These would have had to have been sought for and probably did not occur in areas convenient for slaves to have frequently accessed.

It is possible that slaves or their owners were having to make up for this inability to make colonoware by purchasing Pennsylvania redwares from ships coming into the port cities of Brunswick and, later, Wilmington. They also would have had access to North Carolina Piedmont redwares from places such as Salem. These wares would have been sold in Cross Creek near Fayetteville and shipped down the Cape Fear for sale in the Brunswick area (Bivins 1972). An examination of percentages of redwares from a few South Carolina sites and from sites in the Lower Cape Fear region suggests this is possible. Percentages in South Carolina range from 0 to 3.10 percent at sites yielding more than seventy percent colonoware. At sites with fewer colonowares, the redware percentages range from 0.4 to 13.7 percent. Some redwares in these collections are similar to types that could have been purchased from cargos coming from Pennsylvania and piedmont North Carolina. In the Lower Cape Fear, the percentages range from 6.5 to 20 percent, with a large number consisting of Pennsylvania redwares and North Carolina Piedmont wares (Adams 1998a; Lautzenheiser et al. 1997).

Clearly, the percentage of redwares in ceramic assemblages from the Lower Cape Fear illustrates that they could not make up for the inability to produce colonowares on a large scale. This may suggest a material poverty of kitchenware items for slaves working in the Lower Cape Fear region, which, in some instances, is reflected in the percentage of kitchen-related artifacts (see Table 5.1).

Table 5.1. Percentages of colonowares, redwares, kitchen, and architecture-related artifacts from several sites in North and South Carolina

County, State	Site, Area	Clay Subsoil	Colono-wares	Red-wares*	Kitchen	Archi-tecture	Reference
Berkeley, SC	Average of those listed below	51.0%	84.9%	1.9%	79.8%	14.5%	
Berkeley, SC	Broom Hall 38Bk985, Goose Cr.		76.6%	0.0%	78.3%	15.2%	Trinkley et al. 1995
Berkeley, SC	Lesesne Slave Settlement, Wando		62.0%	0.0%	74.9%	17.6%	Zierden et al. 1986
Berkeley, SC	Early Yaughan, Santee		90.0%	2.5%	84.2%	11.8%	Wheaton et al. 1983
Berkeley, SC	Curriboo, Santee		88.0%	3.1%	76.9%	16.6%	Wheaton et al. 1983
Georgetown, SC	Average of those listed below	51.0%	75.2%	1.3%	77.9%	15.4%	
Georgetown, SC	38Ge291 Overseer, Waccamaw		81.2%	unknown	84.4%	9.3%	Trinkley 1993b
Georgetown, SC	38Ge291 Slave, Waccamaw		78.5%	unknown	75.4%	18.1%	Trinkley 1993b
Georgetown, SC	True Blue Strata 4, Waccamaw		54.5%	2.5%	71.7%	21.7%	Poplin 1989
Georgetown, SC	38Ge340 Slave, Waccamaw		83.1%	unknown	84.7%	11.4%	Trinkley 1993b
Georgetown, SC	38Ge377, Waccamaw R.		78.9%	0.0%	73.2%	16.2%	Adams 1993
Beaufort, SC	Average of those listed below	19.0%	31.8%	1.1%	75.5%	18.3%	
Beaufort, SC	38CH1214, Sea Islands		1.4%	0.0%	84.6%	9.5%	Trinkley 1991
Beaufort, SC	Bonny Shore, Sea Islands		43.6%	0.9%	63.1%	32.0%	Eubanks et al. 1994
Beaufort, SC	Cotton Hope Locus 5, Sea Islands		18.7%	1.3%	77.7%	15.6%	Trinkley 1990
Beaufort, SC	Colleton River, Mainland		63.6%	2.0%	76.5%	16.0%	Kennedy et al. 1994
Charleston, SC	Average of those listed below	19.0%	57.9%	7.8%	75.3%	15.6%	
Charleston, SC	Lexington Slave, Wando		89.0%	0.5%	83.7%	13.6%	Wayne and Dickinson 1990
Charleston, SC	Stanyarne 38CH1107, Sea Islands		66.2%	13.7%	82.9%	6.8%	Trinkley 1995
Charleston, SC	Vanderhorst Str. 5, Sea Islands		56.1%	7.8%	57.4%	26.7%	Trinkley 1993a

Charleston, SC	Wappoo, Mainland		20.4%	9.1%	77.2%	15.4%	Gardner and Poplin 1992
Brunswick, NC	Total for this location	2.5%	2.0%	6.5%	53.4%	22.6%	
Brunswick, NC	Nath Moore's Front, Brunswick		2.0%	6.5%	53.4%	22.6%	Gray 1989
Columbus, NC	Average of those listed below	1.0%	0.4%	13.3%	68.8%	14.5%	
Columbus, NC	31Cb110, NW Cape Fear		0.0%	20.0%	66.4%	15.5%	Adams 1998a
Columbus, NC	31Cb88, NW Cape Fear		1.2%	9.9%	65.1%	15.5%	Lautzenheiser et al. 1997
Columbus, NC	31Cb92, NW Cape Fear		0.0%	10.0%	75.0%	12.5%	Lautzenheiser et al. 1997

*Redware percentages may include domestic and imported wares since this information was not always provided in reports. Those marked as unknown have combined yellow combed and dotted slipwares (Staffordshire) with redwares in analysis.

Conclusions

The historical and archaeological data obtained from the Lower Cape Fear, including the Neale plantation site and Brunswick Town, as well as from various plantations in the South Carolina Lowcountry, provide testimony to the prominent role that the natural environment played in the lives of the slaves. It affected their yearly patterns of labor, their social relationships, and their material culture.

Of particular interest is how it affected colonoware production. The correlation between colonoware production and clay subsoil percentages in various coastal Carolina locations suggests the possibility that demographics may have had relatively little to do with the production of colonoware —that slaves may have produced it anywhere they could to supplement the kitchenwares supplied by the planter. This also suggests that those who could not produce colonoware had to make do with what was provided to them. To some extent, planters or slaves with some money or barter may have tried to partially make up for the lack of a large-scale colonoware industry by purchasing small amounts of relatively inexpensive domestic redwares.

Cultural adaptations and expressions of ethnicity varied in the colonial South, and understanding the totality of the African experience in the region is complex. Determining the variables that affected their pattern of everyday living is not always an easy task. While social variables such as demography may have been important in some aspects of their lives, there are also the realities of actually living on the land and using its resources, which promoted or restricted their ability to carry out craft traditions such as colonoware production on a large scale. Expressions of ethnicity and cultural identity thus developed differently in different regions of the South, in response to these social and natural variations.

Acknowledgments

The archaeology at the Neale plantation was sponsored by International Paper. I appreciate the interest of International Paper and particularly of Environmental Resources Group Leader Joe Zuncich in the project. I would like to thank the following people for their assistance in the preparation of this manuscript: Joe Joseph, Martha Zierden, and Tony Greiner.

6
Guten Tag Bubba: Germans in the Colonial South

Rita Folse Elliott and Daniel T. Elliott

King George I was German, as was George II and George III. The ethnicity of England's eighteenth-century monarchs is often overlooked, yet it undoubtedly played a role in the selection of emigres to the American colonies. Historians estimate that at least 65,000, and perhaps as many as 100,000, Germans immigrated to colonial America (Moltmann 1982:9). The most well-known example of such German immigration involves the Pennsylvania Dutch, although Germans began immigrating to Georgia as early as 1733. The southeastern colonies, especially Georgia and the Carolinas, could boast as much as one-half of their populations as German.

Political boundaries in Europe in the early to mid-eighteenth century were dynamic and contained no specific country called "Germany"; so who were these Germans? The British government defined ethnicity according to language spoken. Immigrants from Alsace, Austria, Bohemia, Herrnhut, Hungary, Moravia, the Palatinate region (the area of Heidelberg by the Rhine River), Salzburg, Saxony, Swabia, Switzerland, Wurttemberg, and Wurzburg were lumped into the category "German" because they spoke the German language. This commonality was cosmetic on one level, however, as the language was divided into High and Low German and contained Bavarian, Silesian, Rhenish-Franconian, and many other dialects. When the German Lutheran minister Johann Boltzius met his new German congregation prior to their trans-Atlantic voyage to Georgia, he could not understand their dialect, nor they his, even though all were "German." German ethnic groups, for the purposes of this study, include all German-speaking emigrants who came to the Southeast in colonial times.

Where did these British-defined German immigrants to the colonial Southeast settle and how did they define themselves, interact with each other, and acculturate? How did they affect southern culture and what markers of ethnicity did they leave in the archaeological record?

This chapter attempts to identify and gather baseline historical and archaeological data on southern German colonial settlements so they can be studied thematically and their role in, and contributions to, southern culture can be recognized and understood. The first section of the chapter, "German Immigration," details the various waves of colonial German immigration and examines the locations of resulting German settlements established in Georgia and the Carolinas. "Being German in the Southeast" explores the various geographic areas in Europe that Germans called home prior to emigrating to America. It also evaluates the criteria used by Germans to define themselves and their ethnicity in America. The search for ethnic patterning of material culture is examined in the section "German Material Culture," as various artifacts and lifeways are described. The conclusion reassesses the thesis of this chapter in light of the overall premise of this volume.

German Immigration

Colonial German settlement in southeastern America began in earnest in 1709 and included areas of Alabama, Florida, Georgia, Louisiana, Mississippi, and what is now North and South Carolina. This chapter focuses on the Germans who settled pre–Revolutionary War Georgia and the Carolinas (Figure 6.1). Towns settled by German immigrants were established for one or more of the following reasons: as havens from religious persecution; as places of economic opportunity to provide trades, land, farms, and freedom from enormous European tax burdens; as places of civil freedoms; as buffers from Spanish and Native American aggression toward already established settlements; and as places to produce raw materials for the British empire. The German perspective was highlighted in a recruiting statement made by Johannes Tobler, who told potential German emigrants, "People are free and everyone, so to speak, a little king, a fact which cannot be changed" (Tobler 1753).

The areas of settlement offered to German colonists in much of Georgia and the Carolinas were often inferior to areas provided for English settlement. This is obvious in the Georgia Trustees' policy of reserving settlement along the prime lands of the Savannah River for the English, rather than Germans. Also, the English were first into much of the central South Carolina region and were able to choose the choicest lands. Settlement of less favorable areas was undertaken by later influxes of Germans. They swelled the ratio of German to English settlers in these environments, since most English immigrants decided that these areas lacked the natural resources necessary for habitation and went elsewhere.

From the establishment of New Bern, North Carolina, in 1709 to the beginnings of the later Moravian towns in the 1770s, nearly two dozen

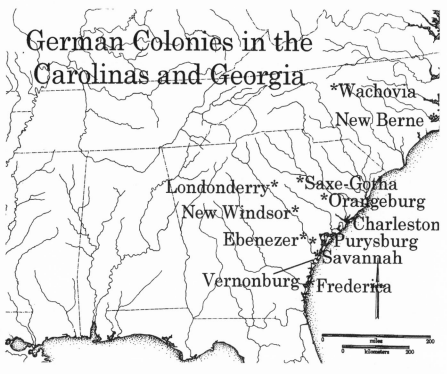

Figure 6.1. German colonies in the Carolinas and Georgia.

predominantly German settlements were established in colonial Georgia and the Carolinas (Figure 6.1). Some settlements encountered a swift demise, or were not populated by a German majority. The earliest documented settlement was in 1674, when a small group of Deutsch Lutherans established the settlement of Jamestown on James Island, South Carolina (Bernheim 1872). It was unsuccessful and was abandoned within a few years. Germans came into Charles Town after 1708 and successfully settled in that city, in addition to English, Irish, and other ethnic immigrants. Other settlements consisted of greater percentages of German colonists and became successfully established in the Carolinas and Georgia.

A total of 1,500 Swiss and Palatinate Germans established the town of New Berne on the North Carolina coast in 1709. There, Swiss Baron Christopher de Graffenreid purchased 10,000 acres and established the settlement at the confluence of the Neuse and Trent rivers. In spite of the geographical distance between the New World and the old, European conflicts and political turmoil found fertile ground in America. The Tuscarora War of 1711 was one such example. That war was an American manifestation of Queen Anne's War in Europe as Spain encouraged the Tuscarora

Indians to attack England through her American colonial settlements. Tuscarora Indian attacks on New Berne left at least sixty Germans dead (Bernheim 1872:72). The New Berne settlement survived the war by remaining neutral and in 1714 its residents successfully petitioned for more land. Although New Berne represents the single largest influx of Swiss-German settlers, the settlers quickly dispersed and most German aspects of the town, other than its name, are gone.

In 1732 the town of Purysburg was established in South Carolina, across the Savannah River from where New Ebenezer would be located four years later. This large, planned town contained four hundred fifty lots, of which only two hundred at most were ever occupied. Germans constituted one-quarter of the five hundred Purysburgers, with Swiss and French making up the remainder (Meriwether 1940:35). The town's architect, Jean Pierre Pury, died soon after Purysburg's founding, and the town suffered for lack of leadership. Purysburg persisted, however, into the early nineteenth century.

In 1734 a group of persecuted Lutheran pietists, expelled from Salzburg by a Catholic prince, journeyed to the colony of Georgia where they settled the town of Ebenezer, on a tributary of the Savannah River. After two grueling years at an ill-suited location that did not allow access to river transportation, and after the deaths of one-third of the original Salzburger settlers from dysentery, typhus, and other illnesses, the colonial trustees allowed the survivors to relocate to a bluff on the Savannah River a few miles away. It had taken the Salzburgers two years to convince the Georgia Trustees and James Oglethorpe to disregard their stated ethnic policies reserving the Savannah River for English settlers (Jones 1969:6). New Ebenezer was peopled with several more boat loads of Germans consisting predominantly of non-Salzburgers. By the 1760s New Ebenezer was a thriving township of eight hundred to a thousand Germans, and townspeople helped establish the satellite communities of Abercorn, Bethany, Halifax, Goshen, New Gottingen, and Zion. Religious and political infighting and alternating occupations of British and American forces during the Revolutionary War permanently crippled the town of New Ebenezer.

In 1735 the Lutheran settlement of Orangeburg was established on a tributary of the Edisto River, adjacent to the town of Amelia in South Carolina. This tributary was commercially unnavigable. Thus, Orangeburg settlers suffered the same riverine transportation problems as did colonists at Ebenezer. In spite of this major hurdle, by 1753 Orangeburg was reportedly as densely occupied as Saxe-Gotha, and inhabited mostly by Germans (Tobler 1753). An estimated eight hundred settlers resided in the township by 1759 (Meriwether 1940:46). Today Orangeburg, which has shifted from the original site, exhibits no obvious signs of its German ethnicity.

In 1735 the Moravians, led by August Spangenberg, established a foreign mission in coastal Georgia at the Irene settlement on Pipemaker's Creek. Their immediate goal was to proselytize among the Native Americans. The increasing threat of Spanish attack in the Savannah area and the efforts of Savannah's citizens to bolster the town's defenses led to friction with the Moravians, who were avowed pacifists. After five years the dozen families living there grew tired of local attempts to force them into military defense of the colony, and they "saw no other prospect . . . but to forsake their flourishing little settlement and emigrate for the North [to Pennsylvania]" (Henry 1859:103).

In 1737 New Windsor was established in South Carolina, southeast of Augusta, Georgia, on the Savannah River. The township was settled predominantly by Swiss Germans, and it maintained a steady population of about three hundred people between 1738 and 1760 (Meriwether 1940:67). The population also included several Indian traders who influenced the local economy.

The township of Saxe-Gotha was established in the Piedmont of South Carolina in 1737. An observer named Hans Riemensperger reported to European Germans, "No township as yet is reported its equal for good land. . . . [It] is only 125 miles from Charleston and on the Great Santee River, and people can go from here at will with heavily laden boats to trade by water when enough boatmen come here to settle and establish themselves. . . . The trail here is cut through the forest wide enough so that people can travel by land in wagons back and forth to Charles Town" (Riemensperger 1740). Riemensperger's recruiting was successful and from 1744 to 1750 a large influx of settlers arrived, mostly from the Rhine area. The Saxe-Gotha congregation consisted of about two hundred eighty people in 1750 (Bernheim 1872:142). In 1759–1760 the Cherokee War affected residents and later the town's church was destroyed during the American Revolution (Bernheim 1872:147).

Between one-half and two-thirds of the Germans immigrating to the colonies did so through indentured servitude. This practice was encouraged by tracts circulated across Europe. Riemensperger, for example, returned to Europe from the Carolinas in 1740 with testimonials signed by German colonists. His tract encouraged emigration by explaining indentured servitude in this fashion: "Also it is well known that in Germany and Switzerland there are poor, unemployed hardworking people who would delight themselves in this gift of land [a 50-acre headright to be received upon release from their indenture], but who cannot afford the expense of the passage across the sea. Arrangements are such that laborers and tradespeople of all sorts and kinds who scarcely know how to make a living in Germany or Switzerland can live in plenty here [in what is now South Carolina] and in a short time make themselves well-to-do" (Riemensperger 1740). Such marketing of the colonies by Riemensperger and others was successful. Recruits who survived the voyage and their five to seven years of indentured servitude were free to establish a household on their own. One example of this is the Georgia coastal town of Vernonburg, settled by Swiss-German indentured servants who had worked off their five-year indenture. At Vernonburg such "redemptioners" were given land and some tools by British colonial trustees to facilitate their independence. Established in 1742, Vernonburg was also a planned settlement that later evolved into a primarily ethnic English village (Elliott and Elliott 1994).

Fort Frederica was a major British outpost located on St. Simon's Island, Georgia. A lesser-known section of the settlement was called the "German Village" and was home to a small contingent of about seventy Germans (Jones 1996). These Germans built most of the houses in Frederica. By 1747, however, all but two families had left Frederica after the fort's military regiment departed. Presumably, the German Village was abandoned at the same time.

By 1750 German colonists, including Lutherans and Reformed Germans, were emigrating from Pennsylvania and Virginia in a steady trickle via the Shenandoah River Valley to settle in the Southeast. In 1753 the Moravians established themselves in an area of the Yadkin River Valley called Wachovia or Wachau near present-day Winston-Salem, North Carolina (see Hartley this volume; South 1999). They established the town of Bethabara that year and then constructed Bethania and Salem nearby in the ensuing thirteen years. The Moravians established three additional settlements in Wachovia between 1769 and 1772 (Bernheim 1872:159). All of these pacifist communities suffered during the American Revolution, but the Moravian element remains vibrant in this region today.

Londonderry was a settlement of several hundred Palatines established in 1764 in the South Carolina Piedmont, near the French town of New Bordeaux, northeast of Augusta, Georgia. The town did not prosper and is one of the least-known German settlements.

Being German in the Southeast

How did these Germans, dispersed across the colonial frontier, define themselves in this foreign land? Apparently there were two major criteria that colonial Germans used to define themselves. The first was geography, or the location of their motherland. Émigrés came from Austria, Bohemia, Herrnhut, Hungary, Moravia, the Palatinate, Salzburg, Saxony, Wurttemberg, and Wurzburg. The majority of Germans who came to America emigrated from the area that is now southern Germany. The second and perhaps most important way colonial Germans defined themselves was by theology. Some of the principal divisions were Lutheran, Reformed (such as Calvinists and Presbyterians), Moravian, Episcopal, and Anabaptist

(Mennonites and Amish). Among these were further divisions according to nuances of orthodoxy. For example, among the Lutherans was a pietist sect represented in its strictest form by Pastor Johann Boltzius and the New Ebenezer settlers.

Germans of various denominations, or even of the same denomination, did not always condone each others' habits. For instance, the Lutheran pietists at New Ebenezer viewed the Moravians, who ironically were the model for Lutheranism, as "disruptive innovators" because of their religious practices and communal living (Jones 1969:4). In spite of differences of opinion among various religious sects, there were some examples of ethnic cooperation. Johannes Tobler wrote back to his countrymen in Switzerland that "there are Germans everywhere who are glad to advise and help new arrivals until they get on their feet" (Tobler 1753). Currently, however, some historians hypothesize that the religious differences among colonial Germans, reflecting growing attitudes in Europe, were much more divisive than previously thought (Fogelman 1999). This hypothesis suggests that later religious polemics manifested throughout New England and the mid-Atlantic region, and the resultant Great Awakening, can be traced directly to the eighteenth-century religious divisions in colonial Georgia.

In spite of the isolation of the frontier and the lack of communication technology that we so heavily depend upon today, the colonial Germans were surprisingly adept at inter- and intra-colonial and global communication. This network involved many of the major "movers and shakers" of the period, in Europe and America. The principal facilitators of missionary communication were European institutions, including the Society for the Promotion of Christian Knowledge, the Society for Promulgating the Gospel, the Moravian home church in Herrnhut, and the Francke Institute. For example, the Francke Institute in Halle (in the former East German Republic) encouraged their Lutheran missionaries to write long and frequent letters about the condition of their settlements. In turn G. A. Francke, aided by Samuel Urlsperger, who was the head of Evangelical Lutheran missions in Augsburg, read, edited, and published these accounts in Europe and/or redistributed them to their other missions in colonial America and around the world. This redistribution served multiple purposes: it allowed the leaders of the outlying missions to receive news on a local, regional, and global level; it allowed them to draw moral support from other missions; it helped raise financial support from benefactors in Europe and other areas; it allowed missionary leaders to petition for specific needs such as medicine, funds, and ministers; it kept Institute leaders current on mission status; and it enabled them to send advice and encouragement in return letters.

German missionaries took the task of communication seriously. Ebenezer's Pastor Boltzius wrote letters directly to General Oglethorpe and other trustees of Georgia, to Samuel Urlsperger, to the Society for the Promotion of Christian Knowledge, which helped sponsor the settlers, and to other influential Europeans (Loewald et al. 1957:219). Boltzius also maintained a diary at New Ebenezer throughout his life, sending entries back to the Francke Institute. These entries constitute eighteen published volumes today and offer a wealth of data to historians and archaeologists about everything from who sinned to how much rain fell on a particular day. Frederica's pastor Driessler also wrote letters to the Francke Institute, many a thousand lines long (Jones 1996:7). Driessler and Boltzius often wrote each other directly, as did Boltzius and Johannes Tobler of New Windsor. Correspondence was also encouraged among the Moravians, whose missionaries kept detailed accounts of their work in the New World. The Moravian leaders Count Zinzendorf and August Gottlieb Spangenberg traveled between headquarters in Europe and Pennsylvania. They sent and received communiques from the North Carolina missions. The North Carolina Moravian records, written well into the nineteenth century, are published in a multivolume series (Fries 1905, 1968).

German colonists acculturated on one level but maintained their identity on another. Eventually, Germans in the Southeast fully acculturated, in that they lost most of their distinctive German cultural traditions and language to become a nearly indistinguishable part of American southern culture. This acculturation was rapid in practices related to survival, such as food and shelter, and much slower in matters such as religion and language. Numerous contemporary testimonials and letters reveal that the New World was constantly compared with the old in terms of environment, botanical and animal specimens, weather, and geography. The limited and irregular shipment of supplies to the far-flung German settlements across the southern frontier, however, demanded that the settlers learn to use available natural resources, no matter how foreign those resources might look or taste. Frederica's Lutheran pastor Driessler wrote of brewing "small beer" by boiling a handful of roasted Indian corn in an iron pot with water, wood, sassafras, and molasses. English beer was too expensive and "as sour as vinegar" and the price of wine was "prohibitive" (Jones 1996:20). Driessler reported, "For lack of tea we have fetched cassina leaves in the forest . . . [for] cassina tea. My family has brewed Indian corn like coffee" (Jones 1996:21). But in true stoic, pietist Lutheran tradition Driessler admitted that while "both [the tea and corn coffee] taste very bad, to be sure, yet we praise the Lord for not letting it harm us" (Jones 1996:21). Driessler reported that both "the Germans and Englishmen eat raccoons and opossum meat like the Indians, but I can't eat any of it because they look frightful like wild cats or half apes" (Jones 1996:21). Frederica's Germans also ate fish (though they were reportedly not as good as German fish), smoked mullet, raw oysters drizzled with orange juice, palmetto stalks, and sweet potatoes. They planted cabbage, greens, herbs, turnips, and watermelons, in addition to apple, orange, and peach trees. The New Ebenezer Germans taught those at Frederica to "boil Indian corn in water and afterwards put the dough on the fire" to make a bread (Jones 1996:21–22). Often the Frederica Germans survived on nothing but boiled rice with bear oil while awaiting provisions from England (Jones 1996:23).

In some ways, acculturation, or the replacement of German traditions and language with English habits, was encouraged by Germans. Johannes Tobler's treatise encouraged other Germans not to "shy away from living among the English; they are, most of them, industrious people and good neighbors" (Tobler 1753). Interestingly, Tobler encouraged German settlement among the English rather than among some Germans. Tobler told European Germans, "Whoever wants to come to America should not go to Pennsylvania. This place is good, to be sure, but it is a cold, wintry land so that the rivers [one and a half miles] wide freeze. . . . Moreover, this province is as densely settled as Germany, and the land is expensive to buy" (Tobler 1753). The fact that Pennsylvania was heavily settled by Moravians undoubtedly influenced this advice given by the Reformed Calvinist, Tobler. The relationship between the English and Germans could be seen in religion, as well. The Germans and English often shared ministers. New Windsor lacked a minister, and made use of Reverend Zublin (or Zubly), who preached in both English and German to accommodate everyone in the area. Zublin's father-in-law, Tobler, reported that "many English people come here on Sunday, so that my living room . . . can hardly contain them" (Tobler 1753). Likewise, Orangeburg's church record book was completed in German and English by two pastors, both named Giesendanner (Bernheim 1872:100–102).

German Material Culture

The questions of acculturation and ethnicity are just two of the many fascinating subjects regarding German colonial sites in the Southeast. Unfortunately, archaeology has been conducted on very few of these sites, resulting in difficulty in determining German ethnic markers in the archaeological record. The only sites examined by archaeologists to date include some of the Wachovia settlements in North Carolina; Dutch Fork, New Windsor, Purysburg, and Saxe-Gotha in South Carolina; and Irene, Old and New Ebenezer, Vernonburg, and Bethany in Georgia (Figure 6.2). Even this list is deceptive, as investigations conducted on some of the sites have been extremely limited in scope, often consisting only of preliminary survey or reconnaissance. The most intensive level investigations have been conducted at settlements of the Moravians at Wachovia's Bethabara and Salem; of the Swiss at New Windsor; of the Lutheran Salzburgers at New Ebenezer; and of the Swiss and Palatines at Vernonburg (Crass et al. 1997,

Figure 6.2. Elderhostelers assist Dan and Rita Elliott in the archaeological excavation of New Ebenezer.

this volume; Elliott and Elliott 1990, 1992; South 1999). Attempts to identify Germans at New Windsor demonstrate the difficulty in identifying ethnic traits from the archaeological record, particularly since these colonists were dominated by the British mercantile system and the importation of German goods was closely controlled (Crass et al. 1999).

One marker of German ethnicity in the archaeological record may be found in ceramics. Jean Pierre Pury's promotional treatise reported, in 1731, "There is not one potter in all the Province [of what is now South Carolina], and no earthenware but what comes from England, nor glass of any kind; so that a pot-house and a good glass house would succeed perfectly well, not only for Carolina but for all the other colonies in America" (Pury 1731). Pury's wish was soon granted. A locally made coarse earthenware has been excavated at New Ebenezer from contexts as early as the 1740s. This pottery consists of a buff-colored paste that has no exterior treatment, or has a slip that is most often a bright yellow, or is covered with a clear lead glaze that appears yellowish green to brown. Vessel forms include large cream pans, saucers, and jars. The New Ebenezer potter, George Gnann, was probably responsible for some of the later vessels, but the maker of the earliest ware has not been identified (Jones 1992). Archaeologists have recovered significant amounts of this drab, coarse earthenware pottery from within a ten-mile radius of New Ebenezer but it is less common beyond that. Morphologically, the Ebenezer coarse earthenware resembles the Moravian slipware manufactured in North Carolina during this period (Bivins 1972). The latter tends to be much more colorful and ornate than the plain, austere wares influenced by the pietistic Lutherans. Some vessel forms are similar, however, such as cream pans and plates.

Another potential marker of German ethnicity may involve architecture. The Moravians and the Georgia Salzburgers both constructed various buildings for communal use. The Moravians in Bethabara, North Carolina, initially constructed hastily built log cabins. The following year, in 1754, they constructed the sleeping hall, a clapboard structure that was converted into a barn within a few years. They erected the dwelling house for strangers, or non-Moravian visitors, that same year; it was built of log construction with a gabled end-chimney and a gabled roof (Idol et al. 1996:2). Moravian drawings and diary accounts offer conflicting information as to what variation of the Alpine-Alemannic architecture was used at Bethabara. Diary accounts support a hewn-beamed and chinked structure. Drawings indicate that the structures would have had solid plank walls held at the corners by grooves in the corner posts (Idol et al. 1996:3). Moravian architecture in North Carolina is marked by extensive use of stone in cellar construction, an attribute not seen in any of the German settlements on the coastal plain where stone is scarce. Orangeburg Germans also used wood and clay construction in their original church, which fell into ruins by the 1770s (Bernheim 1872:124). In comparison, limited excavation at New Ebenezer has uncovered architectural elements that suggest post-in-ground structures with mud and stick chimneys (Elliott and Elliott 1990; Smith 1986). The only surviving colonial house in Ebenezer is a 1750s timber frame and clapboard construction with sills resting on wooden piers. This house, however, has been relocated several times, so the foundation construction is altered. The house site excavated at New Windsor documents post-in-ground architecture and limited use of brick (Crass et al. 1997, this volume). A scarcity of brick is also a hallmark of New Ebenezer, except in the case of their main brick church, which was completed in 1769 (Elliott and Elliott 1990, 1992). The timber frame, pier, and clapboard construction appears to be a carry-over of German architectural style, as Germans struggled to come to terms with the problems of such innate styles in their new termite-infested, humid, southern environment.

German ethnicity might be found in the reed-stemmed, molded tobacco pipes made by the Moravians in the Wachovia settlements. These pipes are most commonly associated with potter Gottfried Aust, who was Bethabara's potter from 1755. Similar pipes have been recovered from other German settlements in Pennsylvania (Walker 1975:107). Only one example was excavated from New Ebenezer. While Moravian pottery also was popular with non-Germans, it may be that these specific pipes can still serve as ethnic German markers. This would be especially true if they are found to have been more popular among Germans than other groups.

A fourth possible indicator of German ethnicity is their use of medicines. Contemporary and modern historians have acknowledged that the Moravians were "ahead of their time in pharmacology and were quick to have their own apothecary and medicinal herb garden" (Moravian Museum of Bethlehem 1999). The colonists at New Ebenezer also had "quite well prepared medicines from England and Halle" (Tresp 1963). In addition to these, they experimented with various herbs and medicines, which they used among themselves and sold to other settlements. Their interest in remedies is apparent in Pastor Boltzius's remark that he wished an old Indian woman had waited to show him the plant of the root she brought him to cure his wife. Boltzius went on to say that "undoubtedly there are many such plants in these woods. My desire to collect some of these for our and our friends' benefit is quite great" (Tresp 1963:23). The pharmacology interests and skills of both the Moravians and the colonists at New Ebenezer may have been associated with their German background. One may argue that the need for medicines on the frontier produced the pharmacological interest apparent in these settlements; however, such desires and skills are not as evident in other, non-German communities. Nor may the interest be compared to the European elitist pursuits of collecting and classifying botanical specimens. Such pursuits were conducted as scholarly hobbies, whereas the German settlers in America were doing pharmacological research as a means of adapting their skills to a foreign and often hostile natural environment. Such German medicinal and scientific pursuits may serve as ethnic markers, located in the archaeological record in the form of medicine bottles, pharmaceutical preparation aids such as mortars and pestles or other equipment, and ethnobotanical remains.

Obviously, German ethnic markers in the southeastern archaeological record are scant, at best. This is due to the lack of archaeological investigation on such sites and the rapid rate of acculturation during the eighteenth and nineteenth centuries. Acculturation appears to have happened swiftly by the late eighteenth century, based on several indicators. The 1790 census records 2,300 people in South Carolina and 7,400 people in North Carolina claiming German nationality (Bureau of the Census 1790). Unfortunately, similar statistics are unavailable for Georgia. These totals reflect less than one percent of South Carolina's population and just under two percent of the total population in North Carolina. Such low percentages (compared with approximately 50 percent during the second quarter of the eighteenth century) suggest that many first-generation immigrants no longer claimed or acknowledged their German origin.

Language is another indicator of acculturation. Before 1800 almost all inhabitants of the Dutch Fork area of South Carolina spoke German; by 1824 none of the schoolchildren could converse in that language (Mayer 1982:6). By 1825 the congregation of New Ebenezer was worshiping in English (Jones 1967:98). This appears to have been a natural development, since English had been taught regularly to the schoolchildren of New Ebenezer during the eighteenth century. The older generation of many communities was not so quick to abandon its heritage. As late as 1891, a German resident in the upper Santee River–Dutch Fork area reported that gatherings of old ladies brought out the "mother tongue" in earnest. These women were children and grandchildren of first-wave German immigrants.

Elderly German residents maintained their ethnicity through their clothing, as well. Historical accounts describe old German men in the Dutch Fork area who "tottered about the yard in their tight knee breeches giving quite a bow-legged appearance to their nether limbs; and while displaying bright silver buckles on their shoes and broad brimmed hats . . . would revel in an overflow of German,—singing songs and telling anecdotes" (Mayer 1982:6–7).

Conclusion

Having suggested that ceramic vessels and tobacco pipes, architecture, and medicinal paraphernalia may be markers of German ethnicity in the archaeological record, we must confess now that we are grasping at straws! Many factors conspire against recognition of ethnic markers. The first such factor is the lack of extensive archaeological investigation on German colonial sites. Directly comparable data sets from the various German colonies do not exist at present. Limited evidence from some excavated German sites suggests that while the Germans were frugal and did not enjoy the same degree of wealth as many Charlestonians, they did strive to accumulate a variety of goods, including some high-status items (Crass et al. 1999). This accumulation would not have been easily achieved in Europe, but was possible in America.

Most of the Germans strove for rapid acculturation in the colonies, as indicated by primary historical documents. Such acculturation is a second factor contributing to the difficulty in recognizing ethnic markers on German colonial sites. A third, and very strong, factor against locating ethnicity on these sites is the nature of the sites themselves. The variability in material culture, inherent in the frequent dual ownership of rural versus urban colonial German sites, makes recognition of isolated German ethnic markers problematic. At New Ebenezer, Germans owned both a house in town and a fifty-acre farmstead outside of town. Excavations on the town lots and farmsteads—often on ones owned by the same people—reveal two drastically different material culture patterns (Elliott and Elliott 1992). One might assume incorrectly that the local pottery of the farmstead and lack of fancy tablewares were a product of German ethnicity, rather than a truer reflection of geography and site function. Likewise, intrasite patterning on these sites does not necessarily reflect ethnicity, as the British authorities dictated the layout of towns such as New Ebenezer and Vernonburg, even stating where on each lot the residence was to be built. The British also maintained tight controls on the material goods that entered and left the colonies. German settlement of colonial sites involved a complex interplay of economic, geographic, political, military, and trade factors. As a result, no one "smoking gun" of German ethnicity has been identified, to date. We have not given up, however, and feel that when these factors are considered along with a much more intensive level of archaeological excavation on these sites and attention is paid to creating comparable data sets, a clearer picture of German ethnicity will begin to emerge.

German immigrants to the southern colonies brought their own particular flavor to the melting pot. Through their unique process of adaptation to a foreign natural environment and exposure to various alien cultural environments, German ethnicity slowly changed. During this change elements of German culture became indelibly entwined into what is popularly avowed to be "southern culture." This chapter has attempted to identify and gather baseline historical and archaeological data on southern German colonial settlements so they can be studied thematically and their role in, and contributions to, southern culture can be recognized and understood. While this chapter has identified the key settlements, players, and ideology of the colonial German immigration saga, the lack of substantial archaeological research on the majority of the German archaeological sites has resulted in prolonging our ignorance of the impact of German culture on the colonial South. The complex nature of German identity and German culture, transplanted into the southern American frontier, necessitates a more thorough, scholarly examination of the German archaeological resources that are vanishing daily. Only then will we be able to fully grasp the meaning of "being southern."

7
An Open-Country Neighborhood in the Southern Colonial Backcountry

DAVID COLIN CRASS, BRUCE PENNER,
AND TAMMY FOREHAND

The past decade and a half has witnessed an increasing scholarly interest in the southern colonial backcountry, the likes of which have not been seen since Frederick Jackson Turner's seminal essay on American exceptionalism and the frontier (Turner 1894). Geographers and social historians have dominated a series of regional conferences, and their dominance is reflected in the scholarly literature (see for instance Beeman 1984; Greene 1988; Hofstra 1990; Hofstra and Mitchell 1993; Mitchell 1991; Nobles 1989; Rutman 1985). In general, studies have focused on geographic, economic, political, and, in some cases, environmental aspects of early colonization of the southern frontier. Little work has been published on what a backcountry settlement looked like on the ground, on how ethnic diversity shaped settlements, or, at a tighter scale, on the internal organization of an individual backcountry farm. This chapter describes a farm located in New Windsor township, the westernmost of the South Carolina settlements founded in the late 1730s.

The colonial townships of South Carolina were relatively short-lived settlements. Various schemes were proposed in the early years of the eighteenth century to protect the western borders of Carolina. However, it was Governor Robert Johnson's proposal for ten such settlements along the Fall Line that met with proprietorial approval, primarily as a result of damage the colony suffered during the Yamasee War of 1715–1718 (see Green et al. this volume), coupled with fears of Spanish and French invasion and a slave insurrection (Figure 7.1). The townships were to be peopled with immigrants recruited in Europe and would serve both to protect the vital rice plantations of the Lowcountry and to furnish raw materials for the English mercantile market.

The Carolina townships met with varying degrees of success (Meriwether 1940). Some, like Saxe-Gotha and Orangeburg, became the bases

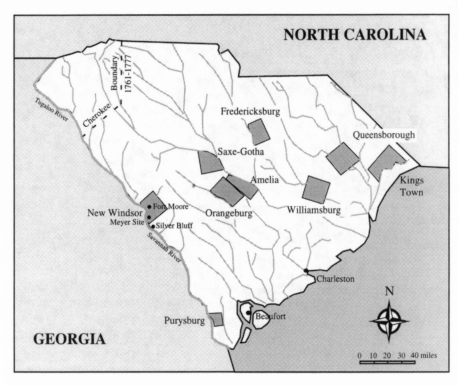

Figure 7.1. The South Carolina townships.

for modern settlements. Others, like New Windsor, attracted just enough
settlers to become recognizable as farming communities, but never coalesced into the backcountry urban centers envisioned by their planners.
The lack of development in New Windsor meant that the archaeological
deposits dating to its initial settlement have remained undisturbed; a characteristic that made it attractive for investigation when the first site was
reported in 1993.

This chapter examines several archaeological sites in New Windsor with
an eye toward their context within the larger settlement and with a special
focus on the home of three Swiss Meyer brothers. We use the concept of
an "open country neighborhood," first employed by geographers of the
Shenandoah Valley, to describe the settlement pattern in New Windsor. Although the architecture of the site reflects the struggle to establish a family
on the frontier and the impermanence typical of that time and place, the
material culture of the Meyers tells a different story, one of rapid integration into a worldwide mercantile system. The relatively impermanent nature of the sites investigated also has important ramifications for field sur-
veys and emphasizes the need for exhaustive archival research and local

informant interviews before efforts are made to locate eighteenth-century frontier settlements on the ground.

The "Discovery" of New Windsor Township

In the spring of 1993, the South Carolina Institute of Archaeology and Anthropology's Savannah River Archaeological Research Program, based at the Savannah River site in Aiken, received reports from landowner Jackie Bartley in nearby Beech Island that she had been collecting pottery from the surface of one of her plowed fields. Curious, she had dug a hole in the area of greatest concentration and had discovered what we later determined was a pit feature full of burned clay and colonial period domestic debris. Bartley had tried for years to interest professional archaeologists in the site; however, she had been unsuccessful in persuading anyone with knowledge of eighteenth-century artifacts to visit her small farm. Jackie Bartley and her husband, Benny, had compiled a treasure trove of primary documents from courthouses in the area, including plat maps, genealogical information, deeds, wills, and probate inventories. After looking over her information, we realized that her contention—that her property was owned in the eighteenth century by three Swiss brothers named Leonard, Ulrich, and Michael Meyer—was probably correct. Moreover, when she took us out to the field where she had gathered her collections, it became apparent that there was a site located in the area. Salt-glazed stoneware, creamware, pearlware, and other eighteenth- or early nineteenth-century markers were abundant on the surface of the plowed field. Over the following months, Bartley took us to two other coeval farm sites as well as a fortified house located on nearby properties.

It is the Meyer household, along with sites settled by the Meyer brothers' neighbors David Zubly and Ulrich Eggar, that is the topic of this chapter. It is worth noting that research at New Windsor also has spawned a master's thesis (Huffman 1997), as well as excavations at one of the largest and most successful trading posts in the colonial backcountry (Crass et al. 1999). Research continues at the settlement under the auspices of the South Carolina Institute of Archaeology and Anthropology. All of this, however, would have been impossible without the help of Jackie Bartley and her husband, Benny, who more than anyone else should be credited with the discovery of New Windsor.

New Windsor's Development

New Windsor was actually not the first English presence in the Middle Savannah River Valley. That honor is claimed by Savannah Town, a trading post established at the Savannah (or Savano) Indian village and inhabited by English and Scots deerskin traders operating out of Charles Town from the 1680s. In the aftermath of the Yamasee War, the Lords Proprietors built Fort Moore nearby (Chesnutt 1989:2; Maness 1986:112). Its traders, soldiers, and Native American inhabitants were joined in 1737 by approximately one hundred fifty German Swiss settlers from Appenzell-Ausserhoden in eastern Switzerland. Primarily pastoralists, the Calvinist Swiss raised cattle for dairy products and wove wool from their sheep. A leading citizen of the New Windsor residents was Johannes Tobler, a one-time governor of Appenzell-Ausserhoden who had lost office in the region's barely suppressed sectarian conflict (Voigt 1921:12–14).

The population of New Windsor grew slowly to about three hundred souls in 1738. In that year, residents began moving across the Savannah River to the newly founded town and fort of Augusta, Georgia, founded in 1737 by General James Oglethorpe. Augusta gradually supplanted New Windsor's previously dominant role in the deerskin trade over the ensuing decades. The 1750s brought guerilla fighting to the area in the Seven Years War (often referred to in Carolina as the Cherokee War), and Johannes Tobler lost his eldest son in an ambush near the Meyer home. Neighboring Fort Moore fell into disrepair by the 1760s, when it was decommissioned by the Commons House of Assembly (Cashin 1986; Maness 1986:241). The American Revolution saw a brief revival of Fort Moore, but by the latter years of the century, New Windsor's population had dwindled to a few farmers. Its small farms gradually gave way to cotton fields as the English, Irish, French, and Scots freeholders and their slaves left the area or established larger plantations in the emerging up-country economy. At about the same time, mapmakers began referring to the area as Beech Island, its modern name. Today the local landscape is dominated by small farms, woodlands, and two industrial sites.

The Meyer Brothers Come to New Windsor

Little is known of Leonard, Ulrich, and Michael Meyer. They apparently came to New Windsor with the first band of settlers in 1737. Michael's 1784 will indicates that he owned four hundred forty acres, four slaves, cattle, hogs, two horses, various tools, and gardens. His furnishings included feather beds, furniture, and books (Abbeville Probate Court 1785, 109:3031). While his landholdings were larger than those of many of his peers, Michael had inherited his brothers' property. Oral tradition in the area holds that Leonard died soon after coming to the New World. Records in Switzerland indicate that Ulrich died in 1755, and his wife, Barbara, died in 1769 (Virginia Strickland, personal communication 1995). The land directly north of the Meyer holding had originally been granted to Conrad Eugster, who died en route to New Windsor in 1737, and his property was purchased by Ulrich Tobler, son of Johannes Tobler. When Ulrich was killed in 1760 during the Cherokee War, his father Johannes took possession of the tract, selling the land that same year to Elizabeth and Ann Meyer, daughters of Michael. When Ann married David Zubly II, whose father was a prominent physician from the township of Purysburg, David assumed ownership of the one hundred–acre tract. His probate is dated 1790, and his wife, Ann, died in 1795.

On the basis of surface collections, shovel tests, and small unit excavations, Zubly's homesite was located adjacent to a Carolina Bay, an upland depression that holds water, sometimes for years at a stretch, and that might have furnished water for cattle or the home itself. The bay was ditched in the 1930s to drain the water; the ditching operation disturbed approximately twenty percent of the site, but much of the site appears to be intact (Huffman 1997:67–78).

The two hundred fifty–acre tract directly east of the Meyer brothers' property was originally granted to Ulrich Eggar, another early arrival in the colony. Sometime prior to 1779 Ulrich's son William inherited the property. The tract was later acquired by Christopher Smithers, who also arrived early in the colony. Smithers sold part of the land to David Zubly II. The chain of ownership grew progressively more complicated until 1806, when it passed into the hands of James Panton (Huffman 1997). Gridded shovel testing and small unit excavation at this site yielded puzzling results. A light scatter of eighteenth-century ceramics on the surface indicated the location of a house; however, shovel testing did not reveal a cohesive distribution of artifacts. Small unit excavation solved the puzzle. The site is located on a field edge, and plowing over the years had buried the site where the farmer turned his tractor. Even so, the artifact yields from Eggar's site were very low. Most dated to the third quarter of the eighteenth century; however, an earlier occupation may be masked by the later, more profuse, artifacts (Huffman 1997:78–89).

The property lines between the three families—Meyer, Zubly, and Eggar—correspond to modern fences, and a field road (Forrest Drive) corresponds to the property line between the Zubly and Meyer families (Figure 7.2). David Zubly II and his wife may be buried in a small cemetery that lies on the south side of their property; their descendants are buried there, and ground-penetrating radar output indicates a number of unmarked interments in the center of the burial ground.

Although the chain of ownership for the three tracts is complex, it is indicative of broader patterns of land ownership in New Windsor, in which family ties, especially between Switzers, were apparently used as a strategy to maintain community cohesiveness. Indeed, plotting surnames from property plat maps on a topographic map reveals that of the sixty-four properties represented, all but two occur in spatially distinct clusters marked by

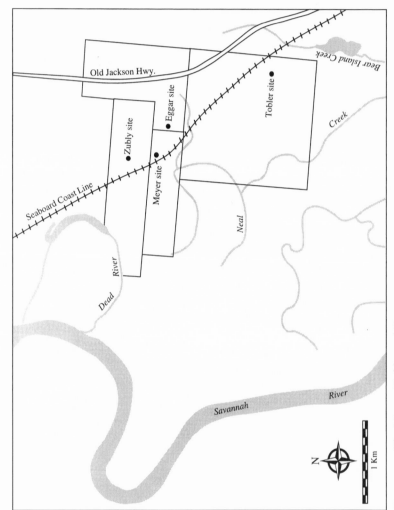

Figure 7.2. The Meyer, Zubly, and Eggar tracts.

Germanic versus non-Germanic surnames, usually along either the Savannah River itself or its tributaries. These spatial clusters apparently broke down rather quickly, but nonetheless, kin ties may have continued to play an important role in land tenure patterns (see also Hofstra 1990 for a similar example from the Shenandoah Valley in Virginia; Elliott and Elliott this volume; Hartley this volume; McCleskey 1998). The settlement pattern throughout New Windsor seems to reflect a process identified first in the Shenandoah Valley, where colonists settled at what geographer Robert Mitchell has called "points of attachment," suitable sites, usually near water and good soils, that then were linked by cleared paths and roads to mills, churches, and other facilities into a "loosely organized, open-country neighborhood" (Mitchell 1998:22). Certainly the Meyer brothers and their neighbors exhibit this pattern. Each house is located approximately two hundred meters from the next; well within eyeshot over plowed fields, but far enough apart to ensure some degree of privacy. New Windsor is somewhat unique in that, although there are no extant colonial structures remaining in the settlement, the links between settlement nodes—field roads, a modern state road that follows the colonial River Road, the Savannah River and its tributaries, and property lines (reflected in fences)—largely remain on the ground. The only exceptions are in the areas of two large industrial plants in the community, which erased the centuries-old landscape features through massive earth moving.

Occupation Period

Excavations at the Meyer brothers' farm (38AK615) began in 1993 with a surface collection and a cruciform shovel test pattern on two-meter centers. Shovel testing and surface artifacts indicated that the site measured approximately seventy meters in diameter. A small test pit indicated the presence of plow scars in the subsoil, and most ceramic sherds recovered from shovel tests were thumbnail-sized or smaller, indicating that the field had been extensively plowed. In addition, artifacts ranging from the prehistoric Middle Archaic period through the late eighteenth century were found on the surface as well, indicating a substantial degree of vertical deflation. After a series of controlled surface collections, the site was mechanically stripped in several phases in order to expose truncated features. Approximately forty centimeters of sandy soil were stripped down to the sandy clay subsoil. Mechanical stripping revealed a roughly U-shaped distribution of 215 truncated features. Some (especially shallow postholes) had been severely truncated; in many cases only the faintest of soil stains indicated the bottoms of the holes. Others—especially deep clay borrow pits and structural postholes—were deep enough to leave distinct patterning, which was in some cases remarkably clear and in others very puzzling.

Several pits yielded ceramic assemblages large enough to furnish reliable dates; most ranged from the 1740s through the mid-1780s; a site mean ceramic date of 1762 was derived from 1,046 sherds recovered from feature contexts. Pipe stem fragments from feature contexts produced formula dates in the 1750s and 1760s, and no cut nails were recovered from the site, indicating that construction ceased no later than the late eighteenth century. The date range corresponds to the sparse archival evidence (which consists of Michael's 1784 will) and local oral tradition, which holds that the brothers left no male heirs to carry the Meyer name forward. However, it should be pointed out that several trash pits did yield pearlware, which appeared after the Revolutionary War (for the most part) and became very popular in the 1790s. This comports with Michael's will as well, which gave his apparently unmarried daughter, Elizabeth, a life estate in the house and garden.

No records have been found for Elizabeth. However, the presence of later ceramic types indicates that she did in fact live in the house for perhaps a decade or so after her father's death. This is borne out by a bit of macrobotanical evidence: chinaberry seeds (or drupes) recovered from a small trash pit containing household refuse, including hand-painted pearlware. Chinaberry trees (*Melia azedarach*) are naturalized into the southern forest, often appearing along road edges and on abandoned homesites, where in the nineteenth and twentieth centuries they were popular as chicken roosts. However, in the eighteenth century they were considered quite exotic; the first were brought to America possibly by Andre Michaux in 1786 on a visit to Charleston, South Carolina (Savage 1986:14). At that time they were known as Persian lilacs or Pride of India trees; descendants of the tree in the Meyer yard still line the road to the site. Taking all of the evidence together, then, it appears that site 38AK615 was initially occupied by the Meyer brothers in the late 1730s and continued in use as a habitation up into the late eighteenth century. The best available evidence also indicates that all three brothers lived at this site. First, there are no other eighteenth-century archaeological sites located on the property taken up by the three brothers. Second, tracts acquired by Michael in 1762 and 1765 appear to have been held only as farmland (Colonial Plats n.d.; Edgefield County Will Book A n.d.; Memorials n.d.; Royal Grants n.d.). Finally, the eldest brother, Leonard, apparently died soon after arriving, and the middle brother, Ulrich, died in 1755.

Site Structure

On the basis of the 215 features left at the site, the Meyer brothers' farm was laid out in a U shape, with the open end facing north, toward the Zubly tract. For ease of interpretation, the portions of the U—the base, and the east and west legs—were designated Areas 1, 2, and 3, respectively. The central part of the U was devoid of features, a point to which we will return later in the chapter (Figure 7.3).

The initial primary residence (Structure A) for the Meyer brothers and their families is indicated by a cluster of pit features and a hearth base (Figure 7.4). No sill lines or postholes were found in the area, and postmolds of varying depths are found surrounding the structure, leading to the conclusion that the home itself was constructed of horizontally laid logs. On the basis of the spacing of the pits, the structure may have had a raised wooden floor (see Deetz and May 1997). A later earthfast addition to the dwelling adjoined the south wall of the cabin. This addition, measuring 258 square feet, was constructed sometime after the early 1760s, based on the presence of a creamware sherd in one of the original postholes. The postholes were spaced at five-foot intervals, indicating that the addition was clapboarded. A structure was added to the east side of the dwelling as well; the irregularly spaced postholes, as well as their relatively small size (13 inches by 10 inches, compared to 16 inches by 13 inches for the southern addition to the house), may point to a lightly built structure, possibly a lean-to with no or only token walls.

The hearth was indicated by a feature in the west wall of the house. Although severely disturbed by plowing, there was a dense concentration of charcoal surrounded by four postholes possibly indicating supports for a fireplace hood. Three pits were clustered around the hearth. The largest would have originally been approximately three feet deep, while the smallest would have been approximately two feet deep. All were filled with dense concentrations of domestic refuse, including a wide range of ceramic types including tin-glazed earthenware, Staffordshire combed yellow and dot wares, white salt-glazed stoneware, Westerwald stoneware, Spanish olive jars, porcelain, and colonoware. Beverage bottle sherds, pipe fragments, flat glass sherds, and sewing pins and buckles were also abundant, as were faunal material, burned daub, and mica. Interestingly, the largest pit exhibited discontinuous stratigraphy, perhaps indicating the presence of internal subdivisions (see Kelso 1984:105 for another example).

What did the exterior of the house look like? Central European folk housing of the time was characterized by Blockbau construction, in which massive timbers were hewn, shaped, and laid horizontally one upon the other (van Ravenswaay 1977:112). The logs may have been square notched, since large amounts of daub were found along the wall lines and in pit features, and both dovetailing and double notching require little or no chinking (Jordan 1985:94). The earthfast addition to the house on its south side may have served as a parlor that was added as the family grew.

A small earthfast structure measuring approximately four and a half feet to a side was located six feet west of the house. Structure B may have

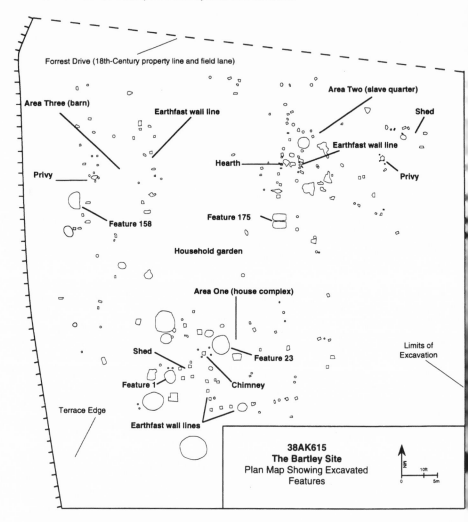

Figure 7.3. Plan map of the Meyer tract features.

served as a storage shed, or speicher, since there were no pits associated with it. The presence of a delft sherd indicates that the shed could have been built at any point in the occupation of the house.

Nine pit features were located in the yard areas associated with the house; four of them were in a cluster just three feet from the west wall that may have defined a yard area. All of the pits contained a mixture of domestic refuse including faunal remains, beverage bottle glass, ceramics, and pipe fragments in equivalent proportions. Several contained more non-domestic artifact classes such as lead shot and bullets, wrought nails, sewing pins, a mouth harp, and whitewash lenses. All contained charcoal

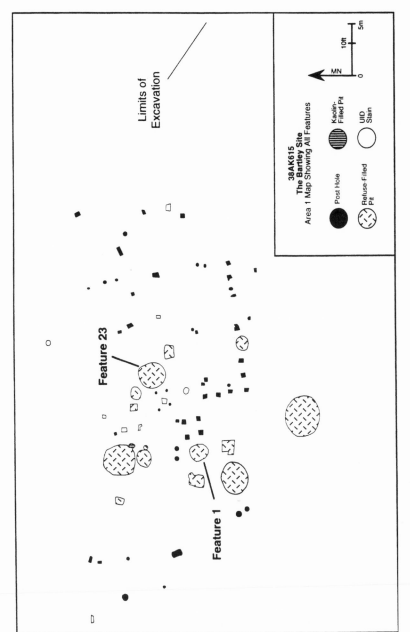

Figure 7.4. Plan map of the Meyer tract, Area 1.

lenses of varying thicknesses, and all were shallow, bowl-shaped holes. Sequencing the pits is difficult; however, Feature 51 contained no creamware or pearlware and thus may date to the earliest phases of occupation, while Feature 203 contained creamware but not pearlware, pointing to a date range in the 1760s through the 1780s. The other pits all contained pearlware types typical of the late eighteenth century, pointing to a date range after Michael Meyer died, perhaps the time his daughter Elizabeth lived in the house.

These pit features may have started as clay borrow pits for daub, after which they were used as cellars. An additional pit, Feature 200, was extremely large—nearly twelve feet across—and would have been nearly four feet deep originally. Three distinct soil strata were present in the feature, the bottom one of which was a coarse sand not found on the site itself. It may have been mined from the Savannah River floodplain just west of the site. A ledge around the edge of the pit sets it apart morphologically from any of the other features. Outdoor root cellars are relatively common on colonial sites in Virginia (Kelso 1984:167) and also are known from Switzerland (Gschwend 1988:160). Johannes Tobler recommended the storage of cabbages, radishes, turnips, carrots, parsnips, and other root vegetables in such a cellar (Tobler 1756:20). The presence of pearlware in the pit indicates that it was filled sometime after Michael died. An intrusive small pit approximately two feet in diameter was located on the southwest margin of Feature 200 and contained a dense concentration of kaolin clay for whitewash, indicating that repairs to the nearby house were being made quite late in its occupation.

Unlike Area 1, the eastern third of the site, Area 2, was very complex. Five potential structures (C through G) were identified, as well as a possible outdoor cooking area and four trash pits. Structure C was defined by two cellars (Feature 175, a and b) of nearly identical morphology separated by an eight-inch wall of clay subsoil (Figure 7.5). Both were six and a half feet long and three and a half feet wide with flat bottoms and straight sides and, when dug, would have been approximately two and a half feet deep. They had identical stratigraphy, consisting of six fill layers; the top three were shared by the two pits. The topmost layer (Level A) was largely charcoal; Level C also had heavy charcoal concentrations, while the other layers were a sandy clay loam. The artifact content of the two pits was also similar. Ceramic types present spanned the occupation of the site, although creamware and pearlware were found only above Level C. In addition to ceramics, personal items such as pins and buckles, and other artifact classes such as beverage glass, bullets, shot, and gunflints, and faunal specimens were recovered from the features. Interestingly, activity-related items such as a splitting wedge, a file, a chisel, whetstones, stable gear, and a brass stopcock were also recovered. Domestic refuse was found only above the

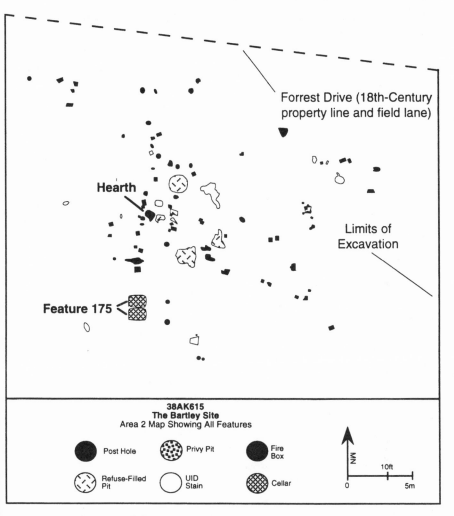

Figure 7.5. Plan map of the Meyer tract, Area 2.

burned Level C, while functional tools like the stopcock and chisel were recovered from the lower stratigraphic levels. No postmolds were identified in the area of Feature 175, leading to the conclusion that the covering structure must have been sill-laid. The morphology of the pits is strongly suggestive of a dairy. The building may have burned sometime before the early 1760s as creamware sherds were recovered from the fill layers above Level C.

An earthfast structure located approximately thirteen feet north of Feature 175 may have been a slave cabin. Measuring fourteen feet long by approximately ten feet wide, Structure D was defined by four corner posts, with smaller posts placed between them. Many of the smaller postmold stains were severely truncated, indicating that more may originally have been present. A square earthen hearth was located in the center of the structure. Defined by a fired-clay collar, it contained ashy fill; no household refuse was recovered from it. However, three pits inside the structure yielded domestic refuse including colonoware sherds, faunal specimens, and metal scraps. An outdoor cooking area adjacent to Structure D was indicated by a cast-iron kettle and an associated pot hook, which were found in a truncated pit. This feature yielded ceramics including Jackfield and creamware, as well as beverage bottle sherds, pipe fragments, brass scrap, and fauna. Three postholes, possibly indicating a tripod over a fire, yielded charcoal and small faunal specimens. A semicircle of trash pits that yielded heavy concentrations of domestic refuse including colonoware lay just east of Structure D, and a remnant hearth that yielded charcoal but not artifacts was located twenty-six feet north of Structure D. Labeled Structure E, this area evidenced no postmold stains, although a light scatter of domestic refuse on the surface was indicative of a household occupation.

A small building that was possibly a shed (Structure F) was located six and a half feet southeast of Structure E. Indicated by the bottoms of three corner posts and a slight stain feature that contained no artifacts, Structure E measured roughly ten feet by six and a half feet. A single colonoware sherd was recovered from one of the postholes. A privy was located in the Structure C yard as well. Indicated by three corner postmold stains, a central pit, and a smaller interior post that may have supported a seat, Structure G measured three feet by two and a quarter feet. The organic-rich pit fill yielded low frequencies of faunal remains, thin metal fragments, and daub. Surrounding Structure D and its dependencies was a welter of posthole stains, most of which were severely truncated. Some seem to have been associated with lightly built fencing, although plow damage was so severe in this area that it is impossible to make any conclusive statements.

Area 3, the western third of the site, was relatively simple to read (Figure 7.6). Structure H was a large, probably open building of approximately forty feet by thirty feet defined by nine postholes. The lack of anything resembling a hearth, the presence of only two trashpits in the area, and the relative paucity of postholes indicate that Structure H may have been a pole barn. Several postholes inside the footprint of the building may represent stalls or feed bins. Structure I was located inside the footprint of the barn, but may have predated it. The single pit and four postmolds were very diffuse and badly truncated but are similar in size and configuration to the privy in Area 2; the fill yielded only daub fragments. Unlike every other building on the site, which are all oriented approximately on magnetic north, the privy seems to have been shifted approximately forty-five de-

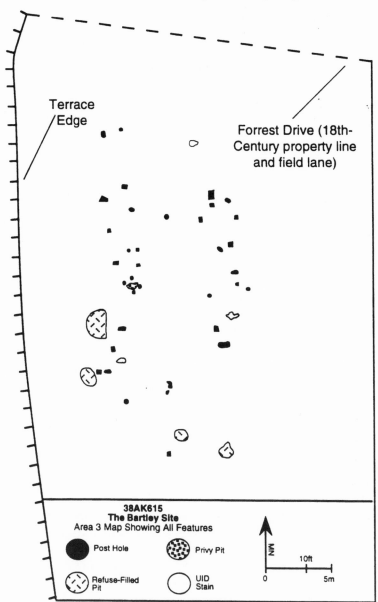

Terrace
Edge

Forrest Drive (18th-
Century property line
and field lane)

38AK615
The Bartley Site
Area 3 Map Showing All Features

Post Hole

Privy Pit

Refuse-Filled
Pit

UID
Stain

MN

10ft

0   5m

Figure 7.6. Plan map of the Meyer tract, Area 3.

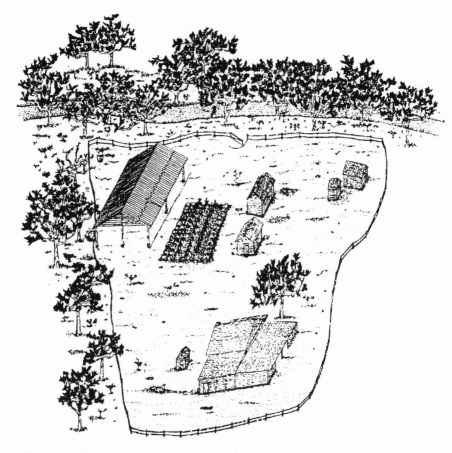

Figure 7.7. Hypothetical reconstruction of the Meyer house and outbuildings.

grees south. Two trash pits outside the barn footprint yielded ceramics (including an Imari-style teacup), a sickle, a snaffle bit, faunal specimens, scissors, hand-wrought nails, and heavy concentrations of charcoal.

Between Areas 2 and 3 was an area devoid of features, and before mechanical stripping, largely devoid of artifacts. This feature faces the field road that then marked (and still marks) the property boundary with the Zubly tract, and we puzzled over it for months until one of our team members went to Switzerland to search for primary documents associated with the New Windsor settlers and to look at vernacular architecture and farmyard proxemics in Appenzell-Ausserhoden (Figure 7.7). While there he observed a number of Swiss farms with household gardens just outside the front door. So, at least preliminarily, we have inferred that the void in the features is indicative of a small garden for household vegetables and flowers. Whether this was really the case or not will probably never be known, but it is intriguing to note that Michael's will left Elizabeth the use of the house and specifically mentioned a garden, so we know one existed.

Conclusion

The Meyer farm gives us a glimpse of life on the eighteenth-century south-eastern frontier. Perched at the farthest edge of the coastal plain, New Windsor was leapfrogged by the founding of Augusta. Its subsequent lack of success means that the archaeological signature of the earliest settlers is relatively undisturbed except for the effects of plowing. Despite deep sub-soil plowing, however, we were able to recover both good spatial data and a robust artifact assemblage. Both the artifacts and the site structure have yielded surprises. The artifact assemblage illustrates the rapid penetration of the nascent English mercantile system even on the edges of the back-country. That even German-speaking settlers in New Windsor, a singularly unsuccessful settlement, had access to and understood the social mean-ing of Chinese porcelain, had a pump organ (at the home of Johannes Tobler), and had libraries at their deaths gives lie to the almost universal disdain with which Lowcountry planters viewed their backcountry neigh-bors (Crass et al. 1999:25–28).

Despite these accouterments, however, the remaining structural evidence at 38AK615, and to a lesser extent that of the Zubly and Eggar tracts as well, speaks of an architecture that was functional first of all, with little to suggest long-term permanency. This may be because colonists in the backcountry built their homes and farms in a series of steps. Tents and small huts often sufficed for the first season, while crops were planted and families became established (Jones 1968:44; Meriwether 1940:165; Reese 1974:51). For instance, research at Kingsmill, Littletown, and Farley's Neck in Virginia indicates that huts were often followed by houses with driven posts, and then by structures with prepared postholes (Kelso 1984: 72). A structure from about 1746 built by Thomas Howell in Saxe-Gotha township consisted of a one-room, framed earthfast dwelling measuring sixteen by seventeen feet with a plank-floored cellar. A raised wood floor may have been supported by interrupted sills, given the lack of earthfast studs between the main support posts. A crib chimney with a brick hearth was built on the gable end of the house; nail lengths indicate that the roof was covered in wood shingles and the walls were clapboarded (Groover 1992:92–99). The Catherina Brown cowpen and its associated house on Steel Creek were built about 1755 by Welsh immigrants. The house ap-pears to have been a one-and-a-half-story frame structure with wood shin-gles, clapboard sheathing, and a wood floor. Two eave-wall chimneys sug-gest that the interior was divided into at least two bays (Brooks 1987: 182–85).

Viewed in the context of houses built at about the same time, the Meyer home appears relatively typical of backcountry yeoman cabins. While we have very little excavated data for either the Zubly or Eggar tract structures, the distribution of artifacts at these sites, as well as at the Johannes Tobler fortified house located nearby, indicates relatively similar site layouts. The house and its appurtenances were clustered within a relatively small circle of about 175 feet. Our crew dug shovel tests that yielded no artifacts in the center of the site (where the inferred garden was). On a straight-line transect with shovel tests dug every thirty meters or so, if the site had been vegetated rather than in an open plowed field, it would have been entirely possible to miss it altogether in a field survey. There is not space in this chapter for a discussion of testing and survey intervals. However, it is worth noting that this open-country neighborhood, where three families began their American experience, never would have been found had it not been for local landowners who take pride in the heritage of their small community, proving once again that perhaps the best stewards of archaeological sites are informed property owners.

The research at New Windsor has made it the best-documented of the South Carolina townships, with forty-two probate inventories for the settlement, as well as other associated documents (Crass et al. 1999:18). However, like most colonial settlements, it was made up of a constantly shifting cast of characters, many if not most of whom left no traces whatsoever in the archival record. The relatively good state of preservation at the Meyer farm, combined with survey and testing results at other sites in the area, indicates that New Windsor township can provide what one geographer has called "history from the ground up" (Robert Mitchell, personal communication 1996). This is a type of historical narrative that bridges anthropology, historiography, environmental science, and geography, resulting in a complex weaving together of strands that offers the potential to communicate, if only faintly, some of the richness and diversity of the early American frontier.

8
Bethania: A Colonial Moravian Adaptation

Michael O. Hartley

Bethania is an extant town in northwestern Forsyth County, North Carolina, and although its antiquity may not be obvious to the casual visitor, there is an aura of age about the place. Older houses are arranged in compact array against stone sidewalks on either side of a central main street. They occupy neat lawns where fences define lots and where outbuildings of various materials and uses stand; glimpses between them and beyond reveal narrow lanes, pastures, fields, and woodlots. Mature shrubs and trees in yards indicate established age, an impression heightened by a conspicuous old brick church at the center of the residential cluster. A cedar-lined avenue climbs easterly from the church to a cedar-covered hill, ending at a well-maintained graveyard surrounded by a freshly painted white board-rail fence. From this hillside vantage, outlying agricultural fields of upland and bottomland increase the sense of compact unity within the residential area, but also suggest an interrelationship between the clustered houses, farmlands, and woodlands. Creeks wind through fertile bottoms and the surrounding ridge tops position the residential area in a tight fold within the broader landscape. This is the impression of Bethania at the close of the twentieth century, a Moravian town established in 1759.

Founded on the frontier of North Carolina during a period of Indian warfare, the village today reflects the needs of its original settlers and their adaptation of an ancient European form. The success of this adaptation is the story of Bethania, the Wachovia Tract, the broader colonial settlement of North Carolina, and the Moravian role in that process.

Ancient Form

The form of Bethania predates its creation on the frontier of Carolina. Study of Bethania has revealed an arrangement of domestic and agricultural divisions of land that has antecedents in a time so remote that the origins of the form are unknown. This form, identified as open-field agriculture, existed in England prior to the time of the Domesday Book as a nucleated village, with typically one street and a set of surrounding fields. It is found in Europe in ancient times as well. Scholars have proposed that elements of this form are seen in the writings of Tacitus on the Germanic tribes, about A.D. 98, in which he described land division with many similarities to the open-field system (Ault 1972:15–16).

Bethania is clearly an example of open-field agriculture. It may also be called a *landschaft*, which "in ancient and medieval thought is the intimate relation of fields and clustered structures," the safety of the familiar in contrast to the danger of the "wilderness" beyond (Stilgoe 1982:7–12). John Stilgoe has argued that this form of outlying fields surrounding a cluster of houses derived from spatial economics, with the more intensely tended garden plots, orchards, and fields that required daily attention lying closer in, while less intensely tended fields lay beyond. Surrounding these were hay meadows, followed by an outer group of pasture fields. The argument for this form in a nonmechanized society involved the economics of time, the walking time required to reach the workplace (Stilgoe 1982:17).

However, in North Carolina, where the common pattern for the farming family was the detached homestead, there were other necessities that led to the selection of this arrangement for Bethania. There was another "economy" involved, that of survival on a hostile frontier, and the need for a form that a corporate theocratic community could adapt to a dangerous land.

Present on the Landscape

A detailed archaeological examination of Bethania greatly heightens awareness of its age and structure as the meaning of the extant landscape reveals itself (Hartley 1993). The system of the residential area and outlots, linked with a carefully designed pattern of roads and lanes, emerges with clarity through study, as does its connection to the environs and region.

During the late 1980s and early 1990s, a series of studies on Bethania were conducted that concentrated on archaeological evidence of land-use patterns, the built environment, and planning issues related to modern development pressure on the community. Inherent in the work was an effort to expand general knowledge and awareness of this historic community. One result of the endeavor was the creation of a five hundred–acre Bethania National Register Historic District, based largely on the significance of the historic land-use patterns (Hartley and Boxley 1990). This nomination was an expansion and amendment to a preexisting fifty-acre

Figure 8.1. Map of Bethania, 1766, by Philip Christian Gottlieb Reuter. Note land divisions, roads, and natural resources. Numbers identify lots and land divisions: No. 1, Residential lots along main street; Nos. 2–5, Orchard lots; Nos. 6–15, Upland fields; Nos. 16–19, 21–27, Bottoms. Symbols identify natural resources and topographic features; for example, a dot in a small circle indicates "good upland," a triangular arrangement of six circles means "many stones," and a capital letter C preceded by a plus sign means "abundance of chestnuts" (collection of Moravian Archives, Winston-Salem, North Carolina; courtesy MESDA/Old Salem, Inc.).

Bethania National Register Historic District, which had concentrated on architecture in the residential core.

There are a number of resources that reveal historic Bethania and its systems (Figure 8.1). Remnants of the colonial town survive and provide direct evidence. Archival information, including historic maps, photographs, and texts, as well as other information, enhances the understanding of these systems. For example, the current U.S. Geological Survey map

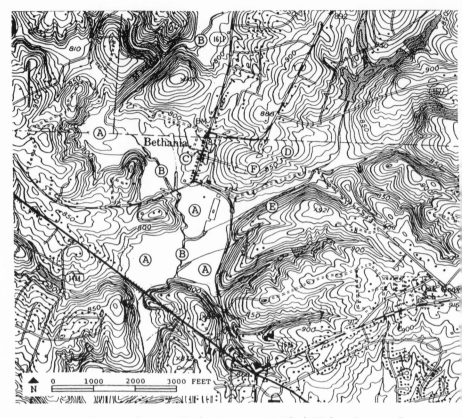

Figure 8.2. Topographic map, Bethania, 1971. *A*, Black Walnut Bottom; *B*, Muddy Creek; *C*, residential cluster; *D*, Bethabara-Bethania roadbed; *E*, cairns of stone; *F*, God's Acre (U.S. Geological Survey, Rural Hall, North Carolina).

covering Bethania provides evidence for distinct natural and archaeological features on the terrain (Figure 8.2). A pronounced feature is the expansive low area or bottom that lies along the north-to-south course of the main waterway. These major natural features, known as the Black Walnut Bottom and Muddy Creek, were important factors in selection of the site for Bethania.

Surrounding ridge tops due east and to the northwest define and enclose the central area of the village. On a south-sloping terrace lies the residential cluster along the village street, Main Street, approximately 1,200 feet from its southern to northern intersections. At the northern intersection, transportation links are seen in an archaeological roadcut indicated by discontinuities in contour lines. This archaeological feature, now abandoned and overgrown, is part of the colonial road that connected Bethania and neigh-

Figure 8.3. Aerial photograph, 1984, of the southern Black Walnut Bottom in Bethania showing demarcation of early strip lots in the field at the center of the photograph. This bottom is part of Bottom Nos. 18 and 19 on the Reuter map in Figure 8.1 (Forsyth County Planning Department).

boring Bethabara three miles away. Bethabara, once a town, is now a collection of stone cellar holes that surround the 1788 church. First revealed archaeologically by Stanley South in the 1960s, Bethabara is an archaeological park today (South 1999).

The relationship of Bethania's residential cluster to the Black Walnut Bottom is clarified by the topographic map. The southern intersection is almost at elevation with the bottomland but remains above floodplain. The bottom was divided into narrow linear fields. Thin dark lines appear in aerial photographs on the surface of the cleared bottom (Figure 8.3). On the ground, these features are shallow but well-defined drainage ditches delineating the early strip lots, an indication of the careful division of this rich agricultural resource.

Along a hillslope at Bear Creek, large cairns of building stone remain stacked, all the more significant in that they are noted in this location on early maps of Bethania (Reuter 1758). An archaeological roadbed nearby was apparently the path to sledge the stone into the nearby residential area.

In God's Acre, the Bethania Moravian Church graveyard, the earliest

Figure 8.4. Aerial photograph, Bethania, 1988. View looking northeast, showing residential cluster along Main Street, eastern orchard lots, outlying upland fields, and the cedars of God's Acre. (photograph by the author).

gravestone is dated 1760. Arrangement in the burial ground shows the typical Moravian pattern in groupings, or choirs, of single men, single women, married men, married women, and children, predominantly with the flat stones of the Moravian tradition. Gravestones bear dates into the immediate present, evidence of strong cultural continuity.

Architecturally, Bethania sustains the image of durability as well. A number of gable-roofed, weatherboarded, log and timber frame houses on stone foundations, as well as outbuildings, reflect their origins in the eighteenth and early nineteenth centuries. They are joined by structures from subsequent periods. Test excavations in the residential area revealed the presence of other colonial buildings no longer extant, such as the pre-1765 Bethania Tavern. The archaeological resources in Bethania are vast and much remains to be learned.

From the air, the Bethania land-use system is clearly visible (Figure 8.4). This shape on the landscape was not random, but was chosen and planned. The form for Bethania had meaning and intention, imposed by those who conceived it and called it into being on the colonial frontier of North Carolina.

Choices on the Frontier

Careful choices, as a means of surviving on the frontier—of adapting—
were characteristic of the Moravians, or *Unitas Fratrum,* in their Wachovia
settlement. Beginning in the 1730s, these Protestants from Central Europe
had gained valuable knowledge from prior experience in the New World:
missions to slaves in the West Indies; attempted settlement in Savannah,
Georgia; and successful settlements in Pennsylvania. While the Pennsylvania settlements were successful, they had been placed in areas already rapidly developing, and the Moravians desired a location where they would
have greater control and autonomy. This pietistic and theocratically organized group desired a large enough tract of contiguous land to provide
them with political and religious control on the scale of a county.

In 1749 while successfully petitioning the English Parliament for recognition as an Episcopal sect, which would grant them particular rights and
privileges in the English colonies, the Moravians came to the attention of
John, Lord Carteret, Earl Granville. The Granville family had held a one-
eighth proprietorship of Carolina and retained the "Granville Tract," effec-
tively the northern half of North Carolina. Granville recognized in the
Moravians a group skilled in settlement and offered them the right to purchase 100,000 acres from his holdings.

Granville's offer to the Moravians, if successfully acted upon, would
provide a much-needed urban anchor for settlement in the interior of
North Carolina. Moravian craftsmen and professionals would supply necessary goods and services, making settlement on the frontier in the western
Granville tract much more attractive to other settlers.

Bishop August Spangenberg, leader of the Moravians in America, arrived in Edenton, North Carolina, from Bethlehem, Pennsylvania, in September 1752 to search for the 100,000 acres. In conferences with Sir Francis
Corbin, Granville's agent in Edenton, Spangenberg was advised to "go to
the 'Back of the Colony,' that is west to the Blue Mountains" to find the
land he wanted (Spangenberg Diary, Sept. 12, 1752, in Fries 1922:33).

The coastal plain of Carolina, anchored on Charles Town and the
Chesapeake, was already heavily settled. This was not the case with the
interior piedmont. A large, permanent town in western Carolina would
provide a needed urban place for settlement on the frontier and could establish the interior anchor on which the colonial process of Carolina could
come to maturity.

On September 18, 1752, Bishop Spangenberg led his party west from
Edenton, keeping careful note of his distance from the important ports of
Charles Town and Wilmington and from the Chesapeake. He ultimately
selected a tract on the upper Yadkin, and at his direction the English sur-

veyor William Churton laid out rectilinear boundaries that took in the majority of the drainage basin of Muddy Creek. He named the tract *Der Wachau*, after an estate of the Moravian European leader Count Nicholas von Zinzendorf; this name became Anglicized to "Wachovia."

Spangenberg came to North Carolina with a plan previously specified by the Moravian leadership. The tract was to be square, twelve miles to the side, was to be bisected by a navigable river, and was to contain a central administrative town surrounded by outlying satellite settlements. He abandoned any hope of locating the tract on a navigable river early in his search, recognizing that there were few of these in North Carolina, and those that did exist were already heavily settled by 1752–1753. Otherwise, he closely followed the plan. His selection gained a variety of resources: good streams for water power, bottomlands suitable for agriculture, and uplands that would also provide fields, as well as timber and stone for construction, game, and other natural resources. The alterations in "squareness" to the tract were implemented to find the best fit to the drainage basin of the creek and its many resources, while still adhering to the basic plan.

In his diary, Spangenberg wrote of a particular concern on the North Carolina frontier. He observed that Indians frequently traveled in large, dangerous groups and were to be feared:

> Every man living alone is in this danger, here in the forest. North Carolina has been at war with the Indians, and they [the Indians] have been defeated and have lost their lands. So not only the tribes that were directly concerned, but all the Indians are resentful and take every opportunity to show it. Indeed they have not only killed the cattle of the whites, but have murdered the settlers themselves when they had a chance. (Spangenberg Diary, Nov. 11, 1752, in Fries 1922:48)

Spangenberg followed this observation with recommendations for initial occupation on North Carolina's colonial frontier.

> Perhaps it would be wise to settle six to ten families together, each in his own house, all working under a capable overseer; and after a time, if anyone wishes to settle on his own farm, as in Pennsylvania, then to try to arrange it for him. (Spangenberg Diary, Nov. 11, 1752, in Fries 1922:49)

The Moravians immediately implemented plans for settlement, and the first group of fifteen Single Brothers traveled from Bethlehem beginning on October 8, 1753, and arrived in Wachovia six weeks later on November 17.

They had come with specific instructions to select a site suitable for the central administrative town, but this was an instance in which Moravian planning went somewhat awry.

The route they followed, the famous Great Wagon Road, was still relatively undeveloped, and the Single Brothers had to widen the track in places to accommodate the large Pennsylvania wagon carrying their tools and supplies. They arrived on the Wachovia Tract in harsh, cold winter weather, and finding an abandoned trapper's cabin on their land a mile and a half from the road, took refuge there. This became the location for the first town in Wachovia, the serendipitous Bethabara, meaning "House of Passage."

Around the cabin the Single Brothers erected a town, clearing land, laying out gardens and fields, and building fences, stables, living quarters, and craft and industrial structures as needed. Forest resources provided material for log buildings. The Moravians knew corner-notched log construction and the plank log, corner posting method, both of which they had used in Bethlehem (Larson 2000). *Fachwerk*, "framework" or half-timber construction using heavy timber framing with wattle and daub or brick infill, was also used, first on the 1756 three-story mill building. However, a sufficiency of trees and the relative speed of log construction made it the preferred choice at that time (Taylor 1981:5–6). By the end of 1755 and the arrival of the first group of Moravian families from Bethlehem, several structures had been added to the complex, including the Single Brothers House and the *Gemein Haus* (church, consecrated February 1, 1756) (Fries 1922:154). These two large buildings were two-story, three-bay log structures with steeply pitched gable roofs and interior chimneys (Fries 1922:122; Taylor 1981:5).

The Bethabara settlement grew, and although its location was unplanned, it functioned as the de facto administrative center of Wachovia. Construction of roads and bridges had commenced upon initial settlement, and the Moravian town became the important focal point for a vast hinterland on the frontier. Supplies, clothing, shoes, and pottery could be found there, as well as a doctor and a minister. In 1755, the Bethabara Memorabilia recorded 426 visitors for the year, including 231 who were fed, 157 there on business, and 38 who needed medical care (Fries 1922:121).

Dispersed settlers also looked to Bethabara as a refuge. This became necessary in the spring of 1759, when, according to a diary from Bethabara, the Indians "began to murder in our neighborhood" (Fries 1922:206). Frontier residents fled into Bethabara, and by May there were one hundred twenty people seeking protection in the Moravian town (Fries 1922:210). Bethabara had been palisaded in 1756, and in 1758 a refu-

gee camp was built at the Bethabara mill, as the Carolina frontier was en-
tangled in the French and Indian War, part of the broader Seven Years War
in Europe. Fear continued into the summer of 1759, when Bishop Spangenberg arrived from Pennsylvania on June 5 to select the site for Bethania
(Crews 1993:6). While the frontier was collapsing under the violence of the
Cherokee, the Moravians set out to accomplish their first expansion in the
Wachovia Tract and build the first planned town.

Bethania, First Planned Town of Wachovia

By June 12, 1759, the site had been selected "according to the Savior's direction" and was inspected (Crews 1993:6). A two thousand–acre Town
Lot was laid out for Bethania, within which the plan was to be implemented. On June 30, the lots, streets, and lanes of Bethania were laid out
by the Prussian-trained Moravian surveyor Philip Christian Gottlieb Reuter. Bethania was located three miles northwest of Bethabara directly across
the Great Wagon Road, at which the two Town Lots linked corners (Figure 8.5).

By July 18, the first family to live in Bethania moved into their newly
built one-story log house; they were accompanied by the men of seven
other Moravian families whose wives were to join them after more houses
were built (Fries 1922:211–12). On July 1 a group of eight German families from the Bethabara refugee camp had applied to be included in the new
town, and they were permitted to join in the settlement of Bethania. On
July 22 these families were also assigned lots (Crews 1993:10–11). There
were approximately thirty people to house in Bethania; about half of these
were children (Fries 1922:208). As at Bethabara, the advantages of log construction made it the preference for Bethania, and within a year, ten one-
story log houses lined the main street and the log *Gemein Haus* stood on
the square (Clewell 1902:66–68; Fries 1925:540).

The pooling of resources on the frontier, with support from the broader
Moravian community in America and Europe, as well as educated leadership and a highly skilled workforce, allowed this rapid and atypical establishment of settlement on the frontier of North Carolina. Bethania came
into existence instantly, as a fully functioning town, without having to pass
through usual frontier patterns of settlement. The step of initial occupation by single men had already been accomplished very quickly at Bethabara; Bethania did not have to repeat it (Hartley 1987:39).

The 1759 plans for Bethania followed Spangenberg's recommendation
that residents of the town have their houses close to one another for support and protection and used a village form drawn from deep European
tradition. Adapting an ancient form to the needs of the Carolina frontier,
the Moravians carefully selected from what they knew.

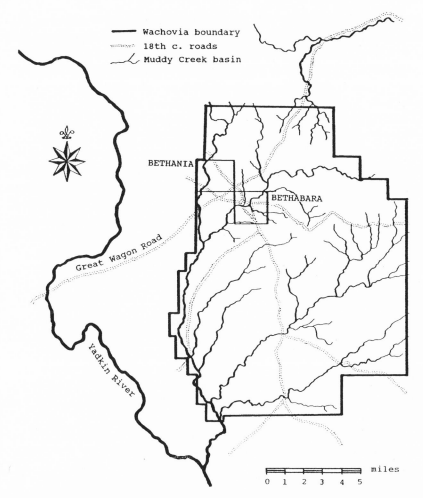

Figure 8.5. Wachovia, ca. 1765, showing Bethabara-Bethania relationship (map by author and Martha B. Boxley, 1988; compiled from information in Moravian Archives, Winston-Salem, North Carolina).

The immediate concern was, of course, the danger from the Cherokee. This concern continued into 1760, and in February of that year a large party of Indians was seen moving toward the Yadkin River. The Moravian towns were set in a state of preparation; refugees again fled into Bethabara and to Bethania, and March was a particularly dangerous month.

Men of Bethania went armed to their evening services. A wounded man, pierced through with two arrows, managed to get to Bethabara, leaving two dead companions on the Yadkin. His life was saved by the Moravian doctor there. Militia ranged out to bury the two dead companions of the wounded man, but finding the Indians out in strength, "so let the burial go and contented themselves with visiting the families who had thought to hold their ground, and bringing them to the fort" (Fries 1922:230). The following night of March 14, the new town was tested.

> The next night Indians were seen in Bethania; the watchman shot at them and drove them off, then there arose a strong wind and on it came the sound as of the howling of a hundred wolves. On the night of the 15th a snow fell, which stopped the activities of the Indians for a few days; otherwise the danger continued. One of the refugees narrowly escaped death on the path between Bethabara and Bethania; two others going out against the advice of Br. Anspach, who was in command at the mill, were attacked and one of them killed. (Fries 1922:230)

The choice of a compact settlement pattern for Bethania by the Moravian leadership, implemented through the selection of an ancient Old World form, proved to be a sound means of weathering a massive Indian assault on the frontier. Moravian foresight, planning, and choices of formal adaptations to the frontier also provided the means of survival for many non-Moravian settlers from isolated cabins and settlements in the outlying regions who fled into Bethabara and Bethania as refugees. The situation proved fatal to many of those who had chosen the more isolated settlement pattern that Bishop Spangenberg had warned against.

The form selected for Bethania was designed to withstand the circumstance of the Cherokee War. At the same time, it was expected to provide long-term security for a community of people and had to function as such. Awareness of western North Carolina as an evolving place is seen in Spangenberg's recognition that the frontier was a temporary context that would eventually become safe enough for dispersed settlement on individual farms by the Moravians. Therefore, the form of Bethania was not only to be a temporary expedient to ensure survival in initial settlement, but it was also required to endure.

In 1760, one of the main participants in the planning of Bethania, the surveyor Reuter, noted several points that had guided him in the layout of the town. Among them was that the town was designed in a regular manner so that it could grow, even if this was not the immediate intention, and the lanes running behind the residential lots would be good for this future development (Reuter 1760).

The land of the Bethania Town Lot was held by the church and leased to members of the congregation (see Figure 8.1). Four categories of land division were included in the plan. The residential category was divided into twenty-four residential lots, clustered with twelve lots along either side of the main street with its central square. Tied to the residential lots were three other categories: orchard lots, bottom lots, and upland lots. Each of the twenty-four residential lots was assigned one of twenty-six orchard lots, sized at two and one-half acres, plus lots in the bottomland and upland. The Black Walnut Bottom contained one hundred thirty acres and was considered by Reuter to be a scarce and valuable resource; it was stipulated that no more than four acres of the bottom be measured off for anyone without specific permission (Hartley and Boxley 1989:18; Reuter 1760). Beyond these four categories, the remaining land of the two thousand–acre Town Lot was held as common land to provide resources such as firewood, construction timber, stone, and game.

The roads of the town were regarded by Reuter as important determinants of direction for growth, if maintained in an orderly manner so that each lot had access. Similarly, the creek on which Bethania was settled, then known as the Dorothea and later as Muddy Creek, was to be a communal resource. Reuter's discussion of Bethania accompanied an ongoing series of maps and survey books illustrating the design that he had fit into the topography of creeks, bottoms, and uplands (Hartley and Boxley 1989:19; Reuter 1760).

Use of the land was also carefully recorded. For example, if an agricultural lot became worn out from a series of plantings, the lot would be taken out of service, or a process of fertilization, probably with manure, begun. Lapses in the control of farm beasts and fowl, with resulting damage to crops, were dealt with by a committee of Bethanians under Moravian authority to oversee matters in the community (Bethania Committee 1764; Hartley and Boxley 1989:26, 29; Reuter 1760).

Early Bethania traded in deerskins and bearskins and produced hides from cattle for export to ports such as Charles Town and Wilmington. Other exports included wheat and various grains, butter, meal, flax, hemp, and Seneca snake root (Hartley and Boxley 1989:29). In 1766, Bethania's inhabitants included sixteen men whose occupations were listed as wheelwright, blacksmith, tailor, cooper, carpenter, baker, weaver (2), shoemaker (3), and farmer (3); nine of the tradesmen were also listed as farmers. There was a schoolmaster/reader as well (Fries 1922:345).

Moravian planning, detailed and prescribed, was not without flexibility. By 1768, Bethania had grown to include almost one hundred persons and residents petitioned Frederic William Marshall, the *Oeconomus* or chief administrator of Wachovia since 1763, for an adjustment to residential lot sizes (Fries 1922:350, 386). The families described the need of additional space for themselves and their livestock; many desired to build more substantial houses, while using their existing homes for shelter during the construction phase (Upper Town Brethren 1768). Marshall responded sympathetically to their request noting that their "houses . . . built of light logs" during the throes of the Cherokee War had become inadequate in size and quality. Significantly, he commented on the changing frontier and its influence on Bethania's arrangement:

> They went to Bethania at the beginning of the war and built the houses close together for the sake of safety. They did so out of necessity. To do the same thing now is not to be thought of, for the land is occupied even far beyond that point. (Marshall, Jan. 1769, Moravian Archives, Winston-Salem, in Hartley and Boxley 1989:31)

Marshall directed Reuter to resurvey the residential lots and to eliminate the central square (Marshall 1769). Reuter redrew the lots in 1769–1770; he also enlarged the Bethania Town Lot to twenty-five hundred acres, gaining favorable land.

Following the restructuring, residents systematically replaced their dwellings. New, larger two-story log houses were built with asymmetrical facades reflecting interiors oriented around massive central chimneys. With antecedents in central European architectural tradition, the typically three-room first-floor plan included entry into a kitchen hall that ran the depth of the house on one side; the other side would have a parlor room with a chamber behind it (Figure 8.6). Additional characteristics included a steeply pitched gable roof with a spacious attic and a stone foundation, often with a stone-lined cellar under the house. Several of these houses survive (Figure 8.7).

Bethania prospered, becoming a successful postcolonial craft and trade center. Because of the hinterland that Bethania served and drew upon in this latter time, it became the western terminus of the longest plank road ever constructed, the Appian Way of North Carolina, in the 1850s. Following linkages established in the colonial period, this road stretched 129 miles from Fayetteville to Bethania. This trade and communication route in the mid-nineteenth century speaks to the ongoing importance of Bethania and the Moravian towns of Wachovia as commercial centers in the backcountry of North Carolina.

Wachovia and Backcountry Settlement

Bishop Spangenberg believed strongly in accumulating as much knowledge as possible in order to successfully plan his actions. He acquired copious information about the condition of Carolina as he began his search for the Moravian tract, and it was out of this developed awareness that he decided

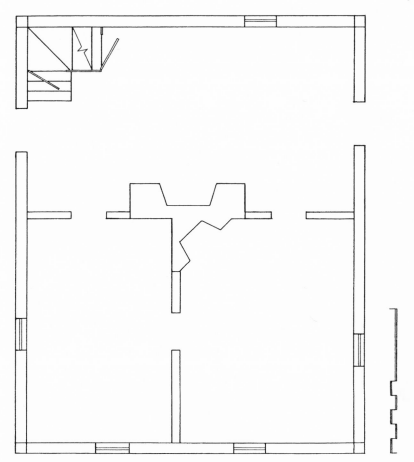

Figure 8.6. A typical floor plan with three rooms around a central chimney (plan by Martha B. Hartley; adapted from a drawing of the 1805 Jacob Shore House in Bethania by John C. Larson and Martha Brown, 1984).

to locate the new Moravian settlement in the back of the colony nearly against the western mountains. Spangenberg indicates in his diary of the search that his intention from the start was to locate on the Yadkin drainage, and he was well aware of potential regional routes of communication and trade.

The Wachovia Tract within colonial Carolina was well placed in regard to regional dynamics (Figure 8.8). The tract lies directly on the main thoroughfare of colonial migration and communication into the backcountry of the Carolinas and Georgia: the Great Philadelphia Wagon Road. When they founded Wachovia, the Moravians immediately extended this road and began to throw out new roads toward Pine Tree (Camden, South Caro-

Figure 8.7. Hauser-Reich-Butner House, ca. 1770, Bethania, locally known as the "Cornwallis House." One of the replacement houses built following the restructuring of Bethania in 1769–70. The original central chimney was removed in the mid-nineteenth century when the house was remodeled; end chimneys were constructed and the interior space rearranged into a four-room plan. The massive stone chimney footing remains in place under the house. Such alterations occurred in other Bethania homes at that time and reflected changes in tastes and attitudes toward domestic arrangement and stylistic display.

Tradition has it that General Lord Cornwallis stayed the night in this house on February 9, 1781, when he and his officers quartered in the houses of Bethania and his army camped in the outlying fields. Cornwallis's pursuit of Nathanael Greene culminated shortly thereafter in the Battle of Guilford Courthouse (photograph by the author).

lina) and from there to Charles Town, South Carolina, and to Springhill (Fayetteville, North Carolina) on the Cape Fear, and thus to Wilmington, North Carolina. The importance of linkages to ports on the seaboard was understood by the Moravians well before the selection of the land for the settlement tract; Bethabara and Bethania, straddling the Great Road, worked to improve these linkages.

The regional placement of Wachovia was also in a position uniquely contiguous to the headwaters of several major river systems of Carolina. In addition to the Yadkin, both the Cape Fear and the Dan River drainages

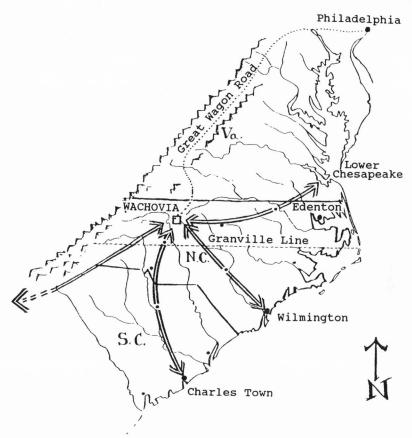

Figure 8.8. Regional context and trade routes, Wachovia, ca. 1760–1775. Wachovia was strategically situated in the backcountry along the Great Wagon Road and at the head of several major river systems of Carolina. This location provided linkages to Charles Town, Wilmington, the Chesapeake, and via the Great Wagon Road through the Valley of Virginia to Philadelphia (map by the author).

have headwaters that in part originate in Wachovia. As colonial routes of communication toward the seaboard tended to follow major drainages, Wachovia was well placed to establish communication from the interior with coastal South Carolina, North Carolina, and the Chesapeake. From a relatively central location, Wachovia's position on the Great Wagon Road also linked it with the backcountry of the Southeast.

As a combined urban center in this position, the Moravian colonial towns of Bethabara and Bethania, and later Salem, were well positioned to support and anchor settlement in the backcountry. Arguably, Bethabara and Bethania together were, as the colonial Moravian towns of Wachovia, a major factor in the settlement and maturation of Carolina. With Charles Town and the Chesapeake, Wachovia provided the final leg of a tripod, supporting settlement on the western frontier of Carolina.

Bethabara and Bethania began the construction of Salem, the planned central town of Wachovia, in 1766. In January of that year, Brethren from the two towns went to the selected site for Salem, raised a log house for shelter, and began the process of building the new town. In a July 1765 letter, Frederic William Marshall had suggested that construction at Salem begin with *fachwerk,* which uses shorter and fewer timbers, requiring less wood (Marshall, July 1765, in Fries 1922:313–15). This medieval construction technique in traditional German form, with structures set on stone foundations and capped with steeply sloping, tiled gable roofs, was used for family houses and institutional buildings in early Salem. Some log construction, and to a lesser extent post and beam and stone rubble construction, was also used during Salem's first decade (Hartley and Boxley 1997:6–7; Larson 2000). The relative peace of the mid-1760s through early 1770s allowed the Moravians to build their new town without the distraction of frontier tensions experienced in the initial period of settlement, and "the architecture of Salem reflected a greater sense of permanency and style indicative of the increased stability in the backcountry" (Larson 2000). Formally occupied in 1772 when administration and crafts moved there from Bethabara, Salem became a service, craft, education, and industrial center in the piedmont.

By the time of formal occupation of Salem in 1772, three other colonial Moravian communities were at various stages of establishment. Known as "Country Congregations," the Town Lots of Hope, Friedberg, and Friedland came into being at the south end of the Wachovia Tract, each with a schoolhouse/church and graveyard. As Spangenberg had predicted, these new settlements were not gathered into nucleated towns, but were dispersed on individual farms. With six colonial Town Lots, Wachovia very closely achieved the plans made by Moravian leadership in the early 1750s, and as the colonial period was drawing to a close, Wachovia was a dynamic system in the western piedmont of Carolina (Figure 8.9).

Conclusion

The system of Wachovia was the outcome of a concept and process that began before the tract was established in 1753. Its placement within the region was not accidental, but was the result of a combination of English and Moravian goals and intentions. From the English perspective, Wachovia provided a strong central place on the western frontier of Carolina to stimulate and anchor new settlement. From the Moravian perspective, the most suitable interior position was selected for trade with the re-

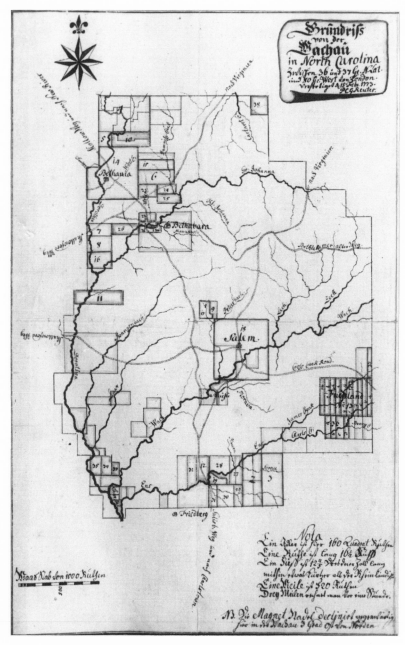

Figure 8.9. Map of Wachovia, 1773, by Philip Christian Gottlieb Reuter, show-
ing the six colonial Town Lots in place: Bethania and Bethabara in the north-
west; Salem in the center; and the southern Country Congregations comprising
Hope (southwest corner, Town Lot not labeled), Friedberg (south center, Town
Lot is above name), and Friedland (Town Lot in southeast) (collection of
Moravian Archives, Herrnhut, Germany; courtesy MESDA/Old Salem, Inc.).

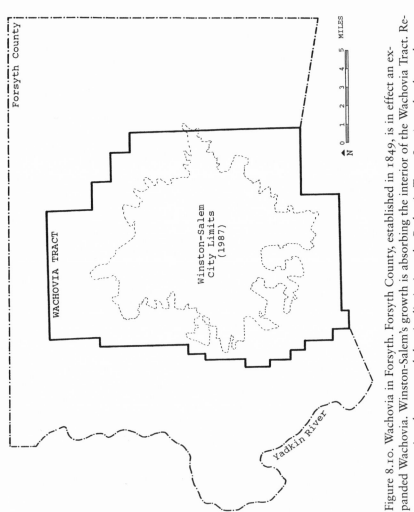

Figure 8.10. Wachovia in Forsyth. Forsyth County, established in 1849, is in effect an expanded Wachovia. Winston-Salem's growth is absorbing the interior of the Wachovia Tract. Recent annexations have moved the city limits into the Bethania Town Lot (map by the author and Martha B. Boxley, 1987).

gion and for insulated cultural stability within the tract. Both interests were served by the choice.

Wachovia exemplifies short- and long-term planning by the Moravians on the frontier of North Carolina. These plans incorporated the establishment of an initial foothold on a hostile frontier, while also anticipating subsequent changes that would be made possible by increased settlement and stability. Moravian foresight and the adaptation of an ancient form for Bethania acknowledged existing conditions while positioning the village for growth in a more stable future.

In those years of initial settlement, it was the strong interrelationship between Bethabara and Bethania that helped to carry Wachovia and the region through the turbulent period of the Cherokee War. Knowledge brought with the Moravians was adapted to the frontier so successfully that Wachovia was also an important factor in the mature occupation of the backcountry in the English colonial period. In time, Wachovia and the Moravian towns determined the structure of present-day Winston-Salem and Forsyth County.

With the formal occupation of Salem toward the end of the colonial period, Bethabara, the House of Passage, had fulfilled its role and begun to fade into the archaeological record; its function was replaced by Salem, which eventually became the city of Winston-Salem. Bethania, its ancient plan firmly placed, has endured into the present. It quietly existed in the countryside of Forsyth County until the 1980s when development pressures began to intensify. Today the little town continues to face many challenges, for now it lies on another frontier, the outskirts of an expanding urban place, Winston-Salem, the county seat of Forsyth County. Forsyth County is in effect an enlarged Wachovia, and Winston-Salem's city limits now almost fill the interior of the Wachovia Tract (Figure 8.10). While it has recently incorporated as a North Carolina town, Bethania again requires careful planning with the kind of wisdom exhibited by Spangenberg to ensure its stability on this new frontier. The town that was sturdily well suited to adaptation in the wild lands of colonial Carolina has now become a fragile remnant in the path of change.

Acknowledgments

Martha B. Hartley is particularly acknowledged for her long participation in the research on Bethania. Her knowledge and recognition of meanings to be found in the little village are greatly appreciated. Her contribution of the architectural component to this chapter is appreciated. John C. Larson of Old Salem, Inc., is gratefully acknowledged for contributions, comments, and counsel provided in the preparation of this chapter as well as during the periods of research. Jennifer Bean Bower and Wes Stewart of the Museum of Early Southern Decorative Arts/Old Salem, Inc., provided the photographic reproductions of the Reuter maps used in this chapter. David Bergstone of Old Salem, Inc., facilitated communication with Moravian Archives in Herrnhut, Germany. The Moravian Archives, Winston-Salem, North Carolina, has, as always, provided invaluable information in the preparation of this work. The thoughts of Spangenberg, Reuter, and other Moravian planners are available because of their ongoing work.

9
Frenchmen and Africans in South Carolina: Cultural Interaction on the Eighteenth-Century Frontier

ELLEN SHLASKO

Historical archaeologists have spent at least forty years studying the relationship between ethnicity and material culture, and these years of experience have shown time and again the complexity of that relationship. When historical archaeologists first began to examine ethnicity, it seemed that finding material evidence of ethnic identity, or "ethnic markers," would be relatively simple. After all, our basic training as archaeologists tells us that different cultures produce different physical remains, and a good part of that training consists of learning the pottery types, architectural styles, and other objects that allow us to recognize and interpret those differences. However, ethnic markers have proved elusive. Even when one is identified, that identification tends to raise more questions than it answers.

This chapter examines the relationship between ethnicity and material culture. It looks at a class of material remains that have been identified as signs of ethnic identity and takes the interpretation of those remains to the next level by acknowledging the complex factors that influence the choices that people make and the options that are open to them. Post-in-trench structures, the material remains examined here, have been found on a small number of sites in the South Carolina Lowcountry. The best known of these sites are Yaughan and Curriboo plantations (Wheaton and Garrow 1985; see Wheaton this volume). Wheaton and Garrow identified the post-in-trench structures at Yaughan and Curriboo as slave quarters and interpreted the unusual building style as an example of an indigenous African construction technique transplanted to the plantations of South Carolina. Their contribution to Singleton's (1985) *The Archaeology of Slavery and Plantation Life*, as well as Leland Ferguson's (1992) subsequent discussion of post-in-trench architecture in his book *Uncommon Ground*, introduced

South Carolina post-in-trench architecture and this interpretation to a wide audience of historical archaeologists.

As suggested above, the identification of post-in-trench architecture as a type of ethnic marker, or "Africanism," immediately raises a number of questions. Why do we find these structures almost exclusively on Lowcountry plantations? What African tradition do these buildings represent? What factors allowed Lowcountry slaves to build post-in-trench structures?

Since the initial discovery of South Carolina post-in-trench architecture almost twenty years ago, additional examples have been identified at the sites of Daniel's Island (Zierden et al. 1986), Lethe Farm (Steen 1999; Steen et al. 1996), and a site discussed below, Waterhorn plantation (Shlasko 1997). The gradually accumulating evidence allows us to take another look at post-in-trench architecture and identify the other variables in the complex equation that links material culture and ethnicity.

Post-in-Trench Architecture

The archaeological remains identified as post-in-trench structures consist of a set of similar subsurface features, although there are differences among the remains found at different sites. In each case, the builders dug a continuous trench (of various widths and depths) tracing the outline of the structure. Upright posts were set in the trench at regular intervals, and the trench was backfilled (Figure 9.1). The archaeological remains, therefore, consist of trenches containing rows of postmolds. The superstructure of these buildings remains a matter of conjecture, with many researchers hypothesizing that the buildings were of some sort of earthen construction, either packed earth or wattle and daub (Ferguson 1992:64). However, there is nothing in the subsurface remains that absolutely precludes the use of plank siding or other wood construction on the trench-set posts.

The post-in-trench buildings vary in size, from approximately thirty-nine by thirteen feet at Curriboo (Ferguson 1992:65), to approximately twenty-five by sixteen feet at Daniel's Island (Zierden et al. 1986), to approximately twenty-six by sixteen feet at Waterhorn. The depth and width of the trenches also varies. At Daniel's Island the trench was forty to fifty centimeters wide and thirty-five to fifty-one centimeters deep (Zierden et al. 1986). At Yaughan and Curriboo, the trenches ranged from 0.8 to 1.5 feet (24 to 46 centimeters) wide and from 1.5 to 2.5 feet (46 to 76 centimeters) deep (Wheaton and Garrow 1985:244). The structures at Waterhorn had trenches that were fifty to ninety centimeters wide and seventy to eighty centimeters deep. In profile, these trenches are straight-sided with flat bottoms (Figure 9.2).

South Carolina post-in-trench buildings appear to be an early to mid-

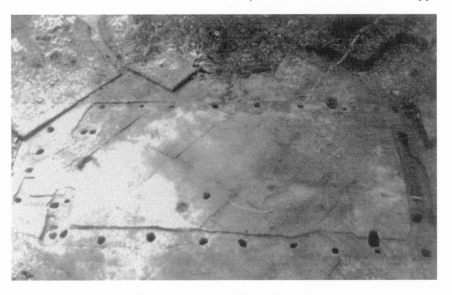

Figure 9.1. Post-in-trench structure at Waterhorn plantation.

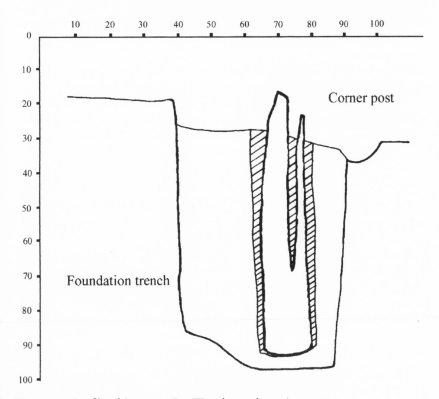

Figure 9.2. Profile of Structure B1, Waterhorn plantation.

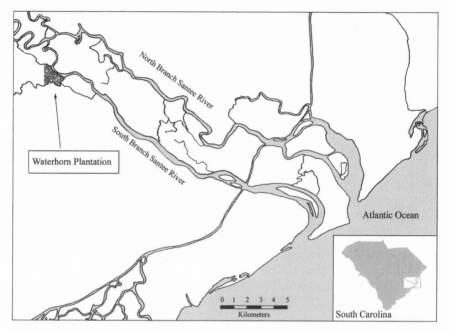

Figure 9.3. Map showing location of Waterhorn plantation.

eighteenth–century phenomenon. The structure at Waterhorn plantation was probably built between 1740 and 1750 and demolished by 1780. Similarly, the post-in-trench structures at Yaughan and Curriboo date to the middle of the eighteenth century (Wheaton and Garrow 1985:243).

Waterhorn Plantation

Originally settled in the mid-1680s, Waterhorn plantation appears to have been a fairly typical Lowcountry plantation. It was located on the south bank of the South Branch of the Santee River in Craven (now Berkeley) County, St. James Santee parish (Figure 9.3). The plantation encompassed approximately five hundred acres of high ground and swamp on a triangle of land, bound on the north by the Wattahan Creek (hence the name) and the Santee River and on the east and south by the Wambaw Creek. The plantation is now a historic area in the Francis Marion National Forest, used primarily for hunting and other recreational activities. Surface remains at the site consist of two mounds of fallen brick that represent the nineteenth-century main house and kitchen, and a standing chimney from a late nineteenth or early twentieth-century tenant farmhouse.

Documentary evidence indicates that Waterhorn plantation was first occupied in the mid-1680s. Daniel Huger I, a French refugee from the town of Loudon, received a land grant for the first two hundred acres of the plantation in 1696 (Salley 1973:464–65). However, the Huger family probably moved to the area between 1686, when they arrived in South Carolina, and 1688, when their son Daniel II was born "in Craven County in St. James Santee River" (Huger n.d.). Like many other early Carolinians (Gray 1958), the Hugers probably raised livestock and sold timber (Salley 1912:225). They also may have participated in the Indian trade (Lefler 1967:19). During the eighteenth century, rice became the main crop produced at Waterhorn.

The Huguenot community along the Santee River was very close-knit, a fact that struck contemporary observers (Lefler 1967:19) and that is evident in the history of Waterhorn plantation. Following Daniel Huger's death and burial at Waterhorn in 1712, his son, Daniel II, sold the property to a fellow Huguenot, James Nicholas Mayrant. Mayrant was connected by marriage to yet another Huguenot family, the Gaillards. When both James Nicholas Mayrant and his wife, Susanna Gaillard Mayrant, died, their estates were left in the care of Elias Horry II, a neighbor and grandson of Daniel Huger I. Eventually, Elias Horry II purchased Waterhorn plantation from the Mayrant children. The property remained in the Horry family until after the Civil War, when it passed to some cousins and then to a string of lumber companies and finally to the U.S. Forest Service (Shlasko 1997). These ties of kinship, proximity, and mutual obligation served to maintain coherence in the French community, despite external pressures for dissolution and assimilation.

The Huguenots

The presence of a Huguenot community in South Carolina resulted from political developments in France in the seventeenth century. Originally guaranteed religious freedom by Henri IV in 1598, French Protestants experienced increasing discrimination and persecution throughout the seventeenth century, culminating in the revocation of the Edict of Nantes by Louis XIV in 1685. Protestants were prohibited from practicing most professions and were forbidden to hold religious services. The government destroyed Protestant churches and used violent means to encourage abjuration of the Protestant faith. In an attempt to control emigration, the Crown confiscated the property of those Protestants who chose to leave France rather than convert (Butler 1983:13–22). Estimates of the number of Protestants who left France vary widely, from as low as one hundred thousand to as high as two million (Butler 1983:23). Those Huguenots who left France scattered among the Protestant countries of Europe. Approximately

fifty thousand refugees went to England, many settling in a large Huguenot community in London (Butler 1983:27).

The South Carolina Huguenots came, in large part, from this English
refugee community. Huguenots were viewed as a skilled and industrious
people, and advertising circulars touting the opportunities to be found in
the new colony were distributed to the London Huguenot community during the 1680s (Butler 1983:91–95). The first boatload of French immigrants arrived in Charleston in 1680, just ten years after the initial settlement of the colony, and Huguenot immigration continued sporadically for
the next few decades (Hirsch 1928). While the total number of French
Protestants in South Carolina was never that large, for a few years at the
turn of the seventeenth century they constituted a substantial minority of
the population, ten to fifteen percent by some estimates (Butler 1983:102).

Like other immigrants, the Huguenots were eligible for land grants
based on the number of people whose passage to South Carolina they sub-
sidized. The initial grant to Daniel Huger I was based on his importation
of six individuals, including himself, his wife, their two daughters, and two
French servants (Salley 1973:464–65). The Huguenot land grants were
clustered in several areas around Charleston, the largest of which was the
area around the Santee River, known as the French Santee. By 1690, there
were an estimated eighty French families living in this community, which
had a local church and plans for a town (Hirsch 1928:15). The area was
overwhelmingly French. In the 1692–1694 election, Huguenots won all six
county seats in the Assembly (Butler 1983:102). During the next decade or
so, a backlash of anti-French sentiment led to the passage of laws and regulations that attempted to strip the immigrants of their political power and
religious autonomy (Butler 1983:103–6).

These repressive measures were one factor in the Huguenot population's rapid assimilation during the eighteenth century. Another factor may
have been the presence of a rapidly increasing African population in the
South Carolina Lowcountry. As the population became increasingly divided across color lines during the eighteenth century, distinctions in the
white population began to blur. French Huguenots, despised in the early
1700s as part of a group that included "Jews, strangers, sailors, servants,
[and] negroes" (in Butler 1983:105), quickly moved into the mainstream
of white society. By the third generation, Huguenots were intermarrying
into the English community and attending English church services. They
became members of a white, free community that stood in clear opposition
to the black, slave population.

Despite their rapid assimilation, the Huguenots brought with them a vibrant culture that became part of the emerging culture of South Carolina.
For archaeologists interested in ethnicity, however, discovering evidence of
that culture has proven to be a frustrating experience.

Africans in South Carolina

Ten years before the first Huguenots arrived in colonial South Carolina, African slaves were among the very first arrivals in the new colony. A substantial portion of the European population came to South Carolina from the Caribbean, particularly Barbados, which had a fully developed economy based on slave labor. When these Europeans came to South Carolina, they brought their social and economic expectations and their slaves with them.

The Africans imported into South Carolina came from the same parts of West Africa that supplied the labor needs of the other colonies. In South Carolina, Africans were put to work clearing land for plantations, preparing forest products for market, herding livestock, and cultivating crops.

The labor demands of the growing colony encouraged the rapid importation of African workers. By 1708, approximately one-half of the South Carolina population consisted of African slaves. By 1720, this percentage had increased to nearly sixty-five percent (Wood 1974:146–47). In certain parts of the colony, particularly the outlying plantation districts, there was an even clearer African majority. In St. James Santee parish, where Waterhorn plantation was located, enslaved Africans made up approximately seventy-four percent of the 1720 population (Wood 1974:146–47).

The contributions Africans made to the colony have been overlooked for most of South Carolina's history. To many researchers, Africans contributed labor, but little else. This view is changing as researchers examine the impact of African expertise, technology, and culture on the emerging society of South Carolina (Carney 1993; Chaplin 1993). Of particular interest has been the role skilled African farmers may have played in the development of South Carolina's staple crop, rice.

Historical archaeologists were among the first to acknowledge Africans as active shapers of their worlds rather than as passive victims of oppression. When Leland Ferguson (1980) identified enslaved Africans as the producers of South Carolina colonoware, he opened the eyes of many researchers to the possibility that enslaved Africans created things and were not simply recipients of European goods. In their analysis of post-in-trench architecture, Wheaton and Garrow (1985) made another important contribution to this movement. Their identification of the Yaughan and Curriboo slave quarters as the manifestations of African ideas, not just African manpower, helped change the way researchers viewed the material remains found on southern plantations.

These and other studies were significant steps forward in the analysis of ethnicity in historical archaeology. By placing enslaved Africans in the center of the analysis, rather than relegating them to supporting roles, these studies gave historical archaeologists a new way of looking at ethnicity and ethnic minorities.

Power Relationships in the Lowcountry

While the recognition of African agency in the material record of Low-country plantations was a critical first step, the identification of these ethnic markers was just that, a first step. Far too often the analysis stops at this first level, degenerating into an endlessly circular argument. Africans lived on plantations. Africans made colonoware. I found colonoware at my plantation site. Therefore Africans lived at that site. This type of analysis leaves something to be desired.

Various researchers have dealt with this dilemma in different ways, expanding their analysis beyond the "artifact A = culture A" equation. For instance, Wheaton and Garrow (1985) took a diachronic approach, using the presence or absence of post-in-trench structures as a key to understanding the timing of acculturation among African-born slaves. Ferguson (1992) went in another direction, examining African religion for clues to the uses and importance of colonoware pottery.

Another type of analysis tries to determine the contexts in which African builders had the opportunity to openly apply their knowledge of traditional building techniques. The relationship between plantation owners and enslaved workers was clearly unequal, with most of the power wielded by the plantation owners. One area in which that power was expressed was the construction of the plantation environment. Many studies have examined the use of landscape design and spatial organization as tools for controlling subordinate groups (Delle 1998; Epperson 1999; Orser 1988), but it is less apparent how much this relationship influenced the construction and design of individual structures. In general, Europeans probably dictated the design and methods used in the construction of plantation buildings, even if they did not participate in the actual labor. Therefore, if we accept that post-in-trench building represents an African tradition of construction, the question becomes: What circumstances on Lowcountry plantations allowed Africans to practice their traditional skills? In other words, on most plantations throughout North America there is no indication of African technology being used, but on *some* Lowcountry plantations we have evidence of African traditional building. What is the difference?

There are very few documentary sources that mention buildings that modern researchers can interpret as African forms. One widely quoted source comes from the Works Progress Administration interviews of former slaves in Georgia (it should be noted that these interviews reflected the conditions of plantation life in the mid-nineteenth century, not eighteenth-century contexts such as those described here). The interviewee says that "Old man Okra" had built himself a clay-walled house, using a wattle-and-daub construction method. The post-in-trench structures found archaeologically could be this type of building. What should be emphasized here, however, is what comes next, which is the destruction of Okra's house under orders from the master, who "said he didn't want an African hut on his place" (in Ferguson 1992:75). The plantation owner would not tolerate the presence of an alien structure in his constructed world and he had the power to enforce his design on the slaves whom he controlled.

In a study of African vernacular architecture in the New World, Jones (1985:196) wrote, "A primary hindrance to blacks infusing more of their traditions into the built environment seems to have been the lack of opportunity. Ultimately, opportunity of expression becomes a question of the application of power." What circumstances, therefore, gave enslaved Africans on certain Lowcountry plantations the freedom to use traditional techniques when constructing plantation buildings? Why did the plantation owners not take one look at these odd-looking structures and order them torn down, the way Okra's master did?

French Colonial Architecture

The English were not alone on the North American mainland. The Spanish and French were also active colonizers during the seventeenth and eighteenth centuries. The French had extensive settlements in North America, not only in Canada, but also along the Gulf Coast and up the Mississippi River. On many of these sites archaeologists have discovered *poteaux en terre,* or post-in-ground, structures. This building technique is described as a "typical French colonial construction technique [that] involved the excavation of narrow wall trenches outlining the basic building shape. Logs, planted upright in these trenches, were joined at the top by hewn sills . . . rubble and stone mortar (*pierrotage*) had been placed between the upright logs to form a solid wall" (Walthall 1991:52). A firsthand account of the construction of these French houses reads:

> These house [*sic*] were formed of large posts or timbers; the posts being three or four feet apart in many of them. In others the posts were closer together, and the intervals filled up with mortar. . . . Over the whole wall, outside and inside it was generally whitewashed with fine white lime, so that these houses presented a clean, neat appearance. . . . Some dwelling houses and the stables and barns were made of longer posts set in the ground, instead of a sill as used in other houses. The posts were of cedar or other durable wood. (in Gums et al. 1991:92)

A few extant structures built in the French vertical-wall style can be found in the French colonial site of Cahokia, including the Cahokia Courthouse and the Church of the Holy Family (Gums et al. 1991:92–103).

The post-in-trench structures from South Carolina seem to fit this description. The builders of Structure B1 at Waterhorn plantation dug a wall trench that outlined the building. They placed posts at regular intervals in the trench. One of these posts, which survived *in situ* (see Figure 9.2), was identified as cedar (Lucinda McWeeney, personal communication 1997). Structure B2 at Waterhorn had a similar trench, although it did not trace a continuous outline of the building (Figure 9.4).

The evidence from the Mississippi Valley shows that the French settlers of North America possessed a tradition of vernacular architecture that closely matches the post-in-trench structures found on South Carolina sites. The *poteaux en terre* construction technique was widely used in the French colonial world, where it served as a form of vernacular architecture in frontier communities.

French and Africans in South Carolina

How does the existence of a French tradition of trench foundation architecture relate to our interpretation of the South Carolina post-in-trench structures? Does this mean that the Lowcountry buildings were built in a French style rather than an African style? Once again, the connection between ethnicity and material culture is seldom so simple. The approach used in this analysis is to see the use of post-in-trench architecture as a reflection of the interaction of two ethnic groups who both had a similar tradition of vernacular architecture.

Interestingly, all of the post-in-trench structures found on South Carolina plantations have been found at sites associated with Huguenot refugees and their families. The settlement and subsequent history of Waterhorn plantation was discussed at some length earlier in this chapter. From the time it was settled in the 1680s, until the end of the eighteenth century, immigrant or first-generation Huguenots owned the plantation. Huguenot families also owned Yaughan and Curriboo plantations and Daniel's Island (Wheaton and Garrow 1985; Zierden et al. 1986). The fifth example of post-in-trench architecture is even more important in this regard, because it represents the only instance of this type of structure to be found outside of the Lowcountry. At Lethe Farm, located in McCormick County in the South Carolina Piedmont, a French settler by the name of John de la Howe built his dwelling house using a type of post-in-trench architecture (Steen 1999, this volume). As of now, post-in-trench architecture in South Carolina is associated as much with Huguenots as it is with Africans.

The house at Lethe Farm is also interesting because it was apparently the home of John de la Howe himself (Steen 1999). One of the arguments for an African origin of post-in-trench architecture is that the first few

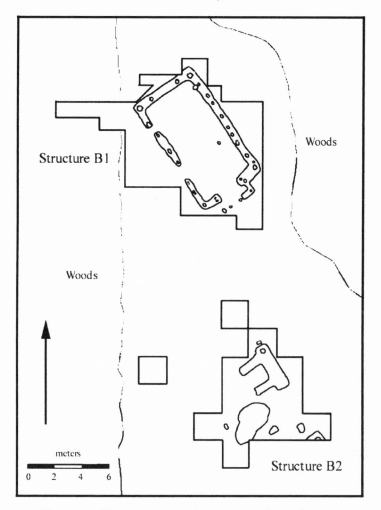

Figure 9.4. Plan view of Structures B1 and B23 at Waterhorn plantation.

structures found were clearly identified as slave quarters (Wheaton and Garrow 1985; Zierden et al. 1986). It was suggested that enslaved Africans, the majority population on Lowcountry plantations, built their own homes in the style with which they felt most comfortable. But at both Lethe Farm and Waterhorn plantation, the post-in-trench buildings are not slave quarters. Structure B1 at Waterhorn, with its integrated chimney, was probably occupied by a white overseer or even the plantation owner on his occasional trips to the plantation. In each of these cases, Europeans were willing not only to have clay-walled structures on their properties, but also to actually live in them themselves.

Conclusion

The presence of French landowners, familiar with post-in-trench and clay-walled houses, may be the factor that gave African builders on Lowcountry plantations the option of creating buildings using techniques they learned prior to leaving Africa. What we are seeing on these plantations are buildings that combined African and French traditions, being used by people who possessed similar ideas about what was appropriate in a dwelling house. This would explain why post-in-trench architecture is not found on more sites in the Southeast, where African laborers constructed houses using other building styles. For instance, in Virginia, even the earliest forms of impermanent architecture consist of framed houses. Sometimes in these houses, posts were set directly into the earth, but in those cases individual postholes were dug for each post (Carson et al. 1988).

As archaeologists explore the relationship between ethnicity and material culture, the complexity of that relationship becomes increasingly apparent. The factors that contribute to the behavioral options and choices that result in physical remains are extremely varied, and picking out the thread of one factor from the interwoven fabric of the final product is difficult, at best. By moving beyond a simple identification of ethnic groups to explore the possibility of ethnic group interaction and power relationships, this study tries to increase our understanding of how different groups of people contribute to the construction of a shared society.

Acknowledgments

The U.S. Forest Service generously supported the excavations at Waterhorn plantation that formed the basis for this research, with additional funding provided by the Archaeological Society of South Carolina. Without the help of numerous volunteers, this research would have been impossible. I would also like to thank Martha Zierden and Joe Joseph for inviting me to participate in this publication and for their kind words and support.

10

John de la Howe and the Second Wave of French Refugees in the South Carolina Colony: Defining, Maintaining, and Losing Ethnicity on the Passing Frontier

CARL STEEN

The French presence in the South Carolina colony was notable and sustained. French immigrants contributed a sizable portion of the colony's early settlement and the French were found in the colonial towns as well as among the Lowcountry's plantations (see Shlasko this volume). As population expanded and settlement pushed into the interior of the colony, the colonial government established a second arc of townships to anchor settlement and guard the coastal region from Native American attacks. The French were again drawn upon as settlers, and the township of New Bordeaux was established with a French presence in 1763 on land that had recently been contested during the Cherokee War.

This second wave of French immigration offered the potential to sustain and revitalize French ethnic identity within the colony. However, this did not occur. While some aspects of French culture can be found in the history and archaeology of this second generation of settlers, French ethnic identity was, for the most part, lost by shortly after the American Revolution. This chapter looks at the French settlement of South Carolina, and in particular the second wave of immigration to the backcountry of the colony, and discusses the definition, maintenance, and loss of ethnic identity through the archaeological and historical analysis of the John de la Howe site.

The French in South Carolina

The permanent European settlement of the South Carolina colony began in 1670 (Jones 1971), when a group of English and Barbadian settlers established Charles Town. The initial group included about one hundred thirty people (Edgar 1998:48). The population grew slowly at first and was focused on Charles Town. In the 1670s and 1680s events in France led to the revocation of the Edict of Nantes, a royal proclamation that had allowed Protestants to practice their religion. The revocation led to an outmigration of French Protestants. Many moved to neighboring lands in Switzerland, Belgium, Germany, and the Netherlands in hope of regaining their ancestral homes. Another destination was the British colonies, including the recently established colony of Carolina (Hirsch 1928). By 1700 some four hundred fifty French immigrants had come to the Lowcountry and settled in and around Charles Town. French enclaves were found in Goose Creek, in the Orange Quarter, and on the Santee River. Many immigrants were tradesmen and merchants, and a number settled in the city of Charles Town (Edgar 1998; Weir 1983).

There were, of course, trials and tribulations as the economy and governance of the colony were established (see Clowse 1971; Edgar 1998; Jones 1971 for in-depth discussion), but in general this first wave of immigrants grew and prospered with the colony. They encouraged friends and family members to immigrate, and eventually joined their British neighbors in the colony's ruling elite. By the turn of the seventeenth century the French Huguenots were firmly established in the Lowcountry, owning land, slaves, and plantations (Shlasko 1997). When the proprietary colony of Carolina became the royal colony of South Carolina in 1719, the second and third generations of French Carolinians were being born, many into Anglo-French families (Hirsch 1928).

The cultivation of rice came to be the colony's most important economic practice during the proprietary period, 1670 to 1719. The French of the Lowcountry experimented with a variety of crops (Clowse 1971), including viticulture and silk production. While early settlement had focused on the Charles Town area, rice was an extremely successful crop and the colonists turned their eyes to suitable lands up and down the coast, and inland. By the 1720s the Indians of the Lowcountry had mostly been enslaved, died of European diseases, or moved to the interior (see Hicks and Taukchiray 1998; Swanton 1946; Waddell 1974) and the expansion of the colony was hindered only by the number of immigrants that could be induced to settle.

During this period a singularly important facet of South Carolina's history crystallized. The lack of settlers was augmented by the importation of slaves. As early as 1708 African slaves became the numerically dominant ethnic population in the Carolina colony (Menard 1995; Wood 1974). Indian slaves, captured in the west and north, made up about twenty-five percent of the population as late as 1730 (Menard 1995). When slaves are referred to in a generic sense herein this grouping includes Africans, African Americans (Mintz 1974), Indians, and offspring of mixed parentage who shared their enslavement. By 1720 there were twice as many slaves as free people in the colony. Further, the plantations were thought to be deadly places for whites, in terms of disease, for most of the year, and those who could escaped to the more healthy environs of the city, leaving their plantations under the control of overseers and slave drivers. In the eighteenth century travelers said the South Carolina Lowcountry looked more like an African country than a European colony (Wood 1974).

At the same time the powerful Indian tribes of the Old West, Georgia and Alabama, were beginning to feel the pressure of the Europeans, and South Carolinians came to fear attacks from both free Indians and slaves. Colonial Governor Robert Johnson proposed a series of townships to be located in the interior of the state in a rough semicircle around Charles Town (Meriwether 1940:17–40; Wallace 1951; Weir 1983). These were to be populated by whites from Europe, who were to be induced to come by free land, and both personal and religious freedom. Each colony had a leader, or organizer, who recruited primarily from the lower classes from their homelands. These populations could be mixed, both economically and ethnically. According to historian Robert Meriwether (1940), two-thirds of the land in Purysburg was granted to people with French names, a quarter to people with German names, and the rest to Englishmen.

Among the Purysburgers were forty Protestants from Piedmont, Italy, and twenty-five Salzburgers. The Piedmontese were actually French Huguenots engaged in silk production there who were induced to bring their expertise with them (Elliott and Elliott 1990, 1994). The people of Purysburg are usually referred to as Swiss, as they came largely from the Alpine regions of Switzerland (see Crass et al. this volume; Elliott and Elliott this volume). But in fact, as stated earlier, many of the immigrants actually came not from the indigenous local populations, but from enclaves settled by refugees after the revocation of the Edict of Nantes. It is estimated that as many as sixty thousand French Protestants found refuge in Switzerland alone (Hirsch 1928:28).

The Purysburgers were placed on the Savannah River at the site of the old Apalachicola Indian town—a major river crossing and trading post. They earned their living trading with the Indians and guarding the colony against them. Meriwether (1940:36) says they received three thousand pounds per year for this responsibility. They grew various agricultural crops as well. Rice, corn, and cattle raising were the most important elements of the agrarian economy, but various other crops like beans, pumpkins, and turnips are also mentioned in the documentary record (Meriwether 1940:36).

French émigrés both earlier and later than the Purysburgers tried to manufacture silk and, indeed, succeeded. However, the people of the lower Savannah River were the most successful. In 1766 the residents of the Purysburg Township gathered over six thousand pounds of cocoons, which yielded about three hundred pounds of raw silk. This amounted to about a third of the silk wound in the government ligature in Savannah (Meriwether 1940:36).

During the period between the establishment of the first wave of townships in the 1730s and the second wave in the 1760s, the interior of South Carolina began to fill in with miscellaneous settlers from all over (Fischer 1989; Meriwether 1940). The townships were usually settled by a core group from a specific area (Meriwether 1940). The western townships—Purysburg, Orangeburg, Saxe-Gotha, and New Windsor—were settled primarily by mainland Europeans. The eastern townships were mostly granted to British immigrants. The people of Williamsburg, for instance, were Scotch-Irish Protestants from Northern Ireland. Kingston and Queensborough were to be settled by English, Welsh, Scots, and Scotch-Irish groups.

Kingston and Queensborough were in fact open to all takers, but there were few, and many came from within the colony itself. These cities provide examples of a phenomenon we see in the second wave of townships as well. Though the townships were established to provide a buffer against the Indians, by the time they were actually settled the Indians were no longer an immediate threat. The Indians of the Pee Dee, for instance, had sold most of their remaining fields to John Thompson in 1737 and moved away (Steen et al. 1998). Instead of taking up land within the township boundaries, settlers obtained the best lands they could, as quickly as they could. By the time the first settlers arrived in Kingston, for example, the Pee Dee River was settled as far north as the North Carolina border, and by 1740 few, if any, Indians remained (Steen et al. 1998).

During this period only two tribes of any size remained in South Carolina. These were the Catawba and the Cherokee. The Catawba were made up of a core group of Catawba and the remnants of dozens of lost tribes from around the Southeast. Among them were Pee Dee, Wateree, and Congaree from within the state, the Sara from Virginia, and the Natchez from Louisiana. The Catawba were "friendly" Indians, fighting on the side of the colonists against their ancestral enemies (Merrell 1992). Yet they were pushed inexorably back, almost to the modern North Carolina border by the 1750s. The greatest impact to their population came not from warfare, however, but from the devastating effects of European diseases. Smallpox epidemics reduced the Catawba to fewer than two hundred people by the 1790s.

The Cherokee, a large and powerful tribe related to the Creeks of Georgia, presented a greater obstacle. The Cherokee lands were mostly in the mountains of North Carolina, Georgia, and Tennessee, but they considered a great deal of the South Carolina Piedmont their territory. Though weakened by disease, they had a larger population than the Catawba and gave ground grudgingly, fighting intermittently, and finally going to war with the colonists in the late 1750s (Meriwether 1940:213–40). Raids and outright massacres on isolated farms and settlements put the backcountry settlers into a panic. Stockade forts and fortified houses were built in a number of locations in response (see Bastian 1982; Elliott 1995; Herd 1981), and both militia and establishment forces were raised.

Using an approach that characterized the colony's relations with Native Americans, and indeed helped shape later national policy, the militia rode into Cherokee territory in force and burned villages and crops, chopped down orchards, slaughtered cattle, and abused men, women, and children, "turning," as the commander of the expedition proudly stated, "five thousand Cherokees into the mountains to starve" (Edgar 1998:207).

The New Bordeaux settlement (Figure 10.1) was established in 1763 on land that had been seriously contested in the Cherokee War. After the Cherokees ceded a large part of the Piedmont in the late 1740s (Wallace 1951), isolated settlers began to filter into the area. At that time the Cherokee considered Little River the boundary of their territory. The first of the European settlers began to dispute this claim. As Figure 10.1 shows, they maintained that the stream we now call Little River was actually the Northwest Fork of Long Cane Creek and that the real boundary was farther west. The earliest land plats in the area assiduously sustain this position (Meriwether 1940).

Early in 1756 an extended family of Scotch-Irish immigrants came down the Great Wagon Road from Virginia to settle in the Little River/ Long Cane Creek area a few miles north of the later New Bordeaux settlement (Gibert 1976; Herd 1981). They were led by Patrick Calhoun, who was father to one of South Carolina's most famous politicians, John C. Calhoun. Patrick became the official surveyor for the area and a leading citizen. By 1758 about 175 land claims had been recorded in the area, many ignoring the Cherokee's definition of their boundary. Calhoun maintained that his group had the permission of the Indians to settle in the disputed zone.

This and countless other instances of encroachment on the frontier led the Cherokees to war. The Long Cane settlements took the first blow. About one hundred fifty Long Cane settlers tried to escape by wagon. A raiding party caught them at a creek crossing and twenty-three of their number were killed on the spot. An equal number were taken hostage. Nine children showed up a few days later, several of whom had been scalped and left for dead, but the remainder were never accounted for. Patrick Calhoun's mother was among those killed (Meriwether 1940:222).

The retaliation by the colony was vicious and led to a quick peace, secured by a 1761 treaty, and the cession of further lands. To secure the land against further threats three new townships were laid out. This was the second wave of townships, comprising Londonborough, Boonesborough, and Hillsborough (Meriwether 1940:116, 251). A bounty was offered to

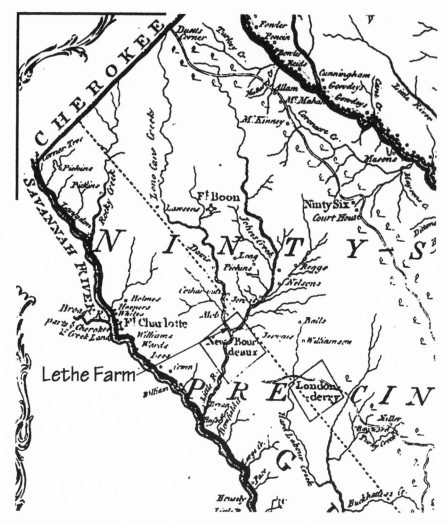

Figure 10.1. The James Cook map, 1773. Detail of Hillsborough/New Bordeaux area.

encourage settlement and beginning in 1762 groups of Palatinate Germans settled in Londonborough, while Irish immigrants settled in Boonesborough, though not in large numbers (Meriwether 1940:251).

In France religious toleration was once again stretched to the breaking point, and a colony of French Protestants was organized by the Reverend Jean Louis Gibert. About 175 people escaped to England and waited until 1763 for transport to the Carolina colony (Meriwether 1940:252). After a trying seven-week journey they arrived in Charles Town in April 1764 (Gibert 1976:10–13). The precise number of settlers is disputed by several authors, but historian Anne Gibert (1976), a descendant of Jean Louis Gibert, sets the number, including later arrivals, at 318.

Since the growing season was already too far advanced for clearing land and raising food at Hillsborough, their ultimate destination, the colonists were sent first to Fort Lyttelton, near Beaufort. There they could raise sufficient provision crops to eke out a living for the time being before moving on to their new home. It should be noted here that the French refugees had abandoned almost all of their possessions, and most came to America penniless. They were almost all in the direst of straits when they arrived in Charles Town, and they were allotted food, shelter, and medicine by the colony and public charities. Many were helped by earlier Huguenot arrivals, like merchant Henry Laurens, a second-generation French Carolinian.

Patrick Calhoun was engaged by the colony to help the French establish their town. He surveyed the township and laid out the town lots (Figure 10.2). The settlers were to receive a one-acre town lot, a four-acre vineyard or olive grove lot, and farmland in the township, as well as seed, provisions, and livestock. The royal governor, William Bull, also directed that a stockade fort be built and that land be set aside for a church, parsonage, and glebe for an Anglican minister, as well as for a parade ground and a public mill. He appointed Pierre Roger as justice of the peace, Daniel Due as captain of the militia, and Pierre Bouttiton as minister.

Calhoun built several houses before the first groups arrived in August and reported that by October the new settlers had completed six houses and prepared the frames for fourteen more (Gibert 1976:29; Meriwether 1940:253). In January 1765 the remaining settlers began to arrive. They brought with them grapevine cuttings, mulberries, and cocoons for silk production.

In 1767 a silk factory was built in New Bordeaux. Although silk production was successful—marketable quantities of silk were produced here, in Purysburg, and in Charles Town—the industry faced the same fate as nearly every other economic pursuit except rice, indigo, and cotton agriculture. The French believed that they could produce silk using the labor of women and children who would tend the worms in addition to doing their regular work. Production at this cottage industry level was sufficient for clothing one's family and provided a small surplus for market (Braudel 1979).

The quality of the product was not in question. In Charles Town Charles Pinckney noted that Pierre Gibert "dressed in a suit made from a mixture of wool and silk, both the growth of his own plantation so handsomely and finely woven and dyed that it would do honor to any manufacture in England" (Davis 1979:148; Gibert 1976:61). But the cost of labor was too high to make the industry profitable, especially after British bounties were eliminated in 1776. Governor William Bull wrote to the Earl of Hillsbor-

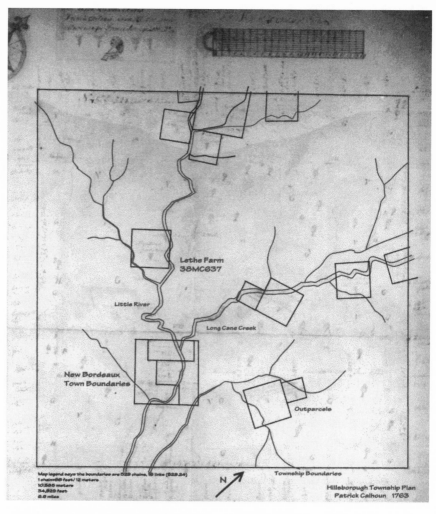

Figure 10.2. Patrick Calhoun's 1763 plan of Hillsborough Township.

ough in 1770: "Silk is a very flattering article as it is of great value. It is raised here of the finest sort with great ease and in great perfection. The only objection . . . [is] . . . if we turn our eyes to countries where it is made in abundance . . . there labor is very cheap, in our province it is very dear" (in Hirsch 1928:203). Both William Moragne and Anne Gibert indicate an ongoing interest in silk production that resembled a hobby, more than a practical pursuit. Hirsch (1928:203) says that the cost of labor "drove the industry into the hands of the well to do and the extremely wealthy classes. They could afford to raise silk for the sake of enjoying a pastime and the love of novelty."

The New Bordeaux settlers also experimented with viticulture, and succeeded in this as well. John Lewis Gervais, a neighbor but not a resident of the township, introduced an innovative method of training the vines to form a *chappelle,* or close bower, instead of winding the vines on stakes or frames. Thus each plant shaded the ground beneath it, preserving moisture and protecting the fruit and blossoms from the cold of winter and the heat of the summer.

Along with Gervais, New Bordeaux resident Jean Louis St. Pierre invested heavily in wine growing. St. Pierre's family had produced wine in Normandy for generations, and he was one of the few settlers who did not arrive utterly destitute. He invested his fortune in obtaining vines and other necessities with the understanding that the sum would be matched by the royal government. After he had given his all, the government backed out of the deal without explanation. Later charges were made that the French government had bribed St. Pierre's biggest supporter, Lord Hillsborough, to withdraw his support.

As was the case with silk, viticulture could not compete with rice, indigo, and cotton as money crops: the value of labor was too high. According to Moragne (1854:24), "They devoted themselves chiefly to the raising of flax, indian corn, and tobacco; but with some silk, indigo and the vine were not wholly abandoned for a generation."

Moragne indicates that the settlers immediately saw the "impracticability of confining themselves to the narrow limits which they had assumed." The length of their stay at the town is not exactly known. Some settlers began to sell their township lands almost immediately. John de la Howe began to assemble Lethe Farm in 1769 from parts of the New Bordeaux Township. The Gibert family, on the other hand, still owns a house in New Bordeaux within a mile of the old town site. Moragne (1854:25) continues, "They were beginning to spread themselves over the neighboring hills and valleys when the war of the Revolution broke out."

The Loss of Identity

The French at New Bordeaux lost their ethnic identity within a couple of generations. Although it has been charged that the concept of acculturation (Steen 1999) overly simplifies a complex process of give and take, in this case it appears that the French took an active and enthusiastic hand in joining the emerging American frontier society. How can we explain this phenomenon?

Material Culture

The French had lost their homes, and in a sense their stake in their French heritage, when they were persecuted, robbed, and driven from their homeland. They had little reason to look back fondly on a country where their neighbors had hounded them out of their ancestral homes and stolen their property. In an immediate sense, and one that is critical for archaeologists, they also lost their material culture. Before the settlers came together in England, many had had to escape by the dark of night, all but empty-handed. Most left behind their homes, furnishings, family heirlooms, and the tools of their trades. When they got to the colony they outfitted themselves as best they could. As their farms began to produce they built more permanent structures and bought furnishings, but there was no local outlet for French goods—they had no way to obtain ethnically significant items on a large scale. For instance, they might obtain a religious item, like a Bible, but not a set of dinner plates. Indeed, English law prohibited the colonies from trading directly with France. So the first generation, as soon as they were able to afford certain goods, say a set of dishes, had to buy from the same stocks as their neighbors. After the American Revolution they were free to trade with France, but few did so.

Only a single site with a French pedigree has received excavations at anything greater than the survey level in New Bordeaux. At John de la Howe's home site, Lethe Farm, excavations around the main house and a detached kitchen building, supplemented by a site-wide shovel testing survey, yielded almost no artifacts of French origin. A few sherds of tin-glazed earthenware are somewhat arbitrarily considered "French" rather than English. Sherds from a Normandy stoneware storage jar are French in origin; these plus a French coin dated 1785 and a Bordeaux wine bottle are the only artifacts that can be segregated. Examining Dr. de la Howe's will and inventory, there is nothing listed that indicates that he spent his first fifty years in France other than a few medical books written in French—and of course he also had volumes written in German, Latin, and English.

The most important thing we found at the site that was clearly French in origin was Dr. de la Howe's house itself. This building was marked by a rectangular mound of clay daub. Beneath this pile of daub and clay the remains of a wall trench and posts are evidence of a French-style *poteaux en terre* structure (Kniffen and Glassie 1986). This is significant because it represents something that the French could bring to the colonies—knowledge of house-building techniques—and that would show up clearly in the archaeological record (Figure 10.3).

We were able to identify the locations of ten structures at the Lethe Farm site other than the main house. All of these were marked by stone foundations. While they may be the remains of French-style *poteaux sur sole* structures (Kniffen and Glassie 1986), which are built on stone and wooden foundations, none yielded any daub, or *bouissilage,* the clay packing that would be used to form the walls.

Thus these appear to be foundations of the German-style log structures that were adopted by the Scotch-Irish in the backcountry. These were com-

Poteaux sur Sole / Post on Sill Construction

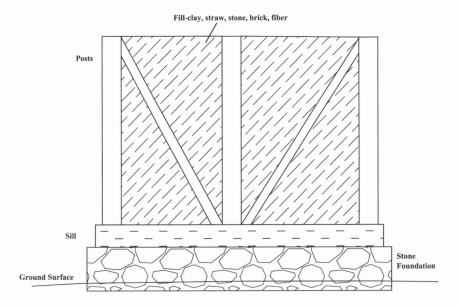

Poteaux en Terre / Trench and Post Construction

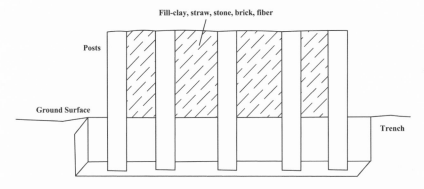

Figure 10.3. Building with clay, French style. *Poteaux en terre/poteaux sur sol* detail.

mon from Pennsylvania to Georgia and points west, spreading with the Western Expansion (Kniffen and Glassie 1986). The nearby Guillebeau House (Lewis 1979), the only standing structure in McCormick County built by a first-generation Huguenot, is a classic example of a one-and-a-half-story, full dovetailed log structure with fieldstone footings and chimneys.

This use by French émigrés of a local architectural style different from that of their native land is a crucial point, because there is some debate over the origin and meaning of wall trench/clay wall construction in South Carolina. In excavations in the Lowcountry wall trench houses have been found at a number of sites, where, as a result of Wheaton and Garrow's interpretation (Wheaton et al. 1983; Wheaton and Garrow 1985), they are usually attributed to African origins. Arguments against this interpretation have been marshaled elsewhere (Steen 1999; Steen et al. 1996). To summarize, briefly, in South Carolina this technique is found most often on plantations with French owners—like Yaughan, Curriboo, Lesesne, and Waterhorn (Shlasko 1997; Wheaton et al. 1983; Zierden et al. 1986). Further, documentary evidence of both clay or cob wall construction and wall trench construction in South Carolina can be attributed to European origins (Steen 1999:97–99).

The arguments in favor of this phenomenon reflecting African roots are that the houses are found in slave settlements (though this may be circular reasoning) and that they at least look like they were built using traditional African construction techniques. At this writing archaeological research in the areas of Africa from whence most South Carolina slaves came is lacking, and there is no physical evidence of similar techniques being in use in seventeenth- and eighteenth-century contexts. In recent works Africanists have warned that there is considerable diversity in the contributory populations that expands exponentially in diachronic terms (DeCorse 1999:132–35).

At Lethe Farm only one building had wall trenches and clay walls, the home of Dr. de la Howe. His slaves were either forced to live in log houses or did so voluntarily. While de la Howe was a singular individual and clearly does not reflect the norm, this and all other evidence points more to a French origin for this architecture than an African origin. This mixing of cultural influences stands as a constant in the development of an American social identity, and in the attendant loss of previous ethnic affiliations.

Livelihood

The French colonists at New Bordeaux also lost their livelihoods. Researchers have accumulated lists of immigrants and their occupations (Davis 1951; Elliott 1984; Gibert 1976; Lesesne 1972). Many had occupations that were doubtless adapted to the new circumstances: wheelwrights, coopers, carpenters, cobblers, tailors, and weavers were surely able to use their skills (Elliott 1984:10–11). There was probably less demand in the backcountry for book binding, wigmaking, and similar occupations.

The largest named category was agricultural: there were sixteen plowmen and thirteen vineyard workers as well as two gardeners and a "worker of soil." Yet even their efforts were transformed by the New World experience. Within a generation there were few who still grew the same crops they had in France, and probably none who did it in exactly the same way. The New Bordeaux settlers moved into a colony whose economy was driven by labor costs and the capitalist principles of supply and demand. Farmers faced the same economic forces as manufacturers and were forced to adapt. As historian Anne Gibert (1976) has noted, many people continued to raise grapes for wine and silk for weaving, but more as an amusement than for market. In this way they were hanging on to a vestige of their traditional lifeways, but this vestige was nonfunctional and soon died out.

Almost all hands in the South Carolina colony were turned to agriculture. There were few towns and almost no manufacturing of any kind—thus labor for wages was rare. In the first twenty years of the New Bordeaux colony the settlers grew corn, flax, wheat, indigo, hemp, and tobacco. They tried to bring in salable amounts of silk and wine as well, but as we have seen, these fell by the wayside before the turn of the nineteenth century. After the introduction of the cotton gin in the 1790s the arable land in the South Carolina backcountry was dedicated to cotton, and a new "aristocracy" of slaveholders and plantation owners began to emerge (Davis 1951; Klein 1990). When the land began to wear out in the early nineteenth century people began to move west, the second generation of French colonists among them. Thus those who adapted to the new agriculture were swept west with the emerging southern plantation society, and were further distanced from their French roots.

Identity

After their occupations the French lost their names. The importance of a name in establishing one's position in social relations is self-evident. Even most of the original settlers Anglicized at least their first names: Jean became John, Pierre became Peter, and so on. In some cases the entire name was translated: Etienne Rhod became Steven Rhodes, Theadore Rossel became Theodore Russel, Jean LeRoy became John King. In the second generation, the first to be born in South Carolina, few parents gave their children French names.

Self-identification is an essential element of ethnic group identification and is a signifier for members and nonmembers. We can extrapolate that the name changing symbolizes both loss of self-identification as members of an ethnic group and the desire to fit in with their neighbors. By giving up their names they were publicly joining the new society.

Language

After their names the French lost their language. In 1854 William Moragne (1854:33) says that when his grandfather, Pierre Moragne, retired he devoted himself to study and "prepared many essays on religious and other subjects, which he designed for publication, but which his immediate descendants did not sufficiently appreciate to make public." In a footnote he adds: "It is but just to state that the third generation, by amalgamating with the English, had so far lost their identity as to present an obstacle to the publication of *anything* in the original language" (emphasis added).

In the appendix of Moragne's address, as if to underline this point, fragments of Pierre Moragne's journal are presented—in translation. Both William Moragne and his sister, Mary, were university educated—he was an attorney and she was a writer—and as such could still converse in French. William Moragne notes that his grandfather spoke almost nothing but French in his lifetime, but also states that his parents had a poor understanding of the language. As Anne Gibert (1976:75) notes, "French rapidly became a second language." Gibert further states that the French volumes found in several inventories of the nineteenth century are more the mark of an educated reader than a sign of survival of the French language among native speakers. In her family in the twentieth century French was learned as a foreign language at school, not at home.

Time and Assimilation

Finally the colonists lost their French ethnicity completely. Mrs. Mary Anne Colvin, the last of the original settlers, died in 1839. Pierre Guillebeau was the last of the children born to original colonists. He died in 1854 at age 90 (Moragne 1854:39). Moragne's address states that in 1854, between death and removals, "at this day not more than forty remain of those descended purely from French parents, while the descendants of those intermarried with the English inhabitants do not exceed one hundred in number." That is, less than a hundred years after being founded, the French enclave had all but disappeared.

Anne Gibert (1976:73) uses her family as an example of how this transpired. Her ancestor, Pierre Gibert, was father of six sons and five daughters. Of eight who married, only one, John Louis Gibert, took a wife from the French community. The other seven married out. As they married outside of the French community they began to move away to join their spouses. Today only a handful of French names remain in McCormick County.

Religion

The religion of the French colonists was not lost entirely, but was adapted to fit their milieu. Huguenots and Presbyterians differed in relatively minor ways theologically, so the transition was not hard. By most accounts the Huguenots of New Bordeaux were upright, and even somewhat severe, Christians. Although the colony was led by Huguenot ministers Jean Louis Gibert and Pierre Bouttiton, and land was set aside for a church, they never actually built a church of their own. Instead they joined their Scotch-

Irish neighbors the Calhouns at Hopewell Presbyterian Church, and later formed their own Presbyterian congregation at Liberty Springs Church. Jean Louis Gibert, Peter Gibert, Pierre Moragne, and others served as elders in these churches, so their membership was obviously not coerced.

Conclusion

In rapid fashion the French settlers of New Bordeaux gave up most elements of their ethnic identity. Their language, their occupations and lifeways, their religion, and even their self-identification were changed in a matter of two to three generations. One could say that they were thoroughly acculturated. This is not a term that I am usually comfortable using, as it indicates the replacement of one culture with another. It implies domination and conquest, suggesting that weaker, inferior cultures are defeated and "captured" by stronger, better ones.

It is an argument that was used to suggest that African Americans were simple, malleable creatures who had no cultural past of their own (Herskovits 1941) and were therefore inferior and deserved to labor in the fields. It should be obvious today that African Americans were never acculturated into some uniform Anglo-European "Georgian" society—rather they hung on to aspects of their cultures, and joined with others to forge a unique creole society. This process of creolization has been discussed by Mintz (1974), Joyner (1984, 1999), Ferguson (1989), and Steen (1993, 1999), while Deetz (1976), Fischer (1989), and Glassie (1968), among others, have examined the ethnic makeup of American society.

The French of New Bordeaux show a different pattern from African Americans, for many reasons. Most important was that they came into the colony under much different circumstances. They also came at a time when colonial culture was changing quickly, and they were free to participate at will. First, sides were being taken in the struggle for power that was decided by the American Revolution. The side one chose was literally a life-and-death matter (Clark 1981; Herd 1981). Gibert (1976) and Moragne (1854) say that the French of New Bordeaux, to a man, took the Revolutionary side. Whether this is completely accurate or not, when the war was over they were no longer French immigrants, but American citizens. So one could say that not only were they acculturated, but also they fought for the privilege.

Second, after the Revolution soldiers received bounties for lands in the west, and the expansion of the frontier into Georgia, Alabama, and Mississippi followed. The children of the first generations of South Carolina backcountry settlers, French, Scotch-Irish, and others, joined in this movement. As much as anything the Western Expansion has defined the American social identity.

Far from being a homogeneous society of whites and blacks, the population of the South Carolina backcountry in the colonial period was an ethnic stew. The French colony at New Bordeaux illustrates a pattern of culture change that many ethnic groups underwent in becoming American. Settlers from Northern Ireland, Scotland, and England were joined by Germans, Swiss, and French. Settlers born in America, both from the northern colonies and from within the South Carolina colony, along with free and enslaved African- and American-born blacks—African Americans—and Indians all combined to forge a new cultural identity.

11

Anglicans and Dissenters in the Colonial Village of Dorchester

Monica L. Beck

The historic manifestations of religious conflict range from mass extermination to actions as subtle as social exclusion. A common feature of religious conflict is that it usually occurs among neighbors, as a result of proximity within the most basic form of settlement, the community. Historian Joseph Wood describes community as a "social web" and notes (1988:160) that "space and place denote common experience, and, in the traditional view, community as experience and community as place were one [therefore] the organization of the common space—the settlement form—reflects in large measure the configuration or spatial structure of the social web."

The focus of this chapter is the social web of the Anglican and Dissenter communities outside of Charles Town, South Carolina, in the eighteenth century, and the landscape created by these people (see Beck 1998; Clement et al. 1999). A closer examination of the community of Dorchester through documents, landscape analysis, and archaeology suggests that coexistence, not conflict, defined the daily lives of these residents. Through an analysis of their settlement pattern and its symbolic meaning, we can investigate the evidence of social conflict, as the historic record suggests, or, perhaps more accurately, we can delineate the spatial negotiations over time of two groups with opposing religious views.

The Conflict between Anglicans and Dissenters

The sources of conflict between the Church of England, or Anglicans, and Dissenters, or those who disagreed with the Church of England, began brewing in the early 1600s and were crystallized by the accession of King Charles I in 1625. Dissenters such as the Presbyterians and Puritans (also known as Congregationalists), Independents, Pilgrims, and Separatists were essentially Calvinists bent on the reformation of the corrupt political power and immoral behavior within the Church of England (Atkins and Fagley 1942:68–76; Kuehne 1996:31–32).

Eschewing the formal rituals and structure of the Church of England, the Puritans saw themselves as a gathering of like minds based on a covenant or an agreement among the congregation. Puritans hoped to work within the established church, while more aggressive groups such as the Separatists or Pilgrims advocated a total break (Atkins and Fagley 1942:68–76; Kuehne 1996:31–32). The Puritans sought the irresistible grace of God, which Anglicans interpreted as a rationalization to reject established order and morality. Anglicans viewed the Dissenter movement as a means to interpret one's own desires as God's will. A purer relationship with God defied traditional obedience to the established order because it defied class distinctions. Anglicans wanted order and obedience, specifically to the established hierarchy of God, king, lords, and bishops, so that traditional power structures would remain (Woolverton 1984:185–86).

Many Dissenters emigrated to the New World in groups, seeking to establish religious enclaves. Anglicans, in contrast, came to the New World singly and as families, often focusing on economic gain over religious freedom. As a result, Anglicans lived scattered throughout the colonies (other than Virginia and the New England colonies), living and working alongside others with predominantly Dissenting religious views. Therefore, the British Anglican leaders were faced with the unenviable task of expanding in the colonies by conversion rather than force. By conducting services, preaching sermons, opening schools, and providing catechetical instruction, the colonial Anglicans hoped to appeal to the very values of what it meant to be a good Englishman (Woolverton 1984:90–105). Where they held power, other strategies could be applied.

In colonies such as South Carolina, Anglicans lacked the power and influence they held in England. Reverend Samuel Thomas, a South Carolina Anglican minister, commented (ca. 1704, in Woolverton 1984:155–56),

> It is sadly evident how destitute our Brethren of the Church of England in South Carolina are of spiritual guides . . . and [in] how much danger they are "to be led aside to error" for as circumstances are at present in this our Province not one person in 20 among those who profess themselves of the Church of England can have benefit of the word and sacraments from a Church of England minister, the Dissenters have at present 4 ministers among them besides one Anabaptist Preacher . . . and I am informed that 3 or 4 more dissenting Ministers are going . . . in the Spring.

The South Carolina Religious Frontier

In South Carolina, the outward battle between Anglicans and Dissenters raged primarily as a political battle from the 1670s through the 1700s (though religion and politics were inevitably intertwined). Although many of the settlers who came to the colonies outwardly supported religious reform, many were toiling as tenants of nobility or were the second and third sons of the landed gentry who responded to the opportunity of easily obtained land in the new colonies. Many of these immigrants continued to see themselves as Englishmen and desired to remain loyal to their King and church.

Political factions emerged, however, as a result of the variety of overlapping national, ethnic, and religious groups who settled the new colony: British, French Huguenots, New England Puritans, African and Barbadian blacks, and Protestants from Ireland, Switzerland, Scandinavia, and Germany. Gideon Johnston, an Anglican minister and commissary to South Carolina, commented that the "contests, that are on foot here, are not between High and Low Churchmen; but between dissenters and the Church" (Woolverton 1984:158).

The Lords Proprietors who established the Carolina colony created a governmental structure that encouraged settlement while allowing them to control the legislative process. In 1669, John Locke and the first Earl of Shaftesbury, Anthony Ashley Cooper, created the original draft of the Fundamental Constitution for the Carolina colony. This guiding document declared that "no person whatever shall disturbe, molest or persecute another for his speculative opinions in Religion or his way of Worship" (Woolverton 1984:157). Although it was never ratified, historian Walter Edgar (1998:43) describes the Fundamental Constitution as "a cleverly written document designed to attract settlers." This document provided for religious toleration and a liberal naturalization process and, when combined with traditional rights regarding land grants, ownership, and titles, would attract many seeking new futures (Edgar 1998:43; Woolverton 1984:157).

As early as two years after settlement, differing political factions emerged. A large group of the initial settlers were Barbadian sugar planters from the West Indies. These settlers opposed the control of the Lords Proprietors. They settled principally in the Goose Creek area and formed a party that included Anglicans and French Huguenots. Edgar (1998:85) notes that the Goose Creek men were referred to as "the Anglican Party, the Church Party, the Barbadians, and the Anti-Proprietary Party" in seventeenth- and eighteenth-century papers. The Proprietors sought to weaken the power of the Goose Creek men by increasing the number of Dissenting settlers. It was their hope that these Dissenters would be defenders of the proprietary government (Edgar 1998:85–88).

The Proprietors selected Joseph Morton, a hard-line Dissenter, as governor in 1682 and refilled positions held by Goose Creek men with Dissenters. Although the Dissenters were in governmental control, they failed to weaken the power of the Anti-Proprietary party. This failure was compounded by the unscrupulous actions of some of the Dissenters chosen by the Proprietors to lead South Carolina; the most notorious, Governor Joseph Blake, used his office and connections with Joseph Morton to make a fortune from customs racketeering (Edgar 1998:90). As a result, the French Huguenots switched sides and the Anti-Proprietary party moved back into power in the 1690s. By this time, political authority began shifting from the Proprietors to the colonial government. The political battle for governmental control was fought by the Dissenters and the Anti-Proprietary party and the prize was both political and economic (Edgar 1998:88–99).

By the 1700s, the focus of the Proprietors began to shift as well. The senior Proprietor by then was an Anglican who supported efforts to exclude from public office those politicians who were not devout members of the Church of England. A simple communion oath was all that was necessary to hold public office and this superficial conformity incensed devout Anglicans. The senior Proprietor sought to enforce conformity in the colony of South Carolina. As a result, the Proprietors began to withdraw support from the Dissenters whom they had encouraged to emigrate and instead supported the previously anti-proprietary faction, the Goose Creek men. The first outward sign that the political tide was changing occurred with the gubernatorial inauguration of James Moore, Jr., an Anglican and acknowledged leader of the Goose Creek men (Edgar 1998:92–93).

Although Moore's election made some Dissenters uncomfortable simply because he was an Anglican, the fact that he was not a religious fanatic and was more interested in military actions in support of Queen Anne's War (1702–1713) eased some of this concern. However, Moore was succeeded in 1702 by Sir Nathaniel Johnson, a High Tory and staunch supporter of the Church of England. It was during Johnson's leadership that the 1706 Church Act established the Church of England as the official church of South Carolina (Edgar 1998:94). Political wrangling continued as the Dissenters lobbied to have the Church Act repealed and Johnson removed from office (Edgar 1998:97; Woolverton 1984:165–66).

The mending of the thirteen-year division between the Dissenters and the Goose Creek men began in 1711 with the political service of Thomas Nairne, a Dissenter leader. Edgar (1998:107–8) credits the increased battles with the Spanish and Native Americans as the catalyst for this new spirit of colonial cooperation. As a result of this cooperative spirit, opposing individuals who once would have undermined each other began to work together. By 1719, the common foe of the South Carolina colonists was the Lords Proprietors, not each other (Edgar 1998:97–108).

The Settlement of Dorchester

It was toward the end of this political and religious battle (one that the Anglicans were winning) that the village of Dorchester was settled by a group emigrating from New England. The records of the Congregationalist or Puritan "First Chyrch at Dorchester" in Massachusetts indicate that on October 20, 1695, Joseph Lord, Increase Sumner, and William Pratt were dismissed from that church for "The gathering of A church for the South Carolina," and two days later,

> ocktober the 22 being ower lecktuer day was sett apart for the ording of Mr. Joseph Lord for to be pastuer to A church gathered that day for to goe South Coralina to settell the gospel ther and the names of the men are thes
>
> Joshua Brooks   of Concord
> Nathaniel Billings   "
> Simon Daken   "
> William Adams   Sudbury
> Increase Sumner   Dorchester
> William Pratt   "
> George Foxe   Reading
> William Norman   Coralina
>
> thes with Mr. Joseph Lord did enter into a most solem Covenant to sett up ordinances of Jesus Christ ther if the lord caryed them safely thither accordin to gospell truth withe a very large profeson of ther faithe. (Salley 1967:191)

With their explicit mission to "settell the gospel" these men formed a scouting party to survey land and apply for grants for the removal of this group to South Carolina. William Norman, listed in the original group, was already a settled Dissenter outside of Charleston. He, as well as other prominent Dissenters, actively recruited settlers from New England and encouraged them to settle in Carolina, perhaps to strengthen the Dissenting voice in the area. The lure of South Carolina was undeniably strong; land was available for the taking. The colony was already known to be religiously tolerant, and it was politically influenced by Dissenters during the late 1600s. However, because of the changing political tide, colonial expansion took on a new meaning; it became a way to expand political strength. William Pratt, who was designated the Elder for the group, wrote in his journal that

Increase Sumnor and I war kindly reseved and entertained by the
Lady Extol and tho two other men war indevering to get into faviour
with the ladey and other neighbers and to obtain the land at asly rever
[and,] that we mit not obtain it, yet thay could not prevail: for as
soon as we came the lady and others of the neighbers did more hily
esteem of us then of the other as thay told us and rejoysed at our
coming (tho ther was no more of the church then increase sumner
and I, and) after we had discorsed secretly with them, thay war not
only very kind to us, but allso used all menes and touk great pains
to obtain our setteling upon ashley rever and that we shuld indever
to perswad our pastr and the Church to settel their. (Salley 1967:
195–96)

Meanwhile, the Reverend Lord and other members of their group were being entertained south of Charles Town by another Dissenting group seeking their settlement. Elder Pratt went on to record:

our minister and church war strongly perswaded by the lieutt generall
blak [who was the governor Blake's brother] and many others to go
to new london [or Willtown located on the Edisto River; see Zierden
this volume] to settel . . . mr lord cald me aside and I had much dis-
cors with him and when he heard what I had to say consarning ashly
rever and consarning new lundon, mr lord was wholy of my mind
and willing to tak up, upon thos condishons that we discorsed about,
at ashly rever, which condishons war keept privet, betwen to or 3 of
us. we keept sumthing secrit from others which was greatly for our
benifit. (Salley 1967:196)

The reasons and conditions that were kept secret then remain a secret
today. Regardless, this group from New England pursued land grants total-
ing 4,050 acres on the north bank of the Ashley River, from the mouth of
Bosho-ee Creek upriver about three miles, not surprisingly, to the boundary of William Norman's land.

Settlement Patterns in the American Colonies

The terms *village* and *community* are often used interchangeably and are
perceived to have the same meaning (see Zierden this volume). The village
—houses, storefronts, and offices arranged around a centrally located commons and church—is the most commonly perceived living pattern associated with colonial period settlement. It is hard to imagine another settlement pattern that would provide settlers of the New World a stronger sense
of security and community (Wood 1988:160–64). Yet, as archaeologist
James Deetz (1990:2) describes, "the classic village-centered three-field sys-

tem" is a visible condition of social order. Communal farming of exterior strips of land allowed people to be farmers while residing within the social confines of a village (Deetz 1990:2). Wood (1988:160) wryly observes that this "conventional view that New England's colonial communities formed compact villages gathered around a central meeting house correlates nicely with an idealized social order attributed to hard-bitten, theocratic Puritans." However, the opportunities of colonial settlement would have created a sense of tension between an individual's desire for the rights of private property, including the related economic potential, and the sense of security derived from an interdependent community (Wood 1988:164).

Although from a shared common heritage, English settlers did not come from homogeneous backgrounds. Seventeenth-century rural England was not composed entirely of farmed fields around nucleated settlements. Instead, dispersed villages were common in many parts of England; thus, the "English village" that New World settlers came from was not necessarily the commonly perceived nucleated village (Wood 1988:164). Archaeologist Kenneth Lewis (1984) argues that the varied social and economic functions offered by a colonial community affected population density. These communities acted as centers of trade and linked the frontier with the colony's entrepôt. *Nucleated settlements* were small yet they remained politically organized and acted as centers of trade. *Seminucleated settlements* were also small and usually they were more dispersed—while they may have had a center, there may also have been outer locations offering some central services, or the center itself may have been disjointed. *Dispersed settlements* contained scattered households that were integrated as cash-crop producers within the larger socioeconomic system (Lewis 1984:23).

Civil and religious liberty was important for settlers who came to the colonies, yet the longing for land was the most compelling reason for settlement and expansion. The abundance of land had an undermining effect on social control, however. New settlers, as well as the relatives of existing settlers, spread inland wherever they could, not necessarily through the enlargement of original towns, but through the settlement of new communities (Wood 1988:160–61). Joseph West, governor of South Carolina from 1674 to 1682, defied the Lords Proprietors a number of times when he sided with the colonists and issued land grants outside of areas that required settlers to build residences in neatly laid-out villages (Edgar 1998: 84–85). These people, then, applied their own adaptive concepts to shape the landscape in a manner that satisfied both economic purposes and explicit expressions of their position in the world (Deetz 1990:3).

The Landscape of Dorchester and the Surrounding Area

Landscape modification represents the most visible aspect of the mediation between the natural and physical worlds (i.e., cultural adaptations), reflecting both social and economic relationships. The meaning of this mediation as expressed on the landscape can be analyzed through an archaeological perspective that focuses on discovering patterns in land use and then interpreting the processes and meanings of the arrangement and relationship between natural properties and cultural remains (Deetz 1990:2; Smith 1993:17; Stewart 1996:12; Zierden 1997a).

By creating landscapes that were useful to them, colonial settlers made powerful cultural statements that were latently symbolic. Many of these "symbols" remain visible in land patterns today (Deetz 1990:1). It is argued by archaeologists Mrozowski and Beaudry (1990:189) that it is

> possible to gain insight into the workings of culture in terms of consciously and unconsciously shared notions of order and causality, of reason and sense in human relations, through archaeology by attending to the affective power of the built environment—the total material expression of landscape and land use.

The following discussion analyzes the implications of the landscape design of Dorchester, from the planned nucleated village to the realities on and in the ground, from initial settlement through the Revolution. It appears that the nucleated village was never the center of the Dissenter community. They apparently established a village to facilitate trade, while emulating their neighbors who capitalized on the possibilities of plantation agriculture. The location of their meeting house and their residences supports this.

The Community of Dorchester

The settlers from Massachusetts who established Dorchester set about to divide the land into something that resembled a New England township (Figure 11.1). This included a commons, farm lots, and land reserved for a mill. The farm lots were initially divided into two divisions consisting of two ranges per division. The first range, located along the river, was divided into twenty-six lots of fifty acres each, while the remaining ranges were divided into lots of forty-five acres a piece. A parcel of fifty acres was designed as a "place for trade" with a small central market square and was named Dorchester. The town was divided into 116 quarter-acre lots neatly arrayed within a grid of streets (Bell 1995:2; Smith 1988:11–12).

Elder Pratt recorded in his journal that on "the 23.day of march in the year 1697. the church and others that wer concarnd did draw loots, the 24th day that all meet together to stak out and mark ther loots in the trading town. on both days when thay meet to gether on thos ocasions ther was love and unity and pece in what was acted" (Salley 1967:199). These lots, like the forty-five- to fifty-acre farm lots, were distributed among the group

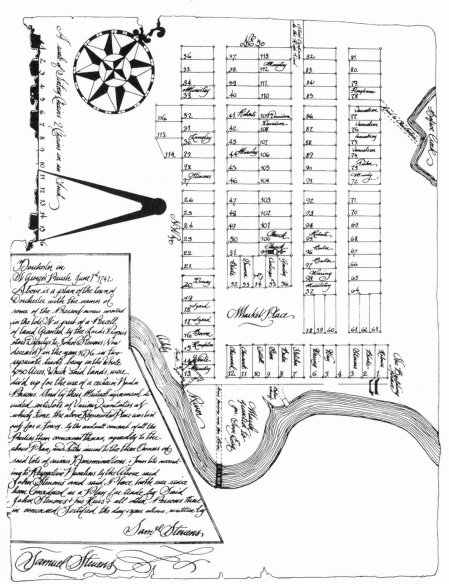

Figure 11.1. A 1742 map of the Village of Dorchester.

by lottery, which, as Sigmon (1992:28) notes, "is the same method used [in 1640] by the land committee [to divide] the . . . lands in Sudbury, MA. . . . It was the [Congregationalist or] Puritan way to allow God to excise His will." Elder Pratt's statement that "others that wer concarnd did draw loots" introduces the question of who actually lived in the town of Dorchester. As yet, no document listing the original settlers and the results of the lottery has been found; however, information derived from subsequent transfers, wills, and conveyances creates a picture of the population of the early town.

Though sparse, there is some historic evidence to suggest that the Dissenters chose to live outside the village as planters. The number of early settlers in the Dorchester area varies. There is documentation that 140 to 158 people sailed from Boston in January 1697. Henry A. M. Smith's research from the early twentieth century traced eighteen Dissenting male heads of households in the settlement before 1720 (Smith 1988); Ray Sigmon (1992) increased this number to twenty-six in his 1971 thesis. There is evidence that at least three non-Dissenting household heads were landholders in the Dorchester settlement early on, and these are most likely some of the "others concerned" in the initial land lottery. The most interesting and telling detail about the original Dorchester settlers is that only five of the twenty-six Dissenting households have any reference, of either willed property or land sales, to town lots. It appears that the overwhelming majority of these early residents chose to settle on their forty-five- to fifty-acre farm lots, many increasing their land holdings to three to four hundred acres through land purchases. Further, of these five Dissenting households associated with specific lots in town, three also owned farm lots and the household members most likely lived outside of the town. Analysis suggests that these settlers used an adapted seminucleated pattern that allowed them to seek their fortunes as planters. Like the Dissenting community at Willtown on the Edisto (Zierden this volume) and the Wappetaw Independent community on the Wappoo (Clement and Grunden 1998), Dorchester manifested a definite sense of community, was situated outside of nucleated centers, and was centered around the church.

The Churches

Church buildings, whatever their denomination, serve an important, and often central, symbolic role in the community and usually dominate the local landscape, both physically and visually. Historian Charles Bolton has suggested that local churches, both the buildings and the collective organizations, "stand at the center of community life." They are the core of "the whole system of values—spiritual, intellectual, and political"—and provide communities with their distinctive texture (Bolton 1982:5).

The church built by the Anglicans at Dorchester supports Thomas Barrie's suggestion that the architecture of churches served as "a symbol of the continuity of the belief systems of a society" and as such "needed to symbolize permanence." Consequently, churches were constructed from more durable materials than surrounding residential architecture. Barrie also voices relationships relevant to the Dissenter's church: "Sacred architecture was typically the result of communal efforts that marshaled the human resources of a particular society and directed them to a common goal" (Barrie 1996:4).

Dorchester Dissenters immediately began the construction of their Meeting House and situated it in the very center of their community (Figure 11.2). However, they did not build it in the village of Dorchester, even though several members of the congregation donated town lots to the ministry. Instead, they chose a location approximately two miles from the village on the road, called the "Broad Path," between the first two ranges of the first division (Sigmon 1992:29). The Meeting House was built on the highest land along this road. In place of their original, temporary wooden structure, the congregation constructed a two-story brick structure that was thirty feet square and was used into the early 1880s (Sigmon 1992:29).

The first Dissenter preacher was Rev. Joseph Lord, who came with the original group from Massachusetts. He remained in the area for over twenty years before returning to New England in 1720, after the Yamasee War. Interestingly enough, Lord was succeeded by Rev. Hugh Fisher, who was described as a Presbyterian minister from Scotland (Cote 1981:147; Stacy 1987:15). Rev. Fisher was the teacher for the Dissenter White Meeting House from 1720 until his death in 1734. Fisher was replaced by Rev. John Osgood, who was born in Dorchester (Cote 1981:147; Stacy 1987:15). Neither Sigmon (1992) nor Smith (1988) mentions village lots associated with Rev. Lord or Rev. Fisher; like their neighbors, they probably resided outside of the village of Dorchester. The name Osgood, however, is associated with a Dorchester lot on the basis of the 1742 map of the village (Figure 11.1). Additionally, the Osgood name has been linked to one of the weavers in the village.

The impressive ruins of the bell tower of St. George's Parish church still have the visual impact the tower must have had during the colonial life of Dorchester (Figure 11.3). The ruins, located on the highest ground in the village, indicate that this Anglican church was located in the very center of the village of Dorchester and begs the question, "What is an Anglican church doing in the center of a Dissenter community?" The Anglican church was built after the area was redefined and designated as St. George's Parish. In 1706 supporters of the Anglican church brought about the passage of the Establishment Act, which established the Church of England as the official church for South Carolina.

Construction of St. George's Church began in 1719. A church commission secured the location and the land for this church, and the place they chose was in the center of Dorchester. Rev. Varnod, the second minister and a prolific writer, described the church in a 1728 letter to the Society for the Propagation of the Gospel as "50 feet long and 30 broad besides the setting out of the chancel 15 foot by five" (Society for the Propagation of

Figure 11.2. The Dissenter's White Meeting House as it looked in 1875.

the Gospel [SPG] n.d., vol. 18). He noted that his home, however, was located approximately a half mile from the church on seventy-five acres of land near the Ashley River. Varnod indicated that his unfinished house measured thirty-four by twenty-five feet (SPG n.d., vol. 18). It is interesting to note that the Anglican glebe and house were located outside the village. The location of the church, though, in the center of the village, expressed the traditional Anglican views of structure and rationalism, active in the church's involvement in the politics, commerce, and social structuring of colonial society. Since most of the Anglican church members were large planters living along the Ashley River and not in the village, the church does not appear to have been situated for the convenience of its members. While one intent may have been to grow, convert, and offer more services to the Dissenter community, the central location more likely reflects the ties of the church leaders to commerce and community, a religious/political/administrative center reflecting hierarchy, order, and tradition.

Figure 11.3. The remains of the bell tower of St. George's Anglican Church.

Spatial Meanings: 1720s to the Revolution

Following initial settlement of Dorchester, it appears that the village was inhabited by both Dissenters and Anglicans and that there was fluidity between the village merchants and surrounding Anglican and Dissenter planters. Lingering political tensions were expressed locally as friction between religious leaders, but there is little evidence that this friction carried over to the general populace. Eventually, the separatist sentiments transitioned into a common pre-Revolutionary unity.

Rev. Varnod described Dorchester in 1728 in this way: "There is a small piece of ground called Dorchester . . . it is the Pleasantest spot of Carolina in the Settlement. There is upon it but 6 Families" (SPG n.d., vol. 18). However, by the 1730s, an increase in newspaper ads for Dorchester merchants suggests that the village was beginning to grow as a commercial center and shipping point for goods to and from Charles Town.

Historic records indicate that several of the initial settlers possessed specialized skills: there were two shoemakers, a shipwright, two families of weavers, a wheelwright, a housewright, a carpenter, and merchants. Three of these settlers can be associated with town lots into the 1720s. While it is difficult to determine who was living in the village, it is also difficult to determine who of these villagers were Anglican or Dissenters. Only two documents from this period offer some information about the religious affiliations of the Dorchester area. The first is a parish census compiled by the Anglican Rev. Francis Varnod in 1728 (SPG n.d., vol. 18) and the second a 1742 map of the village that denotes surnames in some of the village lots (Figure 11.1). On the basis of only these two records, it appears that the religious affiliation of the villagers was predominantly Anglican, or that at least several of the merchants had Anglican partners.

Of the total of thirty-seven surnames noted on the 1742 map, five of these names are listed on the census as Dissenters and nine are listed as Anglicans. For example, Richard Baker, who is noted on the 1742 map on lot 8 (Figure 11.1), was a merchant and operated one of the wharfs in Dorchester; he and his family are documented as Dissenters in Rev. Varnod's 1728 census. Walter Izard and his son Ralph were very wealthy planters who owned a town house on Lots 17 and 18 facing the market square (Figure 11.1). Apparently, the Izards leased the lots to a wealthy man named Dr. Archibald McNeil in the late 1760s. The Izards are designated as Anglicans in the 1728 census and Dr. McNeil was described in the late 1760s as active in the Anglican church. Overall the census indicates that slightly more than half of the parish population were Dissenters (287) and the remaining portion Anglican (260).

The political record indicates that the predominantly Anglican-supported Anti-Proprietary party appeared to be winning the political battle as early as the 1690s. According to Edgar (1998), staunch Anglican and Dissenter foes were working together against the Lords Proprietors by 1719, yet tensions between Anglicans and Dissenters persisted in Dorchester to the 1720s. While Rev. Varnod's rhetoric in several letters to his funding missionary society indicated further community conflict, the spatial distribution of community residents and their respective roles in local political and administrative issues suggest otherwise.

In the South Carolina community for only a few months, Rev. Varnod lamented to the Society for the Propagation of the Gospel in 1723 that he had "the misfortune to be in a place that was 20 years ago all settled by Dissenters, where they have [a] considerable meeting house, together with having been constantly supplied with a teacher when St. Georges Church could have no Minister [,] yet notwithstanding all this we find that our Church is too small for [the] Congregation of this Infant Parish" (SPG n.d., vol. 18). Varnod seemed very pleased to report to the Society in 1728 that, although at the time of his arrival no more than forty either belonged to the Anglican church or attended service, "now Thank God . . . [it] is very much altered for the better for I have about 30 Church families attending Divine Worship every Lords Day" (SPG n.d., vol. 18). Several pages later he noted that "above 240 adults dissenting from the Church of England" attended the Dissenters' meeting house (SPG n.d., vol. 18). From his analysis of this literary religious discourse, Jeffrey Richards (2000) notes that, for Varnod, information worthy of reporting to the Society concerned his ability to build a church. Richards goes on to note that "his discourse has the effect of claiming the space for Anglican rhetoric . . . [while acknowledging] . . . a powerful Dissenter presence in his midst" (Richards 2000:6).

Conflict within the Dissenters' church can also be observed from Rev. Varnod's same 1728 letter. In detailing the religious nature of the parish, Varnod commented that Rev. Hugh Fisher, the Dissenters' "teacher," as Varnod called him, was a professed Presbyterian and "thus these New England People became thereby both Presbyterian and Independants" (SPG n.d., vol. 18). Varnod went on to note that regardless of their current situation, this group had not abandoned all adherence to their former Puritan principals since the "Deacons, and Elders carry that Esteem and Affecton so far as not to allow [Rev. Fisher] to baptize any Children whose Parents are not of the Covenant. A thing I have heard complained of by some Dissenters of his Congregation" (SPG n.d., vol. 18). Varnod continued by including a letter "which Mr Fisher was pleased to favor me with lately" (SPG n.d., vol. 18). In his own words, Fisher explained that the original settlers were Calvinist in their beliefs and they admitted "to communion with them Sober Episcopalians, Anabaptists and Presbyterians" (SPG n.d., vol. 18). However, since Fisher's arrival after Rev. Lord returned to New England, Fisher conceded that the "Government of the Congregation has been Presbyterian for the past 10 yrs, however, holding to their Congregationalist or Puritan views they continued to support their church and their minister by voluntary contribution." Richards's (2000:5) analysis of this passage acknowledges "the full degree and language of resistance within the church itself to Fisher's Presbyterian orientation; and perhaps the measure of Fisher's own attempts to cover up for his Anglican colleague some of the controversy within his own church."

Fisher remained the preacher for the Dissenter community until his death in 1734, and he was succeeded by John Osgood of Dorchester. During this time, the growth within the Dorchester area was reflected in the expansion of Dissenting families who had outgrown the original land grant of 4,050 acres. These young families settled an area nearby called Beech Hill and were serviced by Rev. Osgood on a rotating basis, until the call of abundant land could not be resisted any longer. A portion of this Dissenter community, accompanied by Rev. Osgood, moved to Midway, Georgia, in the 1750s (Bell 1995:10). The draw appeared to be the availability of adequate *communal* land, a concept still attractive to staunch Dissenters; the available lands in the Ashley River area, in contrast, were adequate for the individual-minded Anglicans and those Dissenters who had embraced this philosophy.

Prior to the Dissenter exodus to Georgia, the Dorchester Anglicans continued their struggle for control by pushing for legislation and financial support for an Anglican free school. Legislation for a school was passed in 1724 and a board of commissioners was appointed to govern the institution. The expressed purpose for the school was to teach the Anglican doctrine in an effort to stem the spread of dissent. The commissioners commented that the problem for the Church of England within the parish was the lack of country schools and they complained that without proper Anglican religious instruction, their children would grow up as "Ignorant as the native Indians" (quoted in Bell 1999:3). It is interesting to note that the first group of Dorchester Free School commissioners included a man named Joseph Blake, who was the son of the Dissenter governor Joseph Blake. Although the younger Blake was raised a Dissenter, Varnod's 1728 census lists him as an Anglican. The following board appointed in 1734 included a prominent Charles Town Dissenter (Bell 1999:appendix I). This further supports the generally amicable coexistence of Anglican and Dissenter, as well as the fluidity of church membership by many residents of the Dorchester area. Reasons for membership in, or at least attendance of, both churches may include intermarriage, availability of religious services, commercial or political advantage, or simply convenience.

The board of commissioners struggled for years to raise the funds to construct and operate a free school. At some unknown point, the commission obtained two lots in Dorchester to construct the schoolhouse and the schoolmaster's house, but historic records indicate that the structures were not built until 1758–1760 (Bell 1999:7), long after the most strident Dissenters had moved to Georgia. By this time, the political and religious environment had changed as concepts of unified independence began to take hold.

These lots were located directly across from the main entrance of St. George's Church. The spatial choice of these lots reflects the explicit goal of the school commissioners, which related directly to Anglican control of the school and their desire to impact the future through Anglican indoctrination. Brick mounds are all that is left to represent the presence of the Dorchester Free School and the schoolmaster's house, which is currently under excavation. Unlike the other structures in the village, these buildings were constructed in the center of the lots rather than on the street front. Recent excavation has focused on determining the use of the lot fronts and how the overall complex was used under the management of the schoolmaster (Figure 11.4).

Conclusion

This chapter traces the nature of the religious conflict between Anglicans and Dissenters in colonial South Carolina, particularly in the populated areas of the early eighteenth century, and the historic resolution of this conflict. An initial struggle for political power, sometimes masked in religious rhetoric, eventually gave way to a collective political agenda and climaxed in the American Revolution. In the colonial village and community of Dorchester, this political alliance was preceded by commercial and physical negotiation. An initial interpretation of a contested landscape, supported by the powerful visual symbols of two churches and the sometimes inflammatory rhetoric of colonial religious leaders, has been replaced by one of coexistence and cooperation, with the locations of the two churches instead reflecting differing social agendas.

Though maps and plans would suggest that the settlers of Dorchester embraced the development of an urban center, analysis of land use records and the physical landscape suggests that the Dissenters instead developed a dispersed settlement. Eschewing their allotted town lots, the majority of the early residents settled on their forty-five- to fifty-acre farm lots, adding to these holdings through purchase. They then focused on succeeding in their new home and actively sought the financial rewards arising from plantation agriculture. The seemingly peripheral location of the Meeting House, then, was in fact "central" to the dispersed planter community and located on a prominent land feature adjacent to a major roadway.

Scholars have traditionally interpreted the visually dominating Anglican church, located in the center of the village, as Anglican triumph over the retreating Dissenters, manifest in their move to Georgia. However, a more careful reading of documents from the early eighteenth century, as well as those postdating the departure to Georgia, suggests that instead the village land was simply available to the Anglicans. Their placement of a church in the center of the village embodies their doctrine of hierarchy, order, and tradition—but it did not embody conflict with resident Dissenters. The seemingly peaceful coexistence of Anglican and Dissenter residents in the

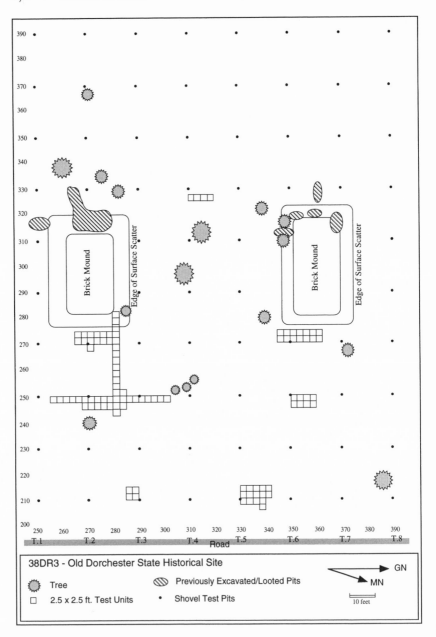

Figure 11.4. Site map of the schoolhouse and schoolmaster's house excavation project.

affairs of daily life and in secular matters stands in contrast to the inflammatory rhetoric found in the correspondence of religious leaders. These letters, which dominate the sparse historical records of Dorchester, may be the only place such conflict existed.

The two church buildings, then, were centers of different types of communities, not necessarily in conflict. As other studies of colonial South Carolina have shown (see Crass et al. this volume; Zierden this volume), most of the European settlers of Carolina quickly got down to the business of profiting from the land and the plantation agriculture system. But the continued coexistence of the two communities, and the eventual departure of some Dissenters, suggests that religious and cultural differences remained.

The late seventeenth-century religious/political conflict between Anglican and Dissenter was replaced by the late eighteenth century with a growing concept of independence and alliance. The evolving message of southern Anglicanism was structure and rationalism. This message appealed to the new Americans who considered themselves English, enlightened, modern, and rational. Within the colonies, Anglican vestries appointed and dismissed their ministers, which amounted to a level of lay control that was unheard of in England. The southern Church of England was controlled by the planters, who wanted an orderly religion whose message would remind everybody of their proper position, along with their duties and limitations, in the colonies (Bolton 1982:4, 13).

Woolverton (1984:181) notes that between 1702 and 1740, more than one-third of the twenty-six Episcopalian ministers who held cures in South Carolina for more than one year were "Calvinists, French, or both." By the mid-1700s, beyond the religious disagreements, there was a growing acceptance of American Protestantism that was supported by the Americanization of both the Church of England and the Dissenters. For example, more signers of the Declaration of Independence were southern Anglicans than any other denomination (Woolverton 1984:232).

A new identity appeared to be forming as the growing concept of Americanism, and independence from England, began to take hold in the 1760s to 1780s. The early rhetoric representing the Anglican and Dissenter conflict has been described by historians of American Congregationalism to have always been "a preacher's movement, the prophet challenging the priest" (Atkins and Fagley 1942:68–69). Further, they argue that this challenge was taken up and lost by the Anglican ministers, for "in the end the Puritan preacher and not the Anglican, in the battle of the pulpits, won the popular mind" (Atkins and Fagley 1942:68–69). Ultimately, it was the Dissenter faiths of Presbyterian, Baptist, and Episcopalian that remained, since it was these denominations that absorbed all previous Anglicans who chose to reside in the newly created independent United States of America.

Acknowledgments

I would like to thank both editors of this volume for their encouragement, patience, and extensive editorial comments of previous drafts of this chapter. I would also like to thank Julia King, Director, Maryland Archaeological Conservation Laboratory; Al Hester, Historic Sites Coordinator, South Carolina State Park Service; Dan Bell, Region I Historic Resource Coordinator, South Carolina State Park Service; Jeffrey Richards, English Department Chair, Old Dominion University; and Keith Stephenson, Research Archaeologist, University of South Carolina, for their discussion, review, and editorial comments of this research project.

12

Frontier Society in South Carolina: An Example from Willtown (1690–1800)

MARTHA ZIERDEN

The thousand-acre Willtown plantation on the Edisto River is marked by an imposing antebellum home on a bluff over the river, surrounded by tidal marshes, low-lying pastures, and climax hardwood forest. About a mile from the river, in the center of the woods, is a knoll of high land covered in large hardwood trees adjacent to swampland, the latter crosscut by dikes and ditches, remnants of eighteenth-century rice production. The only sign of human habitation on the knoll is a deer-hunting stand, constructed in an oak tree, and a dirt road. With the exception of the dikes and the road, the site appears much the same as it did to arriving European colonists, those seeking their fortune through slave-based agriculture. But the wild grapevine and blanket of oak leaves mask evidence of peoples and events of eighteenth-century South Carolina, when various groups interacted, competed, and ultimately formed new identities on the colonial frontier.

American frontiers are implicitly defined from the perspective of the arrival of peoples of European ancestry. But the frontier was a meeting place of peoples of varied ethnic, social, and religious affiliations; it was not so much a place as a phase of interaction within a geographic setting where native and immigrant groups competed, cooperated, and changed in relation to each other (Crass et al. 1997; Hofstra and Mitchell 1993; Mitchell 1991). European domination and Native annihilation was not always a foregone conclusion (see Kupperman 2000).

The founding of new towns on the westward frontier was a common occurrence in the settlement of South Carolina and other colonies. Willtown was part of the first wave of frontier settlement from Charles Town, the point of initial English settlement in 1670. Willtown began in the 1690s as an urban center for protection from Spanish and Native invasion, for communication and worship by Europeans, and for trade with Native

Americans. By the end of the colonial period, it was a community of Euro-American–owned rice plantations, operated by enslaved Africans and Native Americans, part of the larger plantation economy centered in Charleston.

Research at Willtown was commissioned by the owner, Mr. Hugh Lane. Initially, the project was designed to "find Willtown," the original urban enclave. Mr. Lane greeted us with a seemingly simple, yet profoundly challenging question, "Why did Willtown fail?" To begin to answer such a question, both historically and archaeologically, requires an understanding of the panorama of Willtown's existence, both as a nucleated settlement and as a broader community. The serendipitous discovery of James Stobo's rice plantation on the hardwood knoll ultimately contributed more information on the history of Willtown than did research on the town itself.

For the purposes of this study, the Willtown community included the town, the outlying farms and plantations, and the communities of African and Native peoples living with and around European settlers. "Community" is considered to be a basic unit of social organization and transmission, a constantly evolving set of extrafamilial social relations. It can be based on ethnicity, religion, economic or social status, or other social constructs, or on simple geographic proximity (Horn 1994; Lewis 1984). A community, then, may be defined in terms of geographic or social scale, or often both. "Pluralistic" communities are composed of individuals from diverse backgrounds, and the term implies differing social, economic, and political agendas by the community members. In many situations, people live *around* each other as well as *with* each other. There is, as a result, a heightened sense of self/other, where the physical presence of other is a constant issue in defining self. In frontier communities, the relative social status of the varying groups was in flux, and the underclasses in many ways held great sway over the emerging dominant class (see Clement et al. 1999).

The Frontier Town

Although the town did not develop as intended, British colonial leaders initially envisioned Willtown as a nucleated settlement. Built on the frontier that served as a buffer from Spanish and French threat, as well as Indian raids, a close settlement was seen as essential for survival. Willtown was planned with the overlapping and seemingly conflicting goals of promoting Indian trade and protecting Charleston from Indian invasion. Situated on a high bluff on the Edisto River, the site was highly defensible and, for a few decades, well suited for commerce (Figure 12.1; see also Anthony this volume, Figure 4.2).

The earliest settlers, and indeed those often colonizing the expanding

Figure 12.1. Map of the South Carolina coast showing the location of Willtown (based on Stuart map of 1780).

frontier, were religious Dissenters, principally members of the Presbyterian church. Dissenter groups, such as the Willtown Presbyterians, came directly from England or via the northern colonies, and were attracted to South Carolina because of readily available land and religious toleration (Gardner 1969). But religious differences soon developed political overtones in the Carolina colony, and these differences and divisions would guide the political course of the colony through its first half-century. The formation of a Presbyterian congregation in 1704 by the strident and outspoken Archibald Stobo would involve Willtown in the ongoing struggle between Anglicans and Dissenters (Fraser 1989:17; Linder 1996; see Beck this volume).

The Protestant settlers found the Indians with whom they shared the land both a blessing and a curse. Control of the Indians was pursued relentlessly by the English, French, and Spanish as a result of Europe's desire for animal skins and the colonists' desire for Indian slaves. Not surprisingly, Willtown was initially dominated by traders: James Cochran, Commissioner of Indian Trade in 1707; Thomas Bruce of the Scouts; William Scott, an authorized trader; and others (Linder 1996:21–25). It is likely that the stores in Willtown served the Indian trade as much as, or more than, they did the surrounding European settlers. Limited archaeological work in the town area supports this interpretation: Lot 45, documented as occupied in the 1730s and the only one with exclusively eighteenth-century artifacts on the surface, contained two structures of mud-sill construction. Neither appears domestic, and they have instead been interpreted as a store and warehouse, likely for deerskins. The lot is located away from the bluff that was the central part of the planned community, and adjacent to a navigable slough, and the interpretation as commercial property is bolstered by the possession of other lots adjoining this slough by merchants and traders.

More trade, however, was carried out on plantations than in towns. On an informal basis, planters received hides in face-to-face trade for various manufactured goods from Indians who themselves lived in the immediate area and formed as much a part of the community as did the planters (Crane 1981:118). Some planters went so far as to hire an Indian hunter to supply them with skins. Most, however, traded in a haphazard fashion with partners of expedience. Not until after the Yamasee War (1715–1718), when the local groups were largely displaced or decimated, did the overland trade with distant tribes fully usurp the local trade, though the inland trade had been in place since the 1680s (Snell 1973). When Willtown was settled, Indians were the settlers' neighbors—not exactly next door, perhaps, but certainly part of everyday life (see Green et al. this volume).

The effect of the Yamasee War on the Carolina colonists was considerable (Green et al. this volume; see also Merrell 1989; Silver 1990; Snell 1973). This outside threat certainly strengthened the bonds the Europeans felt as Carolinians. A cohesiveness began to develop immediately, despite religious and political differences, as a result of shared hardships on the frontier. It was further strengthened by nearly constant warfare with the French and Spanish and their Indian allies. The friction between Anglicans and Dissenters, while not forgotten, ceased to be a critical concern. Almost immediately, an Act of the Assembly made the legislative body more representative (Fraser 1989; Lesser 1995; Weir 1983).

The Indian trade, too, was altered by the Yamasee War. Local tribes such as the Yamasee, Santee, Congaree, and Pee Dee were virtually extinguished, and survivors left for the interior or for Spanish Florida (Waddell 1974). Though other tribal remnants, known as "neighbor Indians," remained in the area, by 1730 the frontier had been pushed well back from Charleston, and a series of townships became the new buffer (see Crass et al. this volume; Crass et al. 1997). Only Dorchester retained direct ties to the Indian trade, as it remained on a crossroads to the interior (Crane 1981; see Braund 1992; Martin 1994; Merrell 1989).

New economic opportunities arose and changed the direction of Willtown and the composition of local communities. Although the new ways were slow to catch on, the steadily increasing value of rice and the realization of the agricultural potential of inland swamps meant that profits could be made from plantation lands. The principal effect was a rapid rise in the enslaved African population, which created new tension in the white community. By 1730 Africans outnumbered European colonists by a significant amount. Against such odds in the event of an uprising, planters felt little security. By the same token, slaves were emboldened, and in 1739 the largest slave revolt in British North America, the Stono Rebellion, resulted in the deaths of seventy-five Carolinians, black and white. This event involved the Willtown community and took place nearby.

Peter Wood (1974) maintains that the Stono Rebellion was the climax of two decades of changes and adjustments in Lowcountry slave society. The tremendous acceleration of rice agriculture and the escalating importation of new people resulted in major changes in slave life, including less independence and more supervision. As rice cultivation expanded, the polyglot labor force disappeared. Africans became the dominant element in the slave population; Indians, if they remained, were no longer enumerated as such. By the late eighteenth century, planters simply categorized their Indian slaves as Africans, as part of the general trend to equate slavery with African ancestry (Berlin 1998:145).

Fear of armed uprising by this growing population led to increasingly harsh restrictions; the situation became more tense in 1738 when Florida established the town and fort of Mose just north of St. Augustine and announced a royal edict granting liberty to slaves fleeing English settlements (Deagan and Landers 1999).

On Sunday, September 9, 1739, about twenty Angolan slaves under the leadership of Jemmy attacked a store at Stono. Word reached the church at Willtown where Archibald Stobo was preaching to an assembled congregation. John Bee, Jr., an official of the Willtown church, led the men of the congregation in pursuit of the rebels, who had encamped in a field and were beating drums to invite others to join them. By afternoon their numbers were estimated at sixty to one hundred. The militia had the advantage of training and firepower, and the battle was short. The soldiers pursued the stragglers and placed heads on mileposts to deter further trouble (Linder 1996).

Peter Wood (1974) has suggested that the rebellion did not end as suddenly as described; unrest continued in the Lowcountry and rebels remained at large for some time. Planters in the Stono area moved their families to safety, fearing "those concerned in that Insurrection who were not yet taken" (Wood 1974:319). The following year the Negro Act was passed by the Assembly; this would serve as the core of South Carolina's slave code for more than a century (Wood 1974:324).

The Archaeological Evidence

The impact of the Stono Rebellion may be seen on a rice plantation contemporary with Willtown, its archaeological remains discovered outside the platted limits of the town, about one mile from the riverfront. The site lies on the terminus of a hardwood ridge adjacent to inland swamps, heavily diked and ditched for rice production. First granted in 1710, and sold annually from 1717 through 1720, the property evidently saw two building episodes before James Stobo acquired the property in 1741 and built a grand manor house. He left the Willtown area abruptly in 1767, but continued to own and operate the plantation until his death in 1781. While in residence, he stocked his house with the finest consumer goods available, but he constructed it in a manner that suggests a palisaded or fortified compound. Artifacts and documents indicate that the property was home to people of European, African, and Native heritage, living in close proximity and in unequal fashion: Africans and Native Americans bonded and labored in the fields, while the Europeans enjoyed a life of wealth, if not ease. But the arrangement of the house suggests that this balance of power was tenuous, at least in the mind of the planter family. In addition, clear artifactual and stratigraphic data suggest that this existence was indeed fragile, likely falling victim to natural disaster and later the forces of the colonial economy.

The highlight of the site is a large house complex in a highly unusual three-bay plan, with a central courtyard (Figure 12.2). The northernmost room, measuring ten by fifteen feet, contains a brick floor laid directly on the sand (Feature 14) and may be a kitchen, though evidence for a heat source is tenuous. The eastern bay was a two-room plan, sixteen by twenty-four feet, with a brick-floored middling room (Feature 55) and a "best room" with a raised wooden floor (revealed by raised foundations and a lack of brick paving, Features 79 and 95). A back external chimney split the two rooms and heated both (Feature 113). Though not revealed archaeologically, this section was likely multistoried. The third bay, also sixteen by twenty-four, but at a different orientation, was less well preserved and more ephemeral (Features 138, 139, 127). Though there is possible evidence for a chimney, this bay was likely a carriage house and stable. The three-bay plan featured a central courtyard with a prepared surface of coarse sand (Feature 49). Some type of brick wall, or fence with brick foundation, connected Bay 1 to Bay 3 (Feature 102), and another en-

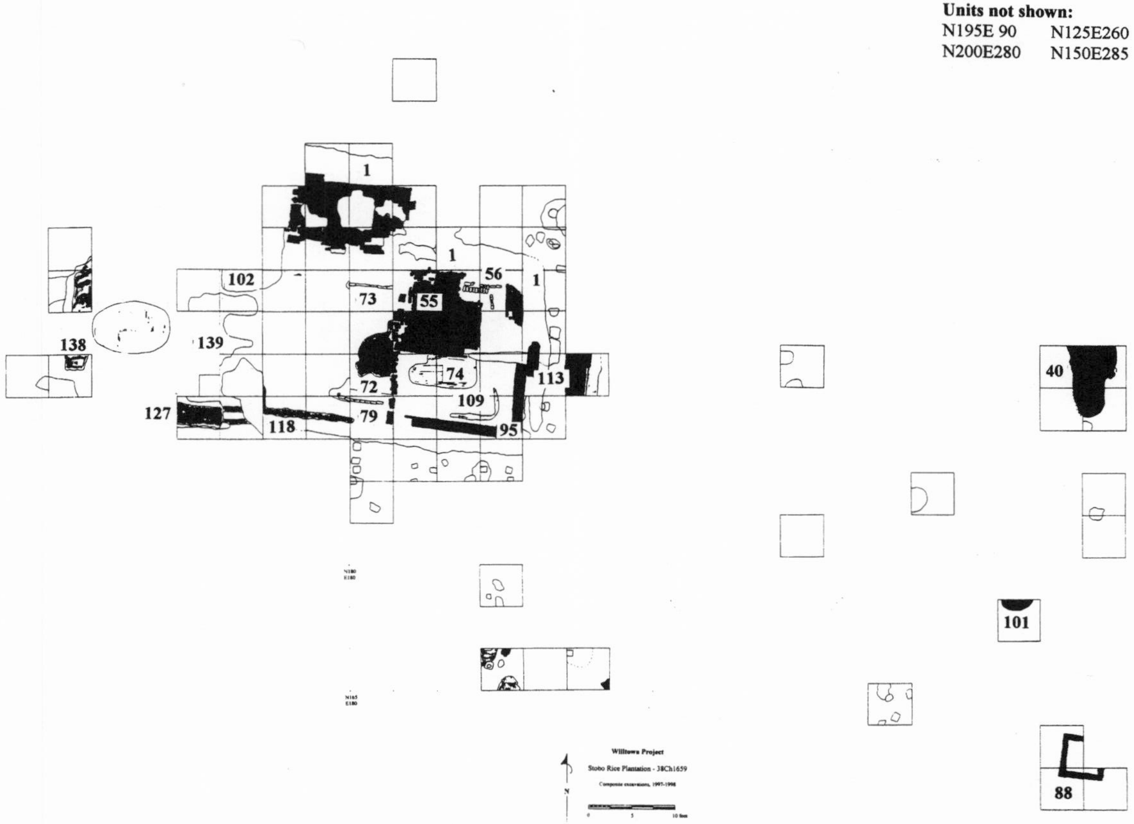

Figure 12.2. Site map of the Stobo plantation, showing feature designations.

Figure 12.3. South profile of unit N215E175, showing the interface of Feature 49 (prepared courtyard surface), Feature 3 (overlying black midden), Feature 2 (layer of demolition rubble), and Feature 1 (robbed wall trench full of demolition rubble).

closed the southern, or fourth, side of the courtyard, and bridged the gap between the northern and western bays (Feature 118). Recovery of door locks in these two locations hints at entry to the compound at these two highly constricted points. Artifacts in the sand courtyard (Feature 49) and beneath the floors of the house support a 1740s date of construction.

Some time after 1765 to 1770, a dense organic midden (Feature 3) accumulated over the kitchen floor, the floors of the east wing, and the courtyard (Figure 12.3). This midden, which is darker and deeper over the northern kitchen and exhibits some evidence of boundaries corresponding to rooms, contains many intact artifacts that signal abandonment rather than discard. The third bay exhibits no such midden accumulation. On top of this midden, and clearly a separate and subsequent event, is evidence of collapse of the building (Feature 2) and the robbing of eighty percent of the walls in a continuous trench around the compound (Feature 1; see Figure 12.2). Pearlware contained in the demolition layer suggests this occurred around 1810, a date corresponding with the general abandonment of inland rice fields and the movement of the settlement and production to the tidal marshes of the riverfront, and the subdivision of James Stobo's estate.

Consulting historical architects suggest that the black midden soil reflects a calamity, one that severely damaged the structure. The characteristics of the midden suggest a storm or flood, but not a fire. It is possible that a large tree unroofed and damaged the home beyond James Stobo's willingness to repair and reoccupy it. The artifact distribution (highly curated objects clustered in the courtyard) suggests at least some cursory attempt to recover damaged valuables. The organic debris, including the tree, then slowly decayed in place, creating the dark midden. The heavily damaged structure may have remained exposed to the elements until new owners decided to reuse the bricks and robbed the walls, producing Feature 1.

However, the demolition rubble contained a significant portion of machine-cut nails, manufactured after 1790. This suggests at least some rebuilding. Architects Willie Graham, Bernard Herman, and Ritchie Garrison (personal communication, 1998) agree that the quantity of nails suggests a "pieced together" repair, but not complete renovations, taking place some years after the 1767 abandonment. The pearlwares in the rubble layers and robbed wall trenches likewise suggest substantial use of the site, but not by those with the money or social ambitions of James Stobo. One proposed explanation for these data is that resident slaves rebuilt and occupied the Stobo house. Tantalizing support for this interpretation comes from an adjoining archaeological site (1,500 feet to the west), tentatively interpreted as the slave community and evidently abandoned in the 1770s.

Stobo's plantation contained artifacts that Willtown did not. The black midden layer that covers the floor, and indeed the underlying courtyard surface, contained a number of artifacts that were normally curated and rarely discarded. This contrasts with the artifact assemblage in outlying units excavated in the yard area (see Anthony this volume, Table 4.2). In the main house area, ceramic and glass vessels are not broken in place, but are mendable over a series of contiguous units (Figure 12.4). There are concentrations of artifact types by room or activity area. Many of the more unusual artifacts were abandoned in the courtyard (Figure 12.5). This supports the current interpretation of sudden destruction, possibly including tree fall and unroofing, with the resulting mass of debris slowly decaying after a cursory attempt to recover usable items. But who attempted to recover them? James Stobo and his family? Or plantation slaves poring through the debris left by the planter family? And who used and discarded the pearlware found in the demolition rubble if the house was uninhabited after 1770?

The artifact assemblage reveals that the Stobo plantation was a community of people of varied economic, social, and religious affiliations. The quantity of artifacts suggests that each group was likely in residence, but that the flow of people through the property and through the general community was widespread. Artifacts speak to the cultural sharing experienced by frontier residents, and in more ephemeral ways to the tensions arising from unequal access to the material and nonmaterial rewards of this exis-

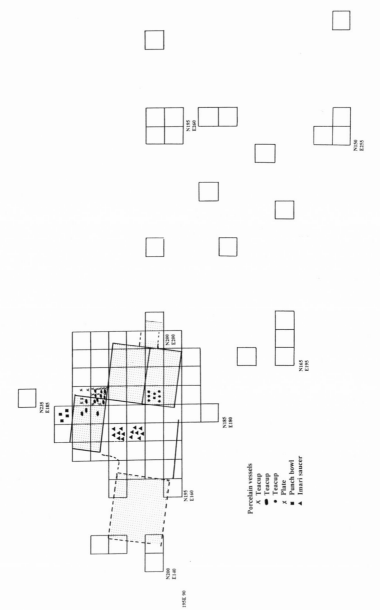

N195
E260

N150
E255

N195
E185

N235
E185

N300
E200

N185
E180

N165
E195

N195
E160

N200
E140

195E 90

Porcelain vessels
x   Teacup
●   Teacup
x   Teacup
■   Plate
■   Punch bowl
▲   Imari saucer

Figure 12.4. Distribution of porcelain vessels.

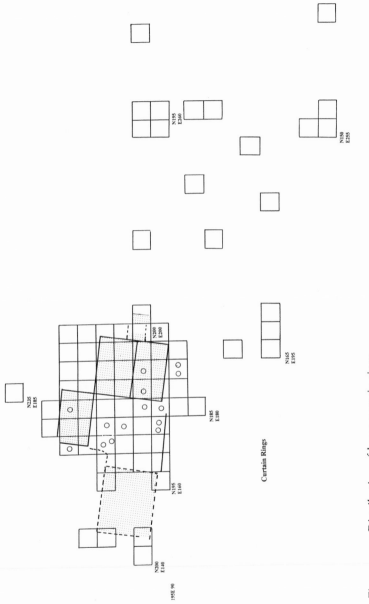

N195
E360

N150
E255

N235
E185

N200
E200

N195
E160

N185
E180

N200
E140

195E 90

N165
E195

Curtain Rings

Figure 12.5. Distribution of brass curtain rings.

Figure 12.6. James Stobo's silver cane tip (photograph by Rick Rhodes, courtesy The Charleston Museum and South Carolina Department of Archives and History).

tence. Thus it is that we clearly see the background, aspirations, and accomplishments of James Stobo, a strident Dissenter and descendant of the patriarch of the Willtown Presbyterian church, in his artifacts. These include extremely expensive and intricately decorated Chinese porcelains, a vast array of wine bottles, silver-plated buttons, a rapier for civilian dress, a monogrammed sterling-silver cane tip (Figure 12.6), elaborate furniture hardware, ornamental flowerpots, and highly decorated horse tack. The elegance of his dress and furnishings is matched by attention to architectural detail, including marble mantles, brass gate hardware, profuse window glass, and brass wall fixtures for lighting.

But Stobo's life was evidently not carefree. The highly defensible layout of his home was matched by a variety of weaponry, including an iron pike. The heavy drudgery of labor required to obtain this wealth and status was reflected in the large range of plantation tools, including hoes for the rice fields, but also a number of hammers, chisels, drills, and other tools.

If Willtown and its surrounding plantations retained a heightened sense of self/other, then sharing and exchange were also unavoidable. If Stobo's house is a material reflection of isolation, then many of the recovered artifacts also reflect interaction and cultural sharing. The artifact assemblage

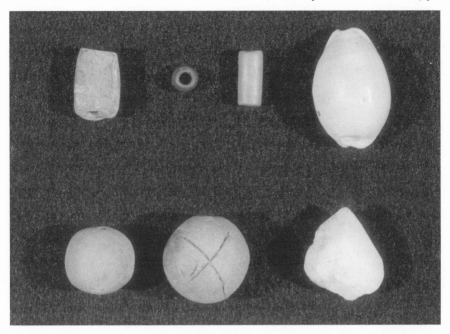

Figure 12.7. African American artifacts. *Top row:* blue glass beads, cowrie shell. *Bottom row:* colonoware sphere marked with an X, quartz crystal (courtesy The Charleston Museum and South Carolina Department of Archives and History).

from Stobo's plantation reflects the lives and activities of site residents other than Mr. Stobo, though these artifacts are fewer in number. The enslaved laborers imported from Africa to work the rice fields left behind quantities of colonoware, some in Mr. Stobo's house, but most outside it (see Anthony this volume). The most dramatic recoveries were those of a quartz crystal and a colonoware sphere with cosmographic markings (Figure 12.7; Leland Ferguson has suggested that an incised X or cross, found on examples of Lowcountry colonoware, may be a religious cosmogram of the Bakongo people. In Africa the Kongo cosmogram has a variety of ritual uses; see Ferguson 1999). The blue beads and cowrie shell may have also belonged to African residents (Russell 1997; Stine et al. 1996). While the items listed above came from the area of the main house, the bulk of the colonoware came from outside. Evidently these ceramics were used principally by people not living in this house.

Though a clear minority, Indian slaves also labored in the rice fields of the Willtown area, as others traded with Willtown residents. Several of the early Willtown planters enumerate a few Indian slaves in documents dating from the 1720s to 1730s. Berlin's recent study (1998) of colonial slavery suggests that descendants of these people may have still been present on

Lowcountry plantations after this time, but were no longer enumerated as Indians. Much of the colonoware in the Stobo assemblage appears to be the product of Native Americans rather than Africans. In his detailed study of the colonowares, Ron Anthony discovered a much higher than expected percentage of wares that appear to be made in the Native style (see Anthony this volume). What is lacking are colonowares made in European forms. The colonowares, then, suggest a strong African and Native presence at the site, and extensive interaction between the two groups, with relatively little influence from the European residents.

Another tantalizing clue to the cultural complexity of the site's demography is faunal remains. Jennifer Webber, Dan Weinand, and Elizabeth Reitz report that cow bones from the area of N165E200 show very unusual hack marks (Webber and Reitz 1999:292). These bones appear to have been repeatedly and forcefully hacked in a random manner, suggesting that if this was done for butchery purposes, it may have been the work of an amateur. Reitz suggests the butcher might have been someone unfamiliar with the animal, or unfamiliar with the tool. Interestingly, these bones were recovered in a concentration of Native American pottery.

The faunal assemblage in general, though, suggests something else. Webber and Reitz found a diet preponderantly European in form, with very little resemblance to those of contemporary African American or Native American sites. The contradiction between these two data sets is puzzling at first, but it is possible that a European diet was modified by the African and Native American residents during preparation, cooking, or consumption to more closely approximate their traditions, in ways that are not visible in the archaeological record.

The most dramatic evidence for cultural interaction is also the smallest. A brass finger ring with a glass setting was recovered just beyond the manor house (Figure 12.8). The glass stone features an image of the crucifixion, with a robed Christ on the cross and two kneeling figures, possibly Mary and Mary Magdalene. Like his minister father, James Stobo was a strident Dissenter who despised papist influences. This ring was likely not his. Nor did it belong to neighboring Anglicans, who during this period were far more Spartan and Protestant in their iconography than in the subsequent century. The scenario constructed so far has the artifact originating with Christianized Indians, possibly from the Apalachee province in Florida (Green et al. this volume; Hann and McEwan 1998). It is further possible that the ring changed hands many times before arriving on the wooded peninsula near the Edisto River. Perhaps it was acquired by African residents before being lost, either by those knowledgeable of its symbolic meaning or by those simply attracted to it, who subsequently assigned it different symbolic value. Recently, historians John Thornton (1991) and Ira Berlin (1998) have explained that the leaders of the Stono

Figure 12.8. Brass finger ring with glass setting, carved with a crucifixion scene (courtesy The Charleston Museum and South Carolina Department of Archives and History).

Rebellion, usually identified as "twenty Angolans," and many other Africans of early eighteenth-century South Carolina, were devout Catholics from the kingdom of Kongo. Thornton suggests that this fueled their desire to rebel and to reach Spanish Florida and the African American community of Mose (Deagan and Landers 1999). Perhaps the ring was always the cultural property of African residents. Though we might pose a variety of plausible scenes, we will never know for sure. That does not negate the power of this singular artifact, however. It remains the signature of the demographic and cultural complexity of the frontier, the meeting point of peoples, belief systems, and iconography.

The Willtown Community

Like many other communities in Carolina and elsewhere, Willtown began on paper and on the ground as an ambitious and well-planned town. Colonial proprietors encouraged the development of urban centers for protection, community, and commerce, though they met with mixed success (see Brownell and Goldfield 1977; Herman 1999; Staski 1982:97; Stilgoe 1982:88–89; Zierden 1997a). Designed by European settlers for protection, trade, and religious toleration, the community seemed poised for economic success. Changes in external threats, in trade and transportation networks, and in political and social mores affected many colonial towns. Further, the development of wildly successful staple crops encouraged dispersed settlement. As the town's role diminished, the Willtown community evolved in purpose and population.

Audrey Horning (1995) has argued that *intent* may define a town as much as size and function. On the basis of these broad definitions, Willtown certainly functioned for a half-century as a town, and perhaps as an urban center. The facts that it was such a prominent landmark on maps of the period, that it was the seat of governmental and religious functions, and that it remained a cognitive landmark long after the vestiges of urban structure had disappeared attest to its intentional role as a town.

As wealth increased in the colony with the intensification of rice production it brought with it the final demise of Willtown as a population center. The movement of the Willtown church in the 1760s to another location, "so that it is very convenient and centrical" (Simmons 1962:151), seems very telling. The Indian trade routes continued to carry traffic past the river bluff, but bypassed the town proper in favor of PonPon (Jacksonborough) a few miles upriver. By 1759 James Stobo had been regranted the entire town, and in 1760 William Elliott received twenty-four lots in the center of the village. The village tract soon became another tidal swamp plantation, with adjacent rivers turned into productive rice land.

Conclusion

If the village of Willtown declined, then the greater *community* of Willtown merely changed. White settlers chose to risk solitary life in the wilderness on newly developed plantations, among potentially threatening African bondsmen and displaced Native Americans, for chances to acquire vast fortunes through rice and indigo production. Forced into new roles, Native Americans were displaced and enslaved, and occasionally resided in small family groups. Imported African laborers, though bound by the laws of slavery, held some leverage through cunning, cultural bonds, and sheer numbers. James Stobo's plantation, then, is very much a part of the story of the Willtown community and of colonial South Carolina. As white and black settlers dispersed, and native groups moved on, the village on the river bluff remained a symbolic, and still occasionally physical, center of the community, where individuals, families, and groups met and interacted for a variety of purposes.

Acknowledgments

Archaeological and historical research at Willtown was initiated and funded by the property owner, Mr. Hugh Lane. Detailed historical research was conducted by Dr. Suzanne Linder. Numerous scholars contributed to the ongoing research through conversations and consultations; those whose work is cited here include Monica Beck, David Crass, Christopher Clement, Chester DePratter, Kathleen Deagan, Bernard Herman, and Willie Graham. Artifacts from the Willtown project are curated and exhibited at The Charleston Museum. The full report on the Willtown project was published by the South Carolina Department of Archives and History in Columbia, South Carolina.

13

"As regular and fformidable as any such woorke in America": The Walled City of Charles Town

KATHERINE SAUNDERS

Charleston, South Carolina, has long been acknowledged as a symbol of southern gentility. The city has achieved international renown both for its history and for its wealth of colonial and antebellum architecture. But the city was not always the picturesque tourist destination it has become and many visitors to the city are surprised to learn that they are wandering the streets of the only English walled city in America. This distinction is often reduced to a footnote in local historical accounts as physical traces of the early fortifications can be glimpsed in only a few locations. Tantalizing clues, however, from archaeological excavations, combined with existing physical evidence and a wealth of documentary sources, offer a new picture of fortified Charles Town; one that highlights the retention of an Old World military and architectural form, skillfully adapted to fit into the peculiar landscape of the New World. As England's southernmost outpost in North America, Charleston began as a city completely encircled by walls, similar in appearance to the medieval walled towns of Europe. Charleston remained fortified until the latter years of the eighteenth century, changing from a "walled city" to a fortified town. These early walls and later fortifications were certainly key in the transformation of this colonial landscape, directing Charleston's growth and development and influencing the city's distinctive architecture (Figure 13.1).

Early Settlement and Defense

The province of Carolina was granted in 1663 by King Charles II of England to eight noblemen, land investors called Lords Proprietors. These investors hoped to claim a share of the New World wealth to be generated during what was then a period of heightened economic and political competition among the major European powers. The proprietary grant for

Figure 13.1. Powder horn, 1762–1764 (collection of the Museum of Early Southern Decorative Arts, Winston-Salem, North Carolina).

Carolina encompassed land stretching roughly from the southern border of Virginia into lands claimed by the Spanish in Florida. Border disputes were common in seventeenth-century America; indeed, much of the Carolina province was often simultaneously claimed by the French, Spanish, and English.

The initial settlement in Carolina under the proprietary grant was located, from 1670 to 1680, to the west of the Ashley River on a small spit of land nearly surrounded by marsh called Albemarle Point. Archaeologist Stanley South excavated at this settlement site in 1969 under the auspices of the South Carolina Tricentennial Commission, in preparation for the opening of the site as Charles Town Landing State Park. South found the principal fortifications here were composed of two main palisade lines above ditches approximately three to five feet in width, each running across the neck of Albemarle Point. These palisades encompassed an area of roughly ten acres. Along the creek that accessed the settlement, the main fortification line was armed with approximately twelve pieces of artillery while "the V-shape of the ditch would provide for an enfilading crossfire against anyone attempting an aggressive landing on the tip of the peninsula" (South 2000:77). In 1672, the settlement at Albemarle Point was described as having houses for around twenty families within the protected area. Approximately ninety other houses and farmsteads were located outside of the palisades, but the fortified ten acres could provide a safe haven for the settlers in the event of an attack (South 2000:6).

The fortifications found at Albemarle Point share some similarities with early seventeenth-century fortified settlements in Virginia. Palisades and trenches at both locations suggest the need for quick and effective defensive measures and a somewhat vernacular approach to the art of fortification. In contrast, the second and permanent location of Charles Town was to become a professionally designed and implemented walled city that would have a more lasting legacy. The move to Oyster Point, site of present-day Charleston, was accomplished by 1680, just ten years after the initial settlement at Albemarle Point. This second location had the advantage of Charleston's harbor and, being a peninsula, it could be more easily defended from French or Spanish threats by sea or from Native American attacks overland.

Old World Plans: New World Realities

Before a town can be defended there must be a town to defend. Toward this end, in 1671 the proprietors sent out the "Grand Modell," a plan for the new Carolina settlement that dictated dimensions for the streets and lots and likely included provisions for the patterning of streets in a Roman-style grid plan. In 1672, John Culpepper, surveyor-general of the province, was directed by the governor to "admeasure and lay out for a town on Oyster Point" (McCrady 1897:163). After an exhaustive survey of other potential sites by the Grand Council, the site choice became official in 1679 when the proprietors made it known to the governor that "Oyster Point is the place we do appoint for the port town of which you are to take notice and call Charles Town" (McCrady 1897:182).

Among the Lords Proprietors, it was Lord Anthony Ashley Cooper, later the Earl of Shaftesbury, who held the primary vision for the urban center that was to become Charles Town. With assistance from his secretary, and later noted philosopher, John Locke, Shaftesbury drafted instructions for the development of a province based upon religious toleration and a hereditary nobility. While the wealth of the province would be derived from profits generated from outlying plantations, Charles Town was to be a defensible port town with houses "placed both orderly and conveniently together" (Cheves 2000:344).

Almost immediately directives from England and the practical considerations of the site would have been at odds. The grid plan, so attractive and rational on paper, now had to be adapted to the physical landscape. The realities of the topography dictated the location of the town on an area of high ground between Vanderhorst's and Daniel's creeks and it was also of importance to future trade that the town fronted the deep and navigable Cooper River. As Oldmixon (1969:465) noted in his early history, *The British Empire in America,* "The Proprietors, as appears by their Constitutions and Instructions to the Governors, thought 'twas almost as easy to build Towns as to draw Schemes." It is likely that it was the adaptation in the early 1680s of the ideal "Grand Modell" by the current surveyor-general, Maurice Matthews, that resulted in a town that took full advan-

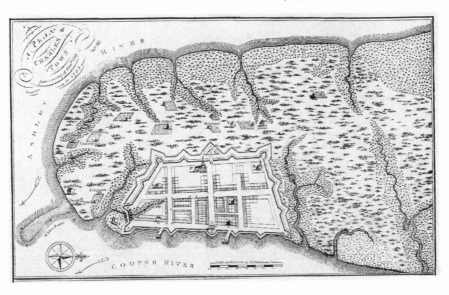

Figure 13.2. The Edward Crisp map of 1704.

tage of its siting and yet remained true to its intended form. Matthews reported in May 1680 that the four principal streets had been laid out and that space had been reserved for important public structures. Matthews's work was so successful that in 1682, Thomas Ashe, a clerk from the ship *Richmond*, noted:

> The town is regularly laid out into large and capacious streets which to buildings is a great ornament and beauty. In it they have reserved convenient places for a church, Town House and other public structures, an artillery ground for the exercise of the militia, and wharves for the convenience of their trade and shipping. (McCrady 1897:183)

New Perspectives: Analyzing the Historical Record

Although good descriptions of the town's earliest appearance exist, Charleston's early fortifications are generally not well understood. The paucity of extant physical evidence and a somewhat limited inspection of the written record have produced an established body of misinformation that has been passed from one historian to another. The generally accepted view has been that Charleston's walls and bastions were complete by 1704, as seen on Edward Crisp's map of that year (Figure 13.2), and that all but the seawall were dismantled a mere thirteen years later, in 1717. Historians generally reference a notation on the "Ichnography of Charles-Town at

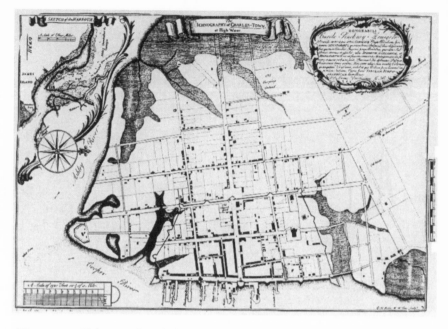

Figure 13.3. "Ichnography of Charles-Town at High Water," 1739, by Bishop
Roberts and W. H. Toms.

High Water" by Roberts and Toms to support this view (Figure 13.3). This
1739 map shows the boundaries of the old walled city area within the
context of the expanded town. The notation explains that the "Double
Lines represent the Enceinte as fortified by the Inhabitants for their defense
against the French Spaniards & Indians . . . after the signal defeat of ye Indians in the Year 1717, at which time the North West and South sides were
dismantled & demolished to enlarge the Town." However, there is no cor-
roborating documentary evidence to support the notion of such a large-
scale civic effort in 1717 to remove the landside walls that enclosed the
town. On the contrary, the Journal of the Commons House of Assembly
references almost constant concern from the late 1690s through the 1750s
that repairs and improvements be made to the walls. Additionally, the Herbert map of 1721 (Figure 13.4) shows all of the curtain walls and bastions
fully intact. If the Roberts and Toms notation is accurate, the 1721 map
should not exist.

After a critical analysis of the available material, it seems clear that construction of the walls was begun in the last years of the seventeenth century, that they were finished in some form after 1707, and that the land-
side walls came down gradually through the early eighteenth century as the

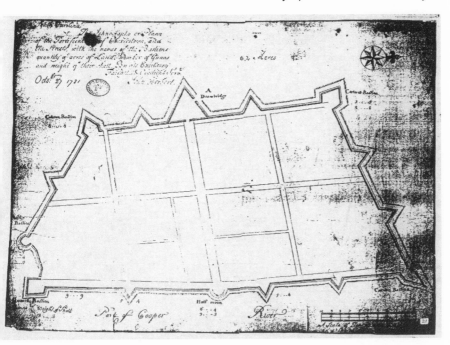

Figure 13.4. The Herbert map of 1721 (collection of the British Public Records Office).

town expanded westward. This gradual removal of the encircling walls did not, however, signal the end to the city's preoccupation with defenses. During the second half of the eighteenth century, new defenses were added and Charleston shifted from "walled city" to "fortified town."

A plan for the walled city of Charles Town was likely developed by professional engineers in England. This plan was overlaid at a later date on the developing street plan with no apparent coordination between the two. This is most clearly borne out by the Herbert map of 1721. This map shows the grid plan and the regularly laid-out streets but shows no street communication between the east and west bastions. In the event of a sea attack, it would have been difficult to transport men and supplies between these key bastions. As with the plan of the town, there seems to have been an effort to take an ideal fortification plan developed off-site and adapt it to existing conditions (Shields n.d.). The two creeks that had helped to determine the siting of the town now provided additional natural barriers to invasion (these creeks are located in the area of present-day Water Street and the market, respectively).

While defensive considerations must have been ongoing from the establishment of the town in 1680, it was not until 1697 that a plan of work on the city walls was described in a report (and thinly veiled appeal for money) to the Lords Proprietors:

> Wee are now hard att worke abt: a fortificacon att Charles Towne which wee hope in a little time to make Serviceable And to Leave it So as when wee can raise Money to Do it with, it may bee made as regular and fformidable as any such woorke in America. (Salley 1916:102)

From this reference and others it seems that work on the walls had begun by 1697 and despite a series of misfortunes including a fire in 1698, a yellow fever epidemic in 1699, and a hurricane in 1700, the colonists were making fair progress by 1702 when England declared war on France and Spain. Work on the fortifications received an adrenaline shot in response to this threat. This type of reactive productivity is a common thread in many of the fortification construction booms and repair efforts throughout the eighteenth century in Charles Town.

The most familiar and most referenced view of Charles Town's fortifications is the map of 1704 by Edward Crisp. This is a textbook drawing of the fortification methods espoused by Vauban, the most famous of all seventeenth-century military engineers. Crisp's detailed view of the walled city has been seductive to many historians who point to it as the culmination drawing of the completed fortifications. In reality, this map lays out in strict geometric fashion an idealized view of what the colonists were hoping for, not what then existed.

In 1706, two years after the date on the Crisp map, an invasion of Charles Town was attempted by a combined French and Spanish fleet. Hoping to find the inhabitants weak in the aftermath of another yellow fever epidemic, an invasion fleet composed of a French frigate and four sloops set sail from St. Augustine in Spanish Florida. By this date, an imposing brick seawall had been completed and proved enough of a visual deterrent that "when [the fleet] came in view of the fortifications, they suddenly bore up and came to anchor" (McCrady 1897:398). After a demand for Charles Town's surrender was received and dismissed by the governor, the invasion party burned some plantations and storehouses in the outlying areas. After a few skirmishes on land and water they departed, leaving around two hundred prisoners in Charles Town. The inhabitants must have been pleased with this outcome. However, in referencing the attempted invasion of the year before, the Commons House in 1707 warned of "ffinishing our ffortifications wch under God hath been our security and will be a ffuture terrour to our Enemies and deter them from giving us any more such visits" (Journals of the Carolina Commons House of Assembly [CCHA] 1707). If the Crisp map of 1704 represents the ideal rather than the reality of Charles Town's fortifications, what did the walled city really look like?

Anatomy of a Colonial Walled City

The earliest architecture of Charles Town was largely obliterated in the numerous fires of the late seventeenth and early eighteenth centuries. However, we may be sure that the encircling walls dictated a certain density to both the town and its architecture. The earliest view of the town is a painting of 1739 called *Charles Town Harbor* by Bishop Roberts. This painting was subsequently engraved in London under the title "An Exact Prospect of Charles-Town, the Metropolis of the Province of South Carolina" (Figure 13.5) and shows a mix of English vernacular styles, namely, "post-medieval and Jacobean, with curvilinear gables and steeply pitched roofs" (Poston 1997:25). Although these particular buildings no longer exist, the high density of lots and buildings within the old walled city boundaries is still visible and tangible.

One of the few buildings to survive from the walled city period is the Powder Magazine (Figure 13.6). Built circa 1712, this small, vaulted brick structure, measuring thirty-three feet square, was located at the edge of the walled city, just inside the northern wall and moat. Now overwhelmed by surrounding structures and sitting squarely in the center of a bustling tourist town, it gives little indication of its critical role in the protection of early Charles Town. Constructed with walls three and one-half feet thick, the Powder Magazine was designed to provide a secure storage facility for the community supply of powder. This military structure and the Palace at Arms, or armory, where weapons were stored, were crucial components of the overall fortification plan. Excavations at the Powder Magazine were undertaken in 1996 by The Charleston Museum for Historic Charleston Foundation. Archaeologist Martha Zierden has noted that, during the proprietary period, the Powder Magazine had a tangible presence; it was "not a symbolic building, but an essential component of a frontier settlement" (Zierden 1997b:168).

The main body of the town's buildings and fortifications was concentrated along the Cooper River waterfront. This was, after all, the very heart of the town; the center of commercial activity in a province dedicated to the proposition of making money. To protect this valuable real estate, construction of the massive brick seawall was begun in the last few years of the seventeenth century. Granville's Bastion and Craven's Bastion were located at either end and the Half-Moon Battery was at its center, providing the formal entrance to the town from the waterside. At least six feet

Figure 13.5. Engraving based on Bishop Roberts's *Charles Town Harbor,* 1739, called "An Exact Prospect of Charles-Town, the Metropolis of the Province of South Carolina."

Figure 13.6. The Old Powder Magazine, ca. 1713 (postcard; collection of Historic Charleston Foundation).

wide at its base, the seawall rose to a height of approximately ten to twelve feet from low water. The seawall and the "great fort," Granville's Bastion, seem to have been the first considerations of the builders. Despite setbacks from hurricane damage in September 1700, which prompted "an Act to prevent ye Seas further Encroachmt upon ye wharf at Charles Town," a report to the proprietors two months later stated that "Sufficient Care is taken to finish our fort & to Mount all our great guns & to Secure & Enlarge ye wharf before Charles Town" (Salley 1916:147). Simultaneous repair and construction of the two harbor-side bastions and the seawall with its redans, or "angles to cleare the Two Batteries," was ongoing for the next several years (CCHA 1701:25). In addition, the commissioners for building the fortifications were directed to "build a brest work at the White Poynt" for six guns and to "finish the halfe Moone, And mount what Gunns they think convenient thereon" (CCHA 1701:28).

Despite historian John Oldmixon's report that "the town was fortified more for beauty than strength" (Oldmixon 1969:510), these harbor-side defenses were built for both high visibility and permanence. Fragments of them remain, providing our only substantial physical evidence of the walled city's fortifications. Granville's Bastion, located at the important southeast corner of the town, was the largest and most heavily armed of the bastions.

In 1925, the walls of Granville's Bastion were revealed by architects Albert Simons and Samuel Lapham during renovation and enlargement of the Missroon House (ca. 1810) at 40 East Bay Street. Simons and Lapham recognized the importance of their find and thoughtfully left documentary photographs, a site drawing, and a detailed account of their findings to future historians. They observed that "the main walls lie about a foot below the present east sidewalk level and the general outline was easily traced. . . . It is five feet wide at its present top, of brick throughout" (Lapham 1925).

Simons and Lapham excavated a good portion of the site, finding a number of cannonballs and a layer of oyster shells and cobblestones around the exterior of the bastion. The excavations around the bastion also allowed Simons and Lapham a rare opportunity to view its overall construction. They found that the brick walls, laid in English bond, extended downward some fourteen feet, sloping out to the water "one inch to the vertical foot" (Lapham 1925), while the interior face was plumb. The walls were constructed atop a grillage or raft foundation, which evenly spread the weight of the brick walls in unstable soil: "This grillage was formed by apparently first layering palmetto logs, one foot in diameter, side by side, paralleling the run of the wall and four feet wider than the same; over these two inch cypress plank were laid, perpendicular to the run of the wall and on this plank the brick work was started" (Lapham 1925). Piles or stakes of red cedar and yellow pine were driven in vertically to prevent shifting of the bottom layer of palmetto logs (Lapham 1925).

Simons and Lapham did not refill the earth removed from the eastern face of the bastion but they did backfill the remainder of the site and covered it in its entirety with new construction. The exposed eastern face can be reached and examined by the intrepid few who can squeeze under the 1925 addition to the Missroon House.

In 1965, another important part of the harbor-side fortifications was unearthed beneath the old Exchange Building (1771). The construction of the Half-Moon Battery, with its brickwork atop a grillage foundation, matches that of Granville's Bastion. This massive battery originally curved out toward the water providing the formal entrance to the town. Behind the Half-Moon were constructed the city watch tower and the Palace at Arms, or armory. Past these buildings, new arrivals to the town found themselves on the Broad Way (now Broad Street), the principal east-west thoroughfare connecting the Half-Moon Battery to the land-side entrance to the town at Johnson's Ravelin.

For the first few decades after establishing Charles Town, the inhabitants had perceived that the greatest threat to their persons and property would arrive under sail. The Upper House of the Commons in 1702 reported that "we are undr no Apprehention of an Inland Invasion" (CCHA 1702:32). A considerably larger amount of debate, wrangling, and, ultimately, work and money were put into the harbor-side defenses than into the inland walls.

Despite one resolution in 1703 that called for "An Entrenchment on ye back Part of ye Towne for the Security thereof" (CCHA 1703:49), most of the early references to the inland walls appear only in acts addressing the need for their repair. The first of these in 1704 stated that "some evil disposed person had been climbing over and breaking them down. A penalty of fining or whipping was provided for all who scaled the walls or went down into the trenches" (Smith 1903:197). Additional acts for repair in 1707, 1714, 1719, and 1721 underscore their secondary status.

We may deduce from the frequent repair references that the inland defenses were constructed of some less durable (and less costly) material than brick. None of the references, however, contain a description addressing their materials or construction. A likely scenario for construction of these landward walls would first involve an entrenchment dug around the perimeter (Lapham 1970). The earth removed would subsequently have been used to construct walls that varied in height from six to ten feet. The ditch then functioned as a moat, filling at high tides. The construction of these landward walls involved combining the mud with oyster shell and other available material and piling it atop a wooden skeleton or frame. This type of construction is referenced in a 1724 repair report to neighboring Fort Johnson:

> The North East Point Ought to be Secur'd with Pine Saplins, Marsh mudd & Oyster Shell a lare of each in the same manner is already done which they find to stand firm and good. (Chicora Foundation 1994:31)

A parapet made of wood likely crowned the ramparts and solid wood planks for flooring would have been employed in the corner bastions and redans where the large, heavy guns would have needed substantial platforms for support.

Wooden elements were also employed in the construction of the ravelin and drawbridge at the land-side entrance to the town. Johnson's Ravelin was constructed here in the first few years of the eighteenth century to defend the land entrance to the town and to provide access from backcountry roads. Referencing the Crisp map of 1704, historians have long believed it to have been a detached earthen structure with at least one drawbridge across the outer moat and another bridge across an inner moat. This type of structure, which Crisp labels "Johnson's Covered Half-Moon Battery," refers to its placement within a moat as a separate structure that could be defended or "covered" by lines of fire from the main curtain walls. In contrast, an attached bastion configuration is seen on the Herbert map of 1721. (When constructed in the attached style, this element is more correctly referred to as a redan.)

The ravelin, drawbridge apparatus, and city gates that were located here were removed in 1750 for purposes of expanding the town westward. A motion in the Commons House of Assembly in May 1750 directed that "the Commissioners for the Fortifications give directions for pulling down the Ravelin at the Gate in King's Street, and making Brick Arches at the place where the Drawbridge is, and to have the same filled up with Earth" (CCHA 1750:105). Earthen components of the west rampart and the ravelin would have been pushed into the moat while parts of the drawbridge and gates were likely salvaged and used elsewhere. The demolition of the ravelin may have been prompted by the planned construction of the Statehouse on the northwest corner of Broad and Meeting streets, which would be completed in 1753. Concern about the difficulty of building over the location of the former moat was expressed in the planning for the Statehouse (see Joseph and Elliott 1994).

Excavations in 1993 for the first time revealed evidence of the moat located to the northwest of the historic Courthouse. Approximately six to eight feet deep during its active use as a moat, it seems to have been backfilled with the earth originally removed for its construction. The feature

Figure 13.7. Hand-hewn cedar piling used in the construction of Johnson's Ravelin, recovered from the Charleston County Courthouse site.

contained extremely sandy unstable soil or fill atop a "thin band of black organic muck," which appears to be an accumulation of the leaf litter and organic material located at the moat base (Joseph and Elliott 1994:32).

Archaeologists thought this was evidence of the moat, but they were cautious about that interpretation until the discovery of four square, hand-hewn cedar pilings in July 1999 brought the picture of the ravelin and moat into sharper focus (Figure 13.7). These pilings, uncovered by workmen in the watery basement of the Old County Courthouse, were approximately nine inches square and adzed to a sharp point. They were driven into the ground at least six to seven feet below the historic ground surface and were placed on two-foot centers forming an approximately seven foot long section of a diagonal wall. This appears to have been a part of the ravelin structure itself. J. W. Joseph (personal communication 2000) has suggested that the posts formed a part of the ravelin wall made of square pilings covered by boards. The substantial size of the pilings and their close spacing would have created an outwork capable of withstanding a heavy artillery assault. When combined with the moat findings of 1993, this new information seems to support the Herbert map's 1721 depiction of the area rather than Crisp's 1704 heretofore accepted view of the detached ravelin since the moat would have abutted the ravelin rather than surrounding it completely.

Design and Execution

Evidence for a well-designed ravelin on the landward side of Charles Town also serves to support the notion of professionalism of design for the fortifications. In the execution of the well-designed plan for a walled city, probably drawn in England, supervision of the earliest fortification construction was almost purely a military matter, with the duty falling in 1703 to Colonel William Rhett and in 1707 to Captain Thomas Walker (Ravenel 1964:18).

These men would have been the first to oversee the large numbers of slaves pressed into service on the fortifications. Enslaved African Americans undoubtedly provided most, if not all, of the intense physical labor needed to complete the works. The Journal of the Commons House of Assembly in the eighteenth century contains a number of references to slave labor on the fortifications; however, most of these references deal only with the monetary compensation due to the owners of the slaves for their use. From the documentary record, it seems that most of the slaves who worked on the fortifications lived in close proximity to Charles Town. However, in times of heightened military threat, the fortification engineers could be empowered to impress "every tenth male Slave, except Tradesmen and Boatmen, who are usually employed on Plantations within fifteen miles of Charles Town" (CCHA 1743:281).

It was not until the 1730s, after the proprietary province came under direct royal rule, that the first in a series of professional military engineers was appointed to design new fortifications and repair old ones. Gabriel Bernard was appointed chief engineer in 1736 at an annual salary of seven hundred pounds but served only one year, dying in Charles Town in 1737 (Ravenel 1964:20). Charles Town's next three engineers were retained almost exclusively to design and build new fortifications in response to internal and external threats and to repair damage wrought to existing fortifications by fire and hurricane.

In 1739, the Stono Slave Rebellion occurred outside of the city. In May 1740, the English war with Spain was proclaimed in Charles Town and in the fall of the same year a great fire "in less than four hours . . . utterly consumed the best and most valuable part of the said Town" doing considerable damage to the fortifications (CCHA 1740:408). Othniel Beale was employed in 1742 to "draw up plans for fortifying the southern and lower eastern portions of the town" as fears of a possible Spanish invasion mounted (Smith 1903:199). Two years later, in 1744, when war between England and France was proclaimed, Beale redoubled his efforts although "these works were termed unsatisfactory by Peter Henry Bruce, chief engineer of the Bahamas" (Ravenel 1964:21).

Bruce was hired in 1745 to survey the state of the existing fortifications and to come up with a plan to put Charles Town in a state of military readiness. His ambitious plan called for a fort or citadel on the landward side of Charles Town, as "the town is quite open on that side to the incursions of the Indians" and to the dangers of a possible slave uprising (Ravenel 1964:23). This was considered too costly but his alternate plan for a moat and earthen rampart across the neck of the peninsula was approved and work begun. Funds for this work were obtained through an additional "Duty of six pence per Gallon of Rum Imported" (CCHA 1745:512).

For the next few years, concerns about defense gave way to concerns over quality of life, such as increased commerce, clean streets, and issues of public health. Then, in 1752, a massive hurricane hit the town. Beale's work along the southern line was almost completely destroyed while "Granvill's [sic] bastion . . . was much shaken, the upper part of the wall beat in" and "the upper part of the curtain line, a solid wall of at least four feet thick, was beat in upon the bay" (Calhoun 1983:5). This damage was left unrepaired for several years until tensions again mounted between England and Spain. After several years of debate between Governor Glen and the assembly over the necessity of his appointment, engineer William Gerard DeBrahm arrived in Charles Town in 1755.

The assembly regarded DeBrahm as a suspicious foreigner, but Glen argued that "Forts and Fortifications Batteries Bastions, Ramparts and Ravelings, all sound well; but if they are empty sounds they will signify little. Let us therefore, not amuse ourselves with words, but let us take the opinion of persons with experience" (DeVorsey 1971:11). DeBrahm repaired the southern waterfront ramparts and worked to strengthen the line across the neck of the peninsula but, as was the case with Peter Henry Bruce, his proposed strengthening of the landward side of town with an elaborate "Citadelle" was considered too expensive. Much of DeBrahm's work, including his plan for a new and improved walled city as seen on his map of 1757 (Figure 13.8), was probably never carried out. This map, showing an expanded Charles Town completely encircled by walls and fortifications, never became a reality, but Charles Town remained fortified through the Revolutionary War years. In fact, it was not until 1784 that the early brick bastions along the Cooper River waterfront were sold out of city ownership at public auction.

Conclusion

Charleston's shift from early walled city to later fortified town paralleled a shift in the priorities of the colony. By the end of the eighteenth century, Charleston was no longer teetering at the southern edge of English influ-

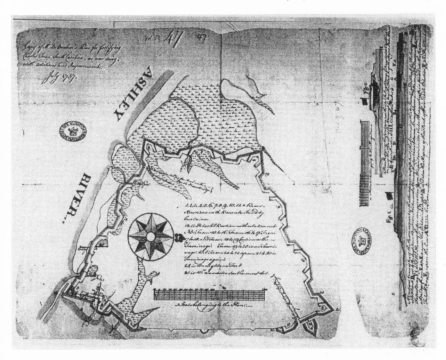

Figure 13.8. Copy of DeBrahm's "Plan for fortifying Charles Town, South Carolina, as now doing, with additions and improvements, July 1757" (collection of the British Public Records Office).

ence in America. Increasingly, the town became a busy and established seaport; still interested in defense but less and less threatened. The fortifications of the second half of the eighteenth century tended to be strategically placed, no longer encircling the town and restricting growth but still important to the defense of the town.

Perhaps because of the lack of above-ground evidence of the fortifications, visitors and even residents of Charleston remain largely unaware of the town's early appearance and history as a walled city. This lack of awareness has been compounded by historians who have traditionally referenced the walled city period as short-lived and, therefore, lacking in influence. When documents, maps, and archaeological evidence are combined, however, a new and different picture emerges. Far from being an insignificant part of Charleston's story, the city walls physically dominated the town for the first half of the eighteenth century, providing defense and influencing the growth and subsequent architecture of the town. The defenses of the town continued to be a real and symbolic military presence throughout the last half of the eighteenth century.

For historians and archaeologists, Charleston's walls and fortifications can speak volumes about a variety of topics. They illustrate the evolution of fortification methods in America; from quick effective palisades to substantial and professionally designed defenses. They illustrate the compromises made to ideal concepts and plans drafted abroad and the translation of those plans to New World realities. The reactivity of fortification building and repair efforts to real and perceived threats tells the story of Carolina within a global context. With regard to military architecture and engineering, there is much that the walls and fortifications of Charleston can tell us about military technology and construction techniques, and about the art of fortification in eighteenth-century America.

Like any true southern lady, Charleston has a graceful and genteel appearance that can obscure a core of practicality and strength. The study of Charleston's history, architecture, and archaeology can only be enhanced by a more thorough exploration of the many facets of its early defenses.

14

From Colonist to Charlestonian: The Crafting of Identity in a Colonial Southern City

J. W. JOSEPH

Throughout the colonial period, Charles Town was the hub for communities and plantations stretching across the Lowcountry and deep into the backcountry of the Carolina colony. Deerskins, naval stores, and agricultural produce flowed into the city for shipment to Europe, the Caribbean, and the northern colonies; goods and immigrants flowed into the city for transport to Lowcountry and backcountry towns and plantations. As noted in the introduction to this volume, the colonial city was a multiethnic entrepôt, and visitors to the town would comment on its diversity of inhabitants and appearance. By the end of the eighteenth century the city's image had changed to a more structured and homogeneous appearance, and city residents defined themselves as Charlestonians, not colonists.

Because goods and people passed through Charles Town on a routine basis, and because Charles Town was both the economic and social center of the region, it follows that changes in the way Charlestonians identified themselves and in the ways they used material things to express their identity would have become known among the Lowcountry and backcountry towns and plantations and would have influenced change there as well. This chapter looks at the changes in ceramics, architecture, and landscape in the city from circa 1720 to circa 1800 to understand how these material expressions of Charles Town changed and what these changes tell us about the ways the colonists identified themselves. These changes are examined through the archaeological analysis of a single site, the Charleston Judicial Center site, 38CH1708. Located on Broad Street between King Street and Courthouse Square, this site is the location of a new County Judicial Center. Archaeological study of the site was sponsored by the Charleston County Department of Capital Projects (Joseph and Hamby 1998).

Like colonial Charles Town in general, the residents of the site were ethnically diverse, including English, Africans, French Huguenots, Dutch, and Italians. This chapter treats them as a whole, looking at broad-scale changes in material culture. The site excavation used machine stripping to clear large surfaces before cultural features were mapped and excavated. More than seven hundred features were recorded at the Judicial Center site and, of these, 140 were excavated. Of the excavated features, two-thirds date to the colonial era. These features and their artifacts provide a look at the changes in material culture that occurred in the colonial city.

Material Culture

Cultural diversity is clearly expressed in the material assemblage of the site, with artifacts originating from a number of locations. French preserve jars and wine bottles, German Westerwald stoneware, Iberian storage jars, delft from Holland and England, faience from France, Chinese porcelain, and Native American and African American colonowares contributed to a cultural mosaic on every table in town. Yet this cultural diversity was a product of the places things were made as much as the people who were using them. In certain instances, artifacts are more clearly indicators of ethnicity, such as in the case of an excavated Dutch kookpot or gortpan, a redware cooking vessel of traditional Dutch form apparently manufactured in the Americas. But such ethnic markers are rare. Looking at broader patterns we begin to see the ways in which the material culture of Charles Town changed and we can begin to evaluate the meaning of these changes.

For the purposes of this chapter I have focused on the vessels identified from ten features spanning the period from circa 1720 to circa 1796. Minimum vessel counts were calculated for each of these features by ceramic type, and within type individual vessels were recognized by attributes such as vessel form, rim treatment, and decoration. Within the collection are more than forty-two types of ceramic. The most common type in the entire collection is underglazed Chinese porcelain, which accounts for seventy-eight of the 574 total vessels. Slipware is the next most common, accounting for sixty-four vessels. If polychrome, blue and white, and plain delft are combined, then delft as a type accounts for fifty-one vessels. Colonoware is fourth on the list, with thirty-seven colonoware vessels identified in the collection. This recipe—porcelain, slipware, delft, and colonoware—is the signature of features predating the 1770s, as the majority of the colonoware (97 percent), slipware (88 percent), and delft vessels (78 percent) are from this period. Only porcelain spans this break, with forty-five of the porcelain vessels (58 percent) predating 1770. The remainder of the colonial collections are made up of refined stoneware vessels, semirefined earthenwares, utilitarian earthenwares, and utilitarian stonewares. This is how things looked before 1770, but not after.

The ceramics from features dating to the 1770s and later are dominated by the products of the Industrial Revolution, the refined earthenwares creamware and pearlware and their many brethren and offspring. Their diversity is misleading, for if we combine the many variants of creamware, pearlware, and other refined earthenwares, then they become the most common type within our collection, with refined earthenwares accounting for 113 vessels. Of these eighty-one (71 percent) come from contexts postdating 1770, and all are from contexts after 1760.

There is a distinct change in the way things looked, in the pottery people used, around 1770; a change that can be attributed to the Industrial Revolution. The Industrial Revolution made durable ceramics affordable the world over. In the British ceramic industry, the origin of the Industrial Revolution was in the efforts to decipher the secrets of porcelain. In attempting to learn how to manufacture porcelain, English ceramicists stumbled upon a socially acceptable alternative in the high-fired earthenwares creamware and pearlware. The ceramics of the Industrial Revolution also provided a setting in which items of a common material could be embellished to achieve differing values, values that were clearly defined, visible, and codified (Miller 1980, 1991). This use of ceramics of the Industrial Revolution to display wealth, an awareness of the latest fashions, and social status was a critical element in the widespread acceptance of these wares.

The products of the Industrial Revolution changed the look of colonial kitchens and dining rooms where it could improve the quality of materials. Creamwares and pearlwares mimicked the appearance of porcelain with their hand-painted and transfer-printed designs and were more durable than slipware and delft, so out these went, and the new products did not erode pewter tableware the way white salt-glazed stoneware did, and so white salt glaze went out as well. Porcelain was still porcelain, and it stayed. But what about colonowares? These were primarily locally made cooking and service vessels for which there was no less-expensive refined earthenware alternative. While iron cooking vessels became more affordable and abundant with the Industrial Revolution, it is doubtful that iron offered as economically affordable a cooking ware as colonoware. Their disappearance was also not a product of the Native American exodus from the Lowcountry, as this had occurred in the late 1710s and colonowares had increased in number since then. The disappearance of colonoware at around 1770 thus does not appear to be entirely a product of the Industrial Revolution, but rather appears to reflect changes both in materials and in the way materials were perceived.

To verify that our minimum vessel counts were not providing a skewed perspective, we looked at all of the colonoware from the site. Fifty features produced a total of 816 colonoware sherds. Grouping these features by mean ceramic date, colonoware as a percentage of all ceramic sherds recovered from these features represents about ten percent of the sherds for features dating to the 1720s, twenty-one percent for features from the 1730s, twenty-nine percent from the 1740s, fifteen percent from the 1750s, seven percent from the 1760s, eleven percent from the 1770s, six percent from the 1780s, and two percent from the 1790s and 1800s. These figures are comparable to the percentages obtained from the minimum vessel count data, in which colonowares contributed twenty percent of the ceramic vessels from the 1720s, thirty percent from the 1730s, twenty-four percent from the 1740s, twelve percent from the 1750s, seven percent from the 1760s, zero percent from the 1770s, ten percent from the 1780s, and zero percent from the 1790s and 1800s. The trend is thus well defined: colonowares are present from the 1720s on, increase in quantity to a peak between the early 1730s and late 1740s, when they account for more than a quarter of the colonial ceramic assemblage, continue to be a strong presence in colonial assemblages in the 1750s and 1760s, when they account for approximately a tenth of the ceramic material, and then rapidly disappear from the ceramic picture during the 1770s and 1780s, leaving only a negligible trace at the turn of the century. Ninety-two percent of the colonoware sherds were recovered from features spanning the period from the early 1730s to the late 1760s.

The vast majority of the colonowares recovered from the site are thin-walled, burnished or polished wares of a type that is generally considered to be of Native American production in assemblages from the South Carolina Lowcountry (Figure 14.1). However, the percentage distribution calls this association into question, as the large numbers of colonoware sherds recovered from features from the 1730s, 1740s, 1750s, and 1760s are from an era with little documented Native American interaction in Charleston. Following the conclusion of the Yamasee War of 1715–1718, Native Americans moved away from the coast into the backcountry of South Carolina, and they would continue to be pushed farther north by European immigration from the 1720s through 1770s. A 1721 Act forbade Native Americans from entering English settlements (Wood 1974:116). The burnished Native American colonowares recovered from Lowcountry plantations have been referred to in some places in the literature as Catawba wares, in reference to Catawba Indian potters who sold their wares in Charleston and the Lowcountry in the 1780s. Between 1730 and 1760, however, the Indian trade was primarily in deerskins and conducted mainly at trading posts strung along the backcountry's frontier. It is doubtful that Native American pottery was being shipped to market from such distance, or that Native American potters were migrating to the coast to make and sell pottery as the Catawba would do several decades later. This is a period of continued and increasing antagonism between colonial settlers and Native Americans who were attempting to maintain a toehold in their home.

Figure 14.1. Examples of colonoware vessels from the Charleston Judicial Center site.

However, these decades did witness significant increases in another segment of the Lowcountry's population associated with colonoware, the Africans. These demographics suggest that the majority of the colonowares from the Judicial Center site were primarily the product of African potters.

The standard dichotomy between Native American and African American colonoware, as developed by Wheaton et al. (1983) and elaborated by Ferguson (1989, 1992) and Garrow and Wheaton (1989), distinguishes two types: a Native American colonoware recognized as thinner, more finely potted, and polished or burnished, and an African-made ware described as thicker, with a less refined body, and with a smoothed, as opposed to polished or burnished, surface. (It should be noted that Ron Anthony has proposed a third type, Lesesne Lustered, whose attributes are intermediate between those of the Native American and African American types. See Anthony 1986 and this volume.) To a degree, the materials that contribute to this taxonomy reflect social variation, as the Native American wares are the product largely of main house contexts, while the

African wares are derived largely from the plantations' African American villages. Since the thicker, less well-made ceramics are found in village contexts, they are thought to be African, while the more finely made wares found in main house deposits have been thought to represent the work of Native Americans. However, population and trade dynamics combined suggest that the majority of colonoware from the Judicial Center site must be of African manufacture, yet these more closely resemble the defined Native American type. Following Crane (1993; see also Anthony 1986 and this volume), I suggest that variation in the appearance of colonoware was the product of who it was being made for, more than who was making it. Enslaved African American potters would have produced for market sale more finely made wares that would have appealed more to European taste (for example, among the colonowares are bowls with coggled and scalloped rims in clear imitation of British slipware—see Figure 14.2 as well as the large bowl in Figure 14.1), while less effort may have been exerted in manufacturing colonoware vessels for personnel use. Better potters may have successfully sold and traded their wares, while less successful potters did not. Vessels that were less successfully fired and finished may also have been retained for personal use as opposed to sale. The dichotomy thus may be one of manufacture and market, not manufacturer, with more finely made wares being intended for market sale and less finished pieces reserved for use within the African community.

It is also a false dichotomy to separate Native Americans and African Americans, as Carl Steen (1999), Ron Anthony (this volume, 1986), Fraser Neiman (1999), and others have noted. Like African Americans, Native Americans contributed to the population of enslaved workers on the colonial plantations, and their numbers were significant in the late seventeenth and early eighteenth centuries, with one source indicating there were more enslaved Native Americans than Africans in South Carolina in 1710 (Wood 1974:116). Rather than viewing colonoware as the result of separate African and Native American production, it is more appropriate to consider it to be a synergistic development from the interaction of African and Native American potters (see Anthony this volume). Many of the enslaved Native Americans were captured during slave raids, and women were captured more frequently than men. This suggests that Native American as well as African American women may have made pottery and passed on their knowledge of pottery making within the enslaved community. A tantalizing discovery from the project was the recovery of historic Native American wares from an early 1720s feature (see Figure 14.2). This feature, a large borrow pit excavated for the recovery of clay used in the construction of a clay-walled house, is associated with African Americans at the site. The Native American wares include several rectilinear stamped designs and all feature a high degree of interior and exterior burnishing.

Figure 14.2. *A*, Colonoware sherd with notched rim; *B*, Native American sherds.

The recovery of historic Native American wares at the Judicial Center site is of interest for several reasons. First, they were recovered from deposits postdating the Yamasee War (see Green et al. this volume) and hence represent either vessels obtained prior to the expulsion of the Native Americans from the coast or the production of enslaved Native Americans. Second, they were recovered from deposits associated with African American slaves and hence represent the interaction of Africans and Native Americans. Third, their burnishing and some of the rim forms resemble both the Catawba wares and the refined colonowares found later in the century and may suggest the independent introduction of these stylistic attributes into the African American colonoware tradition through interaction between African and Native American slaves.

Returning then to our original question of why colonowares disappear near the end of the colonial era, the answer is unclear. If these wares are primarily the product of African American potters, then African Americans, who continued to be a majority population in the late eighteenth century, obviously should have been capable of continuing to produce a large number of colonowares. The products of the Industrial Revolution did not offer an alternative ceramic capable of usurping colonoware's role as a cooking ware, and, indeed, African American cooks, who filled that role in many Charleston households, would express a preference for foods cooked in colonowares well into the nineteenth century (Crane 1993). It is doubtful that economics would be a factor, since colonowares were inexpensively made by a segment of the population actively seeking sources of income. The answer thus does not appear to be one strictly of function or economics, but something else.

Architecture

One of the most interesting discoveries of the excavations was the identification of an earth-walled structure in the rear yard of 96 Broad Street. This building was constructed of clay walls that were set in wall trenches (Figure 14.3): unlike the earth-walled structures found on the plantations (see Shlasko, Wheaton, and Steen, this volume), there were no posts used in the construction and the walls appear to have been formed entirely of earth. The wall material consisted of mixed clay and included occasional wood and brick fragments as well as fibrous material, most likely Spanish moss. North of the structure was a large borrow pit that was dug to obtain the clay used in the building's construction. Artifacts recovered from the lowest stratum of this feature (which include the Native American ceramics noted above) date to the 1720s, as do the limited number of artifacts recovered from the wall trench itself. This structure thus appears to be one of the earliest buildings constructed in this portion of Charles Town, since this area was outside the city walls, which were demolished following the Yamasee War. (In her article in this volume, Katherine Saunders indicates that there is nothing in the colonial records to suggest that the city walls on the interior of Charles Town were demolished in a concerted effort. She thus suggests that the walls were taken down over an extended period of time. I think it is likely, however, that the walls surrounding Broad Street would have been the first demolished, allowing the extension of this main street.)

The earth-walled structure featured a covered entry porch whose signature is left by a series of posts at the front of the structure. Internal space appears to have been divided into two rooms, with a series of post impressions near the center of the building reflecting this interior division. The front room also appears to have functioned as a kitchen. The front wall of the structure is formed of a large clay chimney or oven, within which two ash-filled barrels were identified. The barrels were apparently used to catch ash from the fires in the oven.

This structure appears to have served as a combined kitchen and dwelling, its construction African. Similar earth-walled structures have been re-

Figure 14.3. Earth-walled structure after excavation.

corded within the plantation villages at Yaughan and Curriboo plantations as well as other Lowcountry plantations (Ferguson 1992; Gardner and Poplin 1992; see Wheaton, Shlasko, and Steen this volume) and buildings made entirely of earth are found in a number of settings in West Africa (Vlach 1975, 1978). As Steen and Shlasko have noted in this volume, the use of earth-walled architecture was not strictly African, and variants of earth-walled construction can be found in French, German, English, and Spanish contexts. However, the structure found at the Judicial Center site includes a number of attributes that have been identified by Vlach (1975, 1978) as representative of African architectural style. Key stylistic elements include the rectangular form, two- to three-room internal division without hallways, and the presence of a front porch or covered entryway. Our identification of this building as of African construction is based on both its style and materials.

Other evidence of colonial architecture within the site is limited, although in two instances tabby-floored structures of indeterminate outer wall construction were recorded. With African and European antecedents, tabby was apparently introduced to the New World by the Spanish, who employed *tapia* for low-cost housing in St. Augustine in 1580 (Sickels-Taves and Sheehan 1999:5). Tabby is a mixture of crushed shell, sand, and lime that was poured into wooden forms and hardened into a type of cement (Brooker 1991; Sickels-Taves and Sheehan 1999). It was a common building material for plantation support structures, including village dwellings, and was used in Charles Town for Revolutionary War–era fortifications (Adams 1998b), but apparently was not used with any significant frequency for the construction of dwellings in town.

As Poston (1997:25) notes, there are few surviving examples of colonial architecture in Charles Town. After the fire of 1740 the rebuilt town exhibited a distinctly Georgian character and began the development of what would become the quintessential Charles Town dwelling, the Charleston "single house." In plan a single pile raised Georgian structure turned on its side with two-story porches, the single house is clearly an adaptive architecture, reflecting the integration of Caribbean and English architectural styles to create a house well-suited to the city's climate and urban landscape (Herman 1997a, 1997b). This architectural form became synonymous with the city, with varying materials and scale used to signify social rank within the single house universe.

The archaeology and history of Charles Town's colonial architecture illustrate the use of a variety of building styles and materials, ranging from African earth-walled structures to European half-timbered dwellings to Lowcountry tabby structures to Caribbean transplants built of Bermuda stone. These were eventually replaced by an architecture encompassing both English and Caribbean traditions in an adaptation to the Lowcountry's climate, the Charleston single house. The single house provided a form in which social rank and wealth could be expressed by size and material and, as Herman (1997a) notes, a setting in which social relationships could be negotiated on a number of planes. As with ceramics, its replacement of earlier architectural styles is somewhat a matter of evolution and technology, but not entirely. The earth-walled dwellings also offered adaptive advantages, as their construction provided an insulated architecture that could stay relatively cool during the hot summer months (Ferguson 1992:72). While earth-walled construction may be considered impermanent, it can be a fairly durable medium. In Puerto Rico, an earth-walled variant known as *mamposteria,* which incorporates clay walls with wood, stone, and brick filler beneath a plaster coating, is the predominant building material of houses in Old San Juan, many of which are centuries old. Thus the disappearance of earth-walled structures from Charles Town's landscape, like the disappearance of colonoware, cannot be explained entirely by changes in technology.

Landscape

Archaeological deposits occur within contexts; their meaning is thus derived not only from their contents, but also from their location. One of urban archaeology's concerns is the reconstruction of landscape, particularly in historic cities like Charleston (Zierden 1997a; Zierden and Calhoun 1986; Zierden and Herman 1996). The use of block stripping in combination with a well-preserved colonial occupation surface provided the scale necessary to map and interpret aspects of the colonial landscape. This work revealed that the greatest density of colonial features was found in the immediate rear yards.

For the earliest portion of the colonial period at the site, roughly the era from circa 1720 to circa 1740, the immediate rear yard areas of homes fronting Broad Street contain a large number of features. These features are of a nature normally associated with work yards and include such things as root cellars, storage pits, other pit features, structures, wells, and privies. We were surprised to find these features so near the dwellings on these lots, particularly given the large lot dimensions. However, excavations in extreme rear yard areas failed to uncover any features, while mid yard areas contained late eighteenth- and nineteenth-century deposits, although not in as high a density as areas closer to the dwellings. The highest density of features found on the site was in these immediate rear yard areas, and those features furthermore were among the oldest found.

During the early colonial period more than half of the lot space appears to have been used for agricultural functions, for fields and livestock (see Stewart-Abernathy 1986 for a discussion of urban farmsteads). The raising of livestock on these urban lots is confirmed by the presence of various faunal elements, primarily cranial fragments as well as hooves and other waste bone, indicative of on-site butchering as opposed to market purchase. Calhoun et al. (1984:11) and Weinand and Reitz (1996) note that during the colonial era many Charlestonians raised poultry, hogs, sheep, and cattle on their lots, and that issues regarding livestock management were a constant topic in the local paper and the subject of statutes and regulations. For example, the *South Carolina Gazette* of July 7, 1746, posted a notice that "all goats and swine found running at large in Charlestown shall be forfeited for the use of the poor in St. Phillips Parish" (in Calhoun et al. 1984). Livestock were thus being raised on the urban lots within the site, presumably in penned enclosures.

The presence of a number of root cellars and vegetable storage pits also suggests the growing of vegetables on these lots. While fruits and vegetables could be purchased from outlying plantations and found growing wild in the Lowcountry, many settlers in the colonial city had their own vegetable gardens to supplement produce available at market and as a hedge against times when food was short or prices dear. Colonial root cellars and subsurface storage pits generally took the form of circular to oblong pits, measuring approximately three feet in depth. In several instances remnants of a fiber matting, straw or possibly Spanish moss, were discernible along the sides and floors of these pits. Subterranean pit features for the storage of plants and root crops over the winter are recorded in the historical and archaeological literature. George McDaniel (1982:154–55) reports that shallow "vegetable kilns" were common in the yards of African American homes in Maryland, where they were described as "a circular hole in the ground about two feet deep into which vegetables were stored on a bed of straw and then covered with more straw and a mound of dirt." A variant of this type of subterranean feature was reported by Elizabeth Windom of South Carolina to folklorist Richard Westmacott (1992). Wheaton et al. (1990) and Joseph (1993a, 1997) report the discovery of comparable storage features in nineteenth-century African American house yards.

At 96 Broad Street a fairly substantial outbuilding, the earth-walled structure discussed above, was encountered in the immediate rear yard area, and this structure appears to have served as a kitchen and servants' quarters. Separate kitchens were also found in the immediate rear yard of 92 and 98 Broad Street. Cisterns for drinking water were usually found near one of the rear corners of the main house. Because of Charles Town's coastal location groundwater was brackish, thus cisterns were used to collect rainwater from rooftop gutters for drinking purposes. However, wells were found in the yard area in several of the colonial houselots and it is unclear whether they were used as a source of drinking water prior to cisterns. Cisterns required brick construction; brick was a costly material to obtain in the early colonial period, and cisterns thus may not have become common until the rebuilding of Charles Town following the fire of 1740. Wells may also have been used to collect water for purposes other than drinking, possibly for livestock and crops, as well as for laundry and other household activities. Stables were found just beyond the work yard, bordering the agricultural field and presumably livestock pens.

The image that thus emerges of the early colonial landscape reveals an active work space in the immediate rear yard area consisting of kitchen, servants' quarters, a privy or privies, root cellars, storage pits, possibly a cistern, a well, and other pit features (Figure 14.4, A). This tight clustering of features presumably reflects the devotion of much of the lot space to agricultural functions, but may also reflect cultural preferences. Comparable work yards have been documented in the areas surrounding Afri-

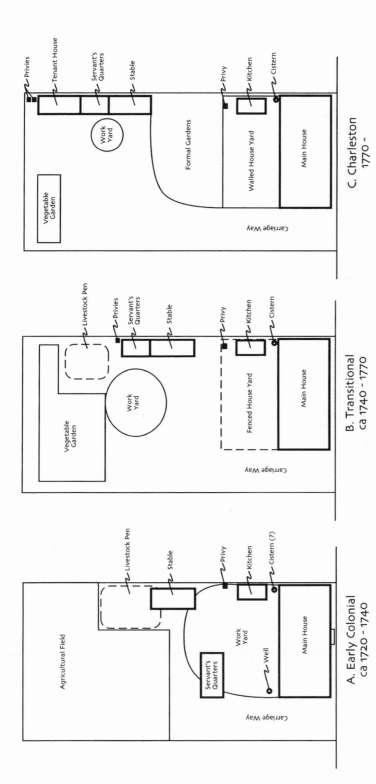

Figure 14.4. Schematic views showing changing landscape plan.

can villages on the plantations (Wheaton et al. 1983) and around antebellum and postbellum nineteenth-century free African American houses
(Joseph 1993a, 2000; Wheaton et al. 1990). Ethnoarchaeologist Kofi
Agorsah (1983) discusses activities that occur in the courtyards of Nchumuru homes, which contain features such as storage pits, hearths, ovens,
work posts, benches, and burials. Indeed, the landscape of 96 Broad Street,
with its earth-walled structure, borrow pit, and storage pits, would have
been decidedly African in appearance.

This pattern appears to have changed at some time near the middle of
the eighteenth century (Figure 14.4, B). The most significant changes are
the removal of servants' quarters from the rear yard area and the relocation
and reduction in the size of the work yard. Servants' quarters now appear
along one edge of the yard, often as additions to earlier structures such as
stables. These additions occurred vertically, through the addition of a second story, as well as horizontally through an expansion of the building.
The work yard area is less readily identifiable and appears to have decreased in both size and intensity of activity. The numerous pit features
recorded for the early colonial period are not as prevalent, and pit features
also appear less regular in form. These changes presumably reflect a decrease in the amount of agriculture taking place within these urban lots. By
mid-century the plantation economy was well established and Charles
Town's markets would have offered a variety of vegetable and animal produce for urban residents. By 1739 a public market was established on the
northeast corner of the square formed by the intersection of Meeting and
Broad streets (Calhoun et al. 1984), a half block from the study area, and
archaeological excavations at the Charleston County Courthouse, which
immediately adjoins the Judicial Center site, revealed a colonial midden indicative of market activities at this location prior to the construction of the
South Carolina State House in 1753 (Joseph and Elliott 1994). Hence the
need for self-sufficiency in the area would have been greatly reduced, and
presumably so too would the amount of land devoted to fields and livestock as urban residents focused their efforts more on mercantile pursuits.

This transition was likely influenced by the dynamics of race in the city.
The year 1740 serves as a benchmark in Charles Town's racial relationships. This was the year after the Stono Rebellion, the first recorded slave
uprising in the Lowcountry (see Zierden this volume), and it was also the
year of the worst fire yet in Charles Town's history, which burned nearly
half the city. The year 1740 thus marked a time to rebuild, and in rebuilding, to rethink and reexpress social and racial relations. The movement of
servants' quarters and work areas away from the main house suggests a
social distancing. Immediate rear yard areas, rather than serving as work
space, appear to have been incorporated into the household setting, and
work and family—support and social—relations appear to begin their

separation. There is some evidence to suggest that rear yard areas at this time were fenced. Fencing may indicate the creation of gardens and other ornamental landscapes that required protection from livestock, but may also reflect heightened concerns for security and separation in the wake of the Stono Rebellion.

This transition would appear to have reached its full expression at some point just prior to the American Revolution (Figure 14.4, C). This period saw the continued development of rear yard areas as an outer domestic sphere, with rental properties and tenements joining servants' quarters on the larger city lots. This infilling reflected the growth of the city and increasing population densities, coupled with a significant reduction in the need for self-sufficiency as the plantation economy now provided ample and affordable foodstuffs to Charles Town. Rear yard enclosures also shifted in nature, from wood fencing to wrought iron to brick walls. These shifts reflect heightening concern over issues of security raised in part by the threat of war as well as by the Revolution's quest for freedom and the contradictory message such a proclamation gave to the Lowcountry's enslaved citizens (Morgan 1983). Zierden and Herman (1996) and Zierden (1997a) observe that the separation and segmentation of Charles Town's landscape would increase after the Denmark Vessey revolt of 1822 and as Charles Town's economy began to stagnate and tensions mounted between North and South. By the eve of the Revolution a landscape in which urban spaces were compartmentalized and boundaries of household security marked by wood and wrought iron fences, and eventually walls, was in place as the model of the urban lot.

Herman (1997a) refers to the landscape of the single house as "embedded" and notes that within the single house compound are a number of landscapes, ranging from the social landscape of the parlor, where "tea table topography" signified and expressed the social relationships of the upper class, to the connected yet separate landscape of the yard and servants' quarters, where saw-but-did-not-see and heard-but-did-not-hear marked the actions of African American servants. This dichotomy, near/distant, together/separate, would be a hallmark of Charles Town culture.

Summary and Conclusion

Charles Town's material landscape changed dramatically over the course of the eighteenth century. A visitor to the town in the 1720s would have seen an array of architectural styles reflecting different cultural traditions, including half-timbered dwellings, Bermuda stone houses, tabby, and earth-walled structures. These buildings would have been set on lots that were organized as urban farmsteads (Stewart-Abernathy 1986), with a considerable amount of space devoted to gardens and livestock pens. Behind the main house they would have found an active work yard with agricultural features such as root cellars and storage pits as well as buildings such as kitchens and servants' quarters. This yard was in many respects African in appearance. In the yard, in the kitchen, and in the main house, they would have come into contact with pottery from various points in Europe as well as from closer to home. In each of these contexts ethnicity would have been visible but the ethnic identity with the highest profile was that of the Africans. In the organization of yard space, in the building of earth-walled structures, in the making of colonowares, in the crops that were grown and the foods that were cooked, images of Africa were present and that presence was obvious and drew the remarks of visitors to the colony. Carolina looked more like an African colony than a colony of Europeans.

On a return trip in the 1770s, on the eve of the Revolution, our visitor would have encountered a dramatically different place. The town had been rebuilt in part in response to fires and hurricanes (Poston 1997), but it had also been rebuilt to express a new identity. Gone was the architectural mosaic; in its place were Georgian dwellings and a particular dwelling that embodied Georgian attributes with a Caribbean flair, the Charleston single house, a building so synonymous with the city that it became its architectural signature. Gone were the earth-walled structures and half-timbered dwellings of the earlier time. The urban landscape had, like the town's architecture, become more formal. Rear yards were now private spaces, fenced, some in wood, some in iron, on the brink of becoming more solidly enclosed by brick. Servants' quarters had been moved well beyond this private space, along rear lot edges, and gardens and livestock pens had significantly shrunk in size and in many cases vanished. In their place were formal gardens, romantic landscapes, designed to signify their owners' place above nature, with it in their control. The ceramics in their kitchens and most importantly on their tables were also different: they were refined English earthenwares with a variety of decorations, laid out in sets, the extent and embellishment of which would signify value and worth to every visitor, as the prices of these things were known, established, defined. Colonowares had vanished from the kitchen, replaced with metal implements. Ethnic identity, of both residents and their servants, was less easily identified, but their wealth and social status was clear and on display and could be read in buildings, in landscapes, and in the plates set on a table.

To a large extent, these changes were the product of Charles Town's economic attainments. It was a mature city now. It was also a bustling and financially vibrant city: the produce of the outlying plantations flowed into its harbor and then out to the world and in exchange the planters brought back the finest that the world had to offer. It was a city built entirely of the nouveau riche, and the nouveau riche, then as now, were conspicuous in their consumption as they made every effort to display how rich they were

(McInnis and Mack 1999; Zierden 1999). To a large extent, the things they displayed were the products of the Industrial Revolution, and hence were different from the things their parents had brought with them to the colonies. They embraced this new material culture; indeed, they demanded it, and they relished its ability to signify their attainments in a language that was clear and less complex than that of their parents' pottery. To a large extent, the material world of Charles Town in the late eighteenth century was simply a product of a vigorous economy coupled to the produce of the Industrial Revolution and wielded by a populace anxious to create their identity on the basis of their economic achievements.

To some extent, however, it was the product of something else. These citizens of Charles Town on the eve of the Revolution were anxious to embrace an identity as Charlestonian and eager to abandon their earlier identities of Huguenot planter, Dutch merchant, or Scottish factor. But there was another identity that became dramatically less visible during this period, one that was neither nouveau nor rich, indeed one that had been the most tangible and indelible in the early ethnic mosaic, that of the Africans. They were still a majority population, yet images of Africa had virtually vanished by the time of the Revolution. Where had they gone, and why?

This same transformation has been charted on the plantations, and one answer offered in those places was that the Africans had acculturated— had joined the creole culture that they helped to form and in so doing had shed their Africaness (Wheaton et al. 1983; Wheaton and Garrow 1985). But as an oppressed segment of society, changes in material culture were not necessarily of their own volition, but rather were the product of the Europeans who attempted to maintain control. What then, was the significance of these changes, or more important, what were they intended to signify?

I have argued elsewhere that on the Lowcountry plantations these changes represented the introduction of a mindset borrowed from the Industrial Revolution emphasizing structure, order, and social hierarchy (Joseph 1993b). Seeing these same changes in a different setting, in another context, leads me to alter this explanation and emphasize the importance of a defined social hierarchy within this developing culture. The culture that emerged in the South during the colonial period was both a caste- and a class-based culture, and as such was dramatically different from the culture that developed in New England. Caste and class are similar cultural concepts, representing the hierarchical stratification of society. Their key distinction is that for caste, social status is ascribed, whereas for class, status is achieved (Mandelbaum 1964:161). Caste was a critical social construct in the establishment of the Carolina colony, which was originally conceptualized as a society led by a hereditary nobility. While this ascribed nobility would not come to fruition, slavery made caste a fundamental tenet of southern culture (Mandelbaum 1964:161). Africans, by their very being, were defined legally as an oppressed segment of society, an oppression that continued even for those fortunate enough to escape the bonds of slavery. In the absence of hereditary nobility, European settlers made class a critical component of the society they developed, with those of sufficient economic attainment occupying the upper class held in Europe by the nobility and emulating the nobility's role and behavior. As caste culture became codified and as social class emerged as the definitive element of southern society, the importance of ethnicity was de-emphasized in deference to social status, both ascribed and obtained. To legitimize this social structure, indicators of ethnicity had to vanish.

In this mind set, Africans were oppressed not because they were Africans; they were oppressed because they were considered to be socially inferior (Jordan 1974; Joseph 1993b). Social inferiority, like social superiority, was indicated through material culture. Africans lived in dwellings that were like the dwellings Europeans lived in, but smaller and less refined. They lived in the back of yards, in positions away from the main house, separate and supportive. They ate from refined earthenware tablewares, but from types that were less expensive and of a lower status than those of the Europeans. I suggest that one of the requirements of a class culture is that all members of the culture must work from a common vocabulary of things whose meaning is defined to all. It is much more difficult to ascribe meaning to things that are different—is an earth-walled house socially superior or inferior to a frame house? Is a colonoware bowl socially inferior or superior to a hand-painted pearlware bowl? The answer is neither, they are simply different, signifying cultural identity, not social identity. Thus within the culture that developed in Charles Town during the eighteenth century, a standardized material culture was required through which social status could be expressed.

Thus the change in Charles Town's material culture and the disappearance of its ethnic diversity must be seen as the product not simply of economic vitality and the Industrial Revolution, but, more important, of the formation of a caste- and class-based culture in which identity was based on ascribed status, social achievement, and rank. What resulted was a shared set of material markers—buildings, landscapes, plates and cups—which in their scale, elaboration, and position reflected the social status of each resident of the larger urban landscape. Within this culture, expressions of cultural identity were discouraged. Thus immigrants to Charles Town shed their traditional ways and joined in a creole culture that stressed social status. African immigrants were forcibly dispossessed of their cultural baggage and required to use, live, and wear things that materially spoke of their social position to other immigrants. This cultural model, based on the social dictates of the plantation economy, was appropriate to other localities in the South, and as a result the expression of cultural variety was eroded from the southern landscape at an early age, not to reappear. The colonists' ethnic diversity was given up as social status—caste and class—became the identifier of Charlestonians.

Acknowledgments

The archaeological excavation of the Charleston Judicial Center site was sponsored by Charleston County's Department of Capital Projects. I am particularly appreciative of the support and interest of Guy Blanton, the director of Capital Projects, and of the oversight, insight, and friendship of county restoration architect Jim Wigley. I am also appreciative of the work of my colleagues on this project: archaeologist Theresa Hamby; analyst Susan Travis; field assistants Matt Tankersley, Martha Wallace, Genevieve Brown, Dione Miller, Alex Caton, and Andrew Agha; historian Mary Beth Reed; ethnobotanist Leslie Raymer; zooarchaeologist Lisa O'Steen; and graphic artists Tracey Fedor and Tony Greiner, who prepared the illustrations that accompany this chapter. In Charleston, Carter Hudgins, Jon Poston, and Katherine Saunders of the Historic Charleston Foundation have been a constant source of information and encouragement. Elsie Eubanks of Charles Town Landing has graciously shared the preliminary results of ongoing excavations of the original Charles Town settlement. Greg Waselkov and James Gibbs provided comments on a draft of this chapter, and I am appreciative of their remarks and especially of James Gibbs's guidance toward clarifying the discussion of class and caste. I am particularly grateful for the visits, ideas, and discussions provided over the course of a lengthy and distended field season by Carl Steen and Martha Zierden.

Bibliography

Abbeville Probate Court
1785   Will of Michael Meyer. Abbeville, South Carolina.

Adams, Natalie P.
1993   *Archaeological Investigations at 38GE377: Examination of a Deep Creek Phase Site and a Portion of the Eighteenth Century Midway Plantation.* Research Series 37, Chicora Foundation, Columbia, South Carolina.

1995   *Management Summary of Archaeological Data Recovery at 38BK1669 and 38BK1670, Berkeley County, South Carolina.* Research Contribution 165, Chicora Foundation, Columbia, South Carolina.

1998a   *Archaeological Investigations at the Neale Plantation (31Cb110), Columbus County, North Carolina.* Technical Report 530, New South Associates, Stone Mountain, Georgia.

1998b   *"Now a Few Words about the Works . . . Called the Old Royal Work": Phase I Archaeological Investigations at Marion Square, Charleston, South Carolina.* Report submitted to Van Valkenburg and Associates, Inc., by New South Associates, Stone Mountain, Georgia.

2001   "Euren Eingang Segne Gott": An Archaeological and Historical Examination of Lot 92, Saxe Gotha Town, Lexington County, South Carolina. Report submitted to American Engineering Consultants, Cayce, South Carolina, by New South Associates, Inc., Stone Mountain, Georgia.

Agorsah, Kofi
1983   An Ethnoarchaeological Study of Settlement and Behavior Patterns of a West African Traditional Society: The Nchumuru of Banda-Wiae in Ghana. Ph.D. dissertation, University Microfilms International, Ann Arbor, Michigan.

Anonymous
1846   Turpentine. *Southern Cultivator* 4:142.

1855 Turpentine: Hints for Those about to Engage in Its Manufacture. *De-Bow's Review* 1855(October): 486–89.

Anthony, Ronald W.

1979 Descriptive Analysis and Replication of Historic Earthenware: Colono Wares from the Spiers Landing Site, Berkeley County, South Carolina. In *The Conference on Historic Sites Archaeology Papers,* vol. 13, pp. 253–68. Institute of Archaeology and Anthropology, Columbia, South Carolina.

1986 Colono Wares. In *Home Upriver: Rural Life on Daniels Island,* by Martha Zierden, Lesley Drucker, and Jeanne Calhoun, pp. 7-22–7-51. Ms. on file, South Carolina Department of Highways and Public Transportation, Columbia.

1989 Cultural Diversity at Mid to Late Eighteenth Century Lowcountry Plantation Slave Settlements. Master's thesis, Department of Anthropology, University of South Carolina, Columbia.

1995 Stono Plantation: Research Orientation and Preliminary Results from the Study of a James Island, South Carolina Plantation. Paper presented at the twenty-eighth annual meeting of the Society for Historical Archaeology, Washington, D.C.

Armstrong, Douglas V.

1999 Archaeology and Ethnohistory of the Caribbean Plantation. In *I, Too, Am America: Archaeological Studies of African American Life,* edited by Theresa Singleton, pp. 173–92. Charlottesville: University Press of Virginia.

Arnade, Charles W.

1959 *The Siege of St. Augustine in 1702.* University of Florida Monographs, No. 3, University of Florida Press, Gainesville.

Ascher, Robert, and Charles Fairbanks

1971 Excavation of a Slave Cabin: Georgia, U.S.A. *Historical Archaeology* 5:3–17.

Atkins, Gaius G., and Frederick L. Fagley

1942 *History of American Congregationalism.* Boston: Pilgrim Press.

Ault, Warren O.

1972 *Open-Field Farming in Medieval England.* London: George Allen and Unwin.

Avirett, James B.

1901 *The Old Plantation: How We Lived in Great House and Cabin before the War.* New York: F. Tennyson Neely.

Baker, Stephen G.

1972 Colono-Indian Pottery from Cambridge, South Carolina, with Comments on the Historic Catawba Pottery Trade. *South Carolina Institute of Archaeology and Anthropology Notebook* 4(1): 3–30.

1975 The Working Draft of the Historic Catawba Peoples: Exploratory Perspectives in Ethnohistory and Archaeology. Ms. on file, Department of History, University of South Carolina, Columbia.

Barrie, Thomas
1996   *Spiritual Path, Sacred Place: Myth, Ritual, and Meaning in Architecture.*
        Boston: Shambhala Publications.
Barth, Frederick
1969   *Ethnic Groups and Boundaries: The Social Organization of Culture Dif-*
        ference. London: George Allen and Unwin.
Bastian, Beverly
1982   *Fort Independence: An Eighteenth Century Frontier Homesite and Mili-*
        tia Post in South Carolina. Atlanta, Georgia: National Park Service.
Beall, Mary Harper
1858   Letter from Mary Harper Beall to Mrs. C. E. Harper, November 19,
        1858. Beall and Harper Family Papers, Southern Historical Collection,
        Wilson Library, University of North Carolina at Chapel Hill.
Beck, Monica
1998   Dissenters and Anglicans within the Colonial Frontier Town of Dorches-
        ter. Paper presented at the annual meeting of the Southeastern Archaeo-
        logical Conference, Greenville, South Carolina.
Beeman, Richard R.
1984   *The Evolution of the Southern Backcountry: A Case Study of Lunen-*
        burg County, Virginia, 1746–1832. Philadelphia: University of Pennsyl-
        vania Press.
Bell, Daniel J.
1995   *Old Dorchester State Park Visitor Guide.* South Carolina Department of
        Parks, Recreation and Tourism, State Park Service, Columbia.
1999   The Dorchester Free School Historical Survey. Unpublished ms. of the
        South Carolina State Parks Service, Charles Town Landing State His-
        toric Site, Charleston.
Berlin, Ira
1998   *Many Thousands Gone: The First Two Centuries of Slavery in North*
        America, 1685–1815. Lincoln: University of Nebraska Press.
Berlin, Ira, and Philip D. Morgan
1993   Introduction: Labor and the Shaping of Slave Life in the Americas. In
        Cultivation and Culture: Labor and the Shaping of Slave Life in the
        Americas, edited by Ira Berlin and Philip D. Morgan, pp. 1–45. Char-
        lottesville: University of Virginia Press.
Bernheim, G. D.
1872   *History of the German Settlements and the Lutheran Church in North*
        and South Carolina. Philadelphia: The Lutheran Book Store.
Bethania Committee
1764   Document of December 2, 1764. In *Minutes of the Bethania Commit-*
        tee, 1763–1772. Unpublished translation of records held by the
        Moravian Archives, Winston-Salem. Bethania Historical Association,
        Bethania, North Carolina.

Bivins, John, Jr.
　1972　*The Moravian Potters in North Carolina.* Chapel Hill: University of
　　　　North Carolina.
Blitz, John
　1999　Mississippian Chiefdoms and the Fission-Fusion Process. *American An-
　　　　tiquity* 64:577–92.
Bolton, S. Charles
　1982　*Southern Anglicanism: The Church of England in Colonial South Caro-
　　　　lina.* Westport, Connecticut: Greenwood Press.
Bourne, Edward G. (editor)
　1904　*Narratives of the Career of Hernando De Soto,* vols. 1 and 2. New
　　　　York: A. S. Barnes.
Braudel, Fernand
　1979　*The Structure of Everyday Life: Civilization and Capitalism, Fifteenth–
　　　　Eighteenth Century,* vol. 1. New York: Harper and Row.
Braund, Kathryn Holland
　1992　*Deerskins and Duffels: The Creek Indian Trade with Anglo-America,
　　　　1685–1815.* Lincoln: University of Nebraska Press.
Brooker, Colin
　1991　Callawassie Island Sugar Works: A Tabby Building Complex. In *Further
　　　　Investigations of Prehistoric and Historic Lifeways on Callawassie and
　　　　Spring Islands, Beaufort County, South Carolina,* edited by Michael
　　　　Trinkley, pp. 110–54. Research Series 23, Chicora Foundation, Colum-
　　　　bia, South Carolina.
Brooks, Richard D.
　1987　*Two hundred Fifty Years of Historic Occupation on Steel Creek, Savan-
　　　　nah River Plant, Barnwell County, South Carolina.* Savannah River Ar-
　　　　chaeological Papers 1, Savannah River Archaeological Research Pro-
　　　　gram, South Carolina Institute of Archaeology and Anthropology,
　　　　University of South Carolina, Columbia.
Brown, Kenneth L., and Doreen C. Cooper
　1990　Structural Continuity in an African-American Slave and Tenant Commu-
　　　　nity. *Historical Archaeology* 24(4): 7–19.
Brownell, Blaine, and David Goldfield
　1977　*The City in Southern History.* Port Washington, New York: Kennikat.
Bureau of the Census
　1790　*State Level Census Data.* Inter-University Consortium for Political
　　　　and Social Research. Historical Demographic, Economic, and Social
　　　　Data: U.S., 1790–1970. Anne Arbor, Michigan. September 9, 1999,
　　　　http://www.fisher.lib.virginia.edu/cgi-local/censusbin/census/cen.pl.
Bushnell, Amy
　1994　*Situado and Sabana: Spain's Support System for the Presidio and Mis-
　　　　sion Provinces of Florida.* Anthropological Papers of the American Mu-
　　　　seum of Natural History No. 74, University of Georgia Press, Athens.

Butler, Jon
  1983   *The Huguenots in America: A Refugee People in New World Society.*
         Cambridge, Massachusetts: Harvard University Press.
Cable, John, Gail Wagner, and Christopher Judge
  2000   *Wateree Archaeological Research Project: 1998 Survey and Testing.* Pal-
         metto Research Institute Occasional Papers No. 1, Irmo, South Caro-
         lina.
Calhoun, Jeanne A.
  1983   *The Scourging Wrath of God: Early Hurricanes in Charleston, 1700–*
         1804. The Charleston Museum Leaflet No. 29, Charleston.
Calhoun, Jeanne A., Elizabeth J. Reitz, Michael B. Trinkley, and Martha A. Zierden
  1984   *Meat in Due Season: Preliminary Investigations of Marketing Practices*
         in Colonial Charleston. Archaeological Contributions 9, The Charleston
         Museum, Charleston, South Carolina.
Carney, Judith
  1993   From Hands to Tutors: African Expertise in the South Carolina Rice
         Economy. *Agricultural History* 67(3): 1–30.
Carroll, B. R. (editor)
  1836   *Historical Collections of South Carolina,* 2 vols. New York: Harper and
         Brothers.
Carson, Cary, Norman F. Barka, William M. Kelso, Garry Wheeler Stone, and
Dell Upton
  1988   Impermanent Architecture in the Southern American Colonies. In *Mate-*
         rial Life in America, 1600–1860, edited by Robert Blair St. George,
         pp. 113–58. Boston: Northeastern University Press.
Cashin, Edward J.
  1986   The Gentlemen of Augusta. In *Colonial Augusta: "Key of the Indian*
         Country," edited by Edward J. Cashin, pp. 27–57. Macon, Georgia:
         Mercer University Press.
Cecelski, David S.
  1997   Oldest Living Confederate Chaplain Tells All? Or, James B. Avirett and
         the Rise and Fall of Rich Lands. *Southern Cultures* 3(4): 5–24.
Chaplin, Joyce E.
  1993   *An Anxious Pursuit: Agricultural Innovation and Modernity in the*
         Lower South, 1730–1815. Published for the Institute of Early Ameri-
         can History and Culture, Williamsburg, Virginia, by the University of
         North Carolina Press, Chapel Hill.
Chesnutt, David R.
  1989   *South Carolina's Expansion into Colonial Georgia, 1720–1765.* New
         York: Garland.
Cheves, Langdon (editor)
  1894   *The Year Book of Charleston.* Collections of the South Carolina Histori-
         cal Society, Charleston.
  2000   *The Shaftesbury Papers.* Reprint of 1897 Edition. Charleston: South
         Carolina Historical Society.

Chicora Foundation
   1994   *The Property Nobody Wanted: Archaeological and Historical Investiga-*
          tions at Fort Johnson, SC. Research Series 43, Chicora Foundation, Co-
          lumbia, South Carolina.
Clark, Murtie Jane
   1981   *Loyalists in the Southern Campaign of the Revolutionary War.* Balti-
          more: Genealogical Publishing.
Clement, Christopher, Monica Beck, and Martha Zierden
   1999   Far from the Madding Crowd: Outlying Settlements in Seventeenth Cen-
          tury Carolina. Paper presented at the annual conference of the Society
          for Historical Archaeology, Salt Lake City.
Clement, Christopher Ohm, and Ramona M. Grunden
   1998   *"Where the Wappetaw Independent Congregational Church Stood ... "*
          Archaeological Testing at 38CH1682, Charleston County, SC. Research
          Manuscript Series 225, South Carolina Institute of Archaeology and An-
          thropology, Columbia.
Clewell, John Henry
   1902   *History of Wachovia in North Carolina.* New York: Doubleday, Page.
Clifton, James M.
   1973   Golden Grains of White: Rice Planting on the Lower Cape Fear. *North*
          Carolina Historical Review 50(4): 365–93.
Clowse, Converse D.
   1971   *Economic Beginnings in Colonial South Carolina 1670–1730.* Colum-
          bia: University of South Carolina Press.
Colonial Plats
   n.d.   Plat for 239-acre grant to Michael Meyer, 6 vol. 6, p. 19. South Caro-
          lina Department of Archives and History, Columbia.
Carolina Commons House of Assembly
   1692–1765 Journals of the Commons House of Assembly, bound in various
          volumes, including 1692–1707/08, 1724–1726, and 1735–1765. South
          Carolina Department of Archives and History. University of South Caro-
          lina Press, Columbia.
Cooper, Margaret, and Carl Steen
   1998   Potters of the South Carolina Lowcountry: A Material Culture Study of
          Creolization. Ms. on file, The Charleston Museum, Charleston.
Cooper, Thomas, and D. J. McCord (editors)
   1836   *The Statutes at Large of South Carolina,* 2 vols. Columbia: A. S.
          Johnston.
Cote, Richard N.
   1981   *Local and Family History in South Carolina: A Bibliography.* Charles-
          ton: South Carolina Historical Society.
Covington, James W.
   1968   Stuart's Town, the Yamasee Indians and Spanish Florida. *Florida An-*
          thropologist 21:8–13.

Crane, Brian
1993 Colono Wares and Criollo Ware Pottery from Charleston, South Carolina and San Juan, Puerto Rico in Comparative Perspective. Ph.D. dissertation, University of Pennsylvania, University Microfilms, Ann Arbor, Michigan.
Crane, Verner W.
1928 *The Southern Frontier, 1670–1732.* Durham, North Carolina: Duke University Press.
1981 *The Southern Frontier, 1670–1732.* Reprint. New York: W. W. Norton.
Crass, David C., Tammy Forehand, Bruce Penner, Chris Gillam
1997 *Excavations at New Windsor Township, South Carolina.* Savannah River Archaeological Research Heritage Series 3, Institute of Archaeology and Anthropology, University of South Carolina, Columbia.
Crass, David C., Bruce R. Penner, and Tammy R. Forehand
1999 Gentility and Material Culture on the Carolina Frontier. *Historical Archaeology* 33(3): 14–31.
Crews, C. Daniel (translator and editor)
1993 *Bethania: A Fresh Look at Its Birth.* Winston-Salem, North Carolina: Moravian Archives.
Davis, Mary K.
1979 The Featherbed Aristocracy: Abbeville District in the 1790s. *South Carolina Historical Magazine* 80:136–55.
Davis, N.
1951 The French Settlement at New Bordeaux. *Transactions of the Huguenot Society of South Carolina* 56:52.
Dawdy, Shannon
2000 Preface. Creolization. *Historical Archaeology* 34(3): 1–4.
Deagan, Kathleen
1983 *Spanish St. Augustine: The Archaeology of a Colonial Creole Community.* New York: Academic.
1999 Historical Archaeology and Multicultural Engagement in the Formation of the Atlantic World. Paper presented at the College of Charleston Faculty Seminar on the Atlantic World. Ms. on file, The Charleston Museum, Charleston, South Carolina.
Deagan, Kathleen, and Jane Landers
1999 Fort Mose: Earliest Free African American Town in the United States. In *"I, Too, Am America": Archaeological Studies of African-American Life,* edited by Theresa A. Singleton, pp. 261–82. Charlottesville: University Press of Virginia.
DeCorse, Christopher R.
1999 Oceans Apart: Africanist Perspectives on Diaspora Archaeology. In *"I, Too, Am America": Archaeological Studies of African-American Life,* edited by Theresa A. Singleton, pp. 132–55. Charlottesville: University Press of Virginia.

Deetz, James
  1976   *In Small Things Forgotten: The Archaeology of Early American Life.*
         New York: Doubleday.
  1990   Landscapes as Cultural Statements. In *Earth Patterns: Essays in Land-*
         scape Archaeology, edited by William M. Kelso and Rachel Most,
         pp. 1–4. Charlottesville: University Press of Virginia.
Deetz, J. Eric, and Jamie E. May
  1997   Architectural Determinates in Root Cellar Placement. Paper presented
         at the Annual Conference of the Society for Historical Archaeology,
         Corpus Christi, Texas.
Delle, James A.
  1998   *An Archaeology of Social Space: Analyzing Coffee Plantations in Ja-*
         maica's Blue Mountains. New York and London: Plenum.
DePratter, Chester B.
  1989   Cofitachequi: Ethnohistorical and Archaeological Evidence. In *Studies*
         in South Carolina Archaeology: Essays in Honor of Robert L. Stephen-
         son, edited by A. C. Goodyear and G. T. Hanson, pp. 133–56. Anthro-
         pological Studies 9, Occasional Papers of the South Carolina Institute
         of Archaeology and Anthropology, University of South Carolina, Co-
         lumbia.
  1994   National Register of Historic Places Registration Form for the Yamasee
         Town of Altamaha, National Park Service, U.S. Department of the Inte-
         rior. Document on file at the South Carolina Department of Archives
         and History, Columbia.
DePratter, Chester B., and William Green
  1990   Origins of the Yamasee. Paper presented at the Southeastern Archaeo-
         logical Conference, Mobile, Alabama.
DeVorsey, Jr., Louis (editor)
  1971   *DeBrahm's Report of the General Survey in the Southern District of*
         North America. Columbia: University of South Carolina Press.
Drucker, Lesley M., and Ronald W. Anthony
  1979   *The Spiers Landing Site: Archaeological Investigations in Berkeley*
         County, South Carolina. Resource Studies Series 10, Carolina Archaeo-
         logical Services, Columbia, South Carolina.
Dunlop, William
  1929   Capt. Dunlop's Voyage to the Southward, 1698. *South Carolina Histori-*
         cal and Genealogical Magazine 30:127–33.
Ebanks, R. C.
  1974   Letter to the Editor. *Jamaica Journal* 7(2-3): 2.
Edgar, Walter
  1998   *South Carolina: A History.* Columbia: University of South Carolina
         Press.
Edgefield County Will Book A
  n.d.   Will of Elizabeth Meyer, Jr., on p. 25. Edgefield County Probate Court,
         Edgefield, South Carolina.

Ekirch, A. Roger

   1981   *"Poor Carolina": Politics and Society in Colonial North Carolina, 1729–1776*. Chapel Hill: University of North Carolina Press.

Elliott, Daniel T.

   1984   *An Archeological Survey of Compartment 252, Long Cane District, Sumter National Forest*. USDA Forest Service, Columbia, South Carolina.

   1995   *Clark Hill River Basin Survey*. LAMAR Institute, Watkinsville, Georgia.

Elliott, Daniel T., and John S. Cable

   1994   *Cultural Resources Survey of the Bull Point Tract, Beaufort County, South Carolina*. Report prepared for Metropolitan Properties, Inc., by New South Associates, Inc., Stone Mountain, Georgia.

Elliott, Daniel T., and Rita F. Elliott

   1990   *Seasons in the Sun: 1989 and 1990 Excavations at New Ebenezer*. LAMAR Institute, Watkinsville, Georgia.

   1992   City House, Country House: A Comparison of Salzburger Material Culture in Colonial Georgia. Presented at the annual meeting of the Society for Historical Archaeology, Kingston, Jamaica.

Elliott, Rita Folse, and Daniel T. Elliott

   1994   *Vernonburg Village, An Archaeological Study*. Prepared for the Georgia Department of Natural Resources, Atlanta, by LAMAR Institute, Watkinsville, Georgia.

Epperson, Terrence W.

   1999   Constructing Difference: The Social and Spatial Order of the Chesapeake Plantation. In *"I, Too, Am America": Archaeological Studies of African-American Life*, edited by Theresa A. Singleton, pp. 159–72. Charlottesville: University Press of Virginia.

Espenshade, Christopher T.

   1996   The Changing Use Contexts of Slave-Made Pottery on the South Carolina Coast. Paper presented at the conference African Impact on the Material Culture of the Americas, Winston-Salem, North Carolina.

Eubanks, Elsie, Christopher T. Espenshade, Marian Roberts, and Linda Kennedy

   1994   *Data Recovery Investigations of 38BU791, Bonny Shore Slave Row, Spring Island, Beaufort County, South Carolina*. Brockington and Associates, Atlanta.

Fairbanks, Charles

   1974   The Kingsley Slave Cabins in Duval County, Florida, 1968. In *The Conference on Historic Sites Archaeology Papers 1971*, pp. 62–93. Institute of Archaeology and Anthropology, Columbia, South Carolina.

Ferguson, Leland

   1980   Looking for the "Afro" in Colono Indian Pottery. In *Archaeological Perspectives on Ethnicity in America*, edited by Robert Schuyler, pp. 14–28. Farmingdale, New York: Baywood.

   1985   Struggling with Pots in Colonial South Carolina. Paper presented at the annual meeting of the Society for Historical Archaeology, Boston.

1989 Lowcountry Plantations, The Catawba Nation, and River Burnished Pottery. In *Studies in South Carolina Archaeology: Essays in Honor of Robert L. Stephenson,* edited by Albert C. Goodyear III and Glen Hanson, pp. 185–91. Anthropological Studies 9, Occasional Papers of the South Carolina Institute of Archaeology and Anthropology, University of South Carolina, Columbia.

1992 *Uncommon Ground: Archaeology and Early African America, 1650–1800.* Washington, D.C.: Smithsonian Institution Press.

1999 "The Cross Is a Magic Sign": Marks on Eighteenth-Century Bowls from South Carolina. In *"I, Too, Am America": Archaeological Studies of African-American Life,* edited by Theresa A. Singleton, pp. 116–31. Charlottesville: University Press of Virginia.

Fewkes, Vladimir J.
1944 *Catawba Pottery-Making, with Notes on Pamunkey Pottery-Making, Cherokee Pottery-Making, and Coiling.* Proceedings of the American Philosophical Society 88, Philadelphia.

Fischer, David H.
1989 *Albion's Seed.* New York: Oxford University Press.

Fletcher, Joshua N., and Bruce Harvey
2000 *Cultural Resources Survey of the Hasell Point Tract, Beaufort County, South Carolina.* Report prepared for D'Amico Management Associates by Brockington and Associates, Inc., Mt. Pleasant, South Carolina.

Fogelman, Aaron Spencer
1999 Shadow Boxing in Georgia: The Beginnings of the Moravian-Lutheran Conflict in British North America. *Georgia Historical Quarterly* (Savannah) 83(4): 629–59.

Franklin, Maria, and Garrett Fesler (editors)
1999 *Historical Archaeology, Identity Formation, and the Interpretation of Ethnicity.* Williamsburg, Virginia: Colonial Williamsburg Research Publications.

Fraser, Walter
1989 *Charleston! Charleston! The History of a Southern City.* Columbia: University of South Carolina Press.

Friedlander, Amy
1985 Establishing Historical Probabilities for Archaeological Interpretations: Slave Demography of Two Plantations in the South Carolina Lowcountry, 1740–1820. In *The Archaeology of Slavery and Plantation Life,* edited by Theresa A. Singleton, pp. 215–38. New York: Academic.

Fries, Adelaide L. (translator and editor)
1905 *The Moravians in Georgia, 1735–1740.* Raleigh, North Carolina: Edwards and Broughton.

1922 *Records of the Moravians in North Carolina,* vol. 1. North Carolina Historical Commission, Raleigh.

1925 *Records of the Moravians in North Carolina,* vol. 2. North Carolina Historical Commission, Raleigh.

1968   *Records of the Moravians in North Carolina* (reprint ed.). State Department of Archives and History, Raleigh, North Carolina.

Gardner, Harold
1969   The Dissenting Sects on the Southern Colonial Frontier, 1720–1770. Ph.D. dissertation, University of Kansas, University Microfilms, Ann Arbor, Michigan.

Gardner, Jeffrey, and Eric Poplin
1992   *Wappoo Plantation (38CH1199/1200): Data Recovery at an Eighteenth Century Stono River Plantation in Charleston County, South Carolina.* Mt. Pleasant, South Carolina: Brockington and Associates.

Garrow, Patrick H.
1985   Evidence for Acculturation at Yaughan and Curriboo Plantations. Paper presented at Seminar on Problems and Promises in Plantation Research, Charleston, South Carolina.

Garrow, Patrick H., and Thomas R. Wheaton
1989   Colonoware Ceramics: The Evidence from Yaughan and Curriboo Plantations. In *Studies in South Carolina Archaeology: Essays in Honor of Robert L. Stephenson,* edited by Albert C. Goodyear III and Glen T. Hanson, pp. 175–84. Anthropological Studies 9, Occasional Papers of the South Carolina Institute of Archaeology and Anthropology, University of South Carolina, Columbia.

Gartley, Richard T.
1979   Afro-Cruzan Pottery: A New Style of Colonial Earthenware from St. Croix. *Journal of the Virgin Islands Archaeological Society* 8:47–61.

Gibert, Anne C.
1976   *Pierre Gibert, Esq.: The Devoted Huguenot.* Published by the author.

Glassie, Henry
1968   *Pattern in the Material Folk Culture of the Eastern United States.* Philadelphia: University of Pennsylvania Press.

1975   *Folk Housing in Middle Virginia.* Knoxville: University of Tennessee Press.

Gold, Robert L.
1965   The East Florida Indians under Spanish and English Control: 1763–1765. *Florida Historical Quarterly* 44:105–20.

Gomez, Michael
1998   *Exchanging Our Country Marks: The Transformation of African Identities in the Colonial and Antebellum South.* Chapel Hill: University of North Carolina Press.

Gray, Anna
1989   "Be Ye Friend Or Foe": An Analysis of Two Eighteenth Century Sites. Master's thesis, Department of Anthropology, College of William and Mary, Williamsburg, Virginia.

Gray, Lewis Cecil
1958   *History of Agriculture in the Southern United States to 1860.* Gloucester, Massachusetts: Peter Smith.

Great Britain Public Record Office

1924   *Journal of the Commissioners for Trade and Plantations.* His Majesty's
        Stationery Office, London.

Green, William

1992   *The Search for Altamaha: The Archaeology and Ethnohistory of an
        Early Eighteenth Century Yamasee Indian Town.* Vol. 21 of *Volumes in
        Historical Archaeology,* edited by Stanley South. South Carolina Insti-
        tute of Archaeology and Anthropology, University of South Carolina,
        Columbia.

1995   Strange and Erie Things: Longhouses along the Savannah River. Paper
        presented at the Fiftieth Annual Iroquois Research Meeting, Rennselaer-
        ville, New York.

1998   The Erie/Westo Connection: Possible Evidence of Long Distance Migra-
        tion in the Eastern Woodlands during the Sixteenth and Seventeenth
        Centuries. Paper presented at the Southeastern Archaeological Confer-
        ence, Greenville, South Carolina.

Green, William, and Chester B. DePratter

2000   Ten Years of Yamasee Archaeology in South Carolina: A Retrospective
        and Guide for Future Research. Paper presented at the Southeastern Ar-
        chaeological Conference, Macon, Georgia.

Greene, Jack P.

1988   *Pursuits of Happiness: The Social Development of Early Modern British
        Colonies and the Formation of American Culture.* Chapel Hill: Univer-
        sity of North Carolina Press.

Gregorie, Anne King

1925   *Notes on Sewee Indians and Indian Remains of Christ Church Parish,
        Charleston County, South Carolina.* Contributions from The Charleston
        Museum 5, Charleston, South Carolina.

1926   Indian Trade of Carolina in the Seventeenth Century. Master's thesis, De-
        partment of History, University of South Carolina, Columbia.

Groover, Mark D.

1992   *Of Mindset and Material Culture: An Archaeological View of Conti-
        nuity and Change in the Eighteenth Century South Carolina Back-
        country.* Vol. 20 of *Volumes in Historical Archaeology,* edited by Stanley
        South. South Carolina Institute of Archaeology and Anthropology, Uni-
        versity of South Carolina, Columbia.

Gschwend, Maxmillian

1988   *Bauernhauser der Schweiz.* Schweizer Baudokomentation, Blauen, Swit-
        zerland.

Gums, Bonnie, William R. Iseminger, Molly E. McKenzie, and Dennis D. Nichols

1991   The French Colonial Villages of Cahokia and Prairie du Pont, Illinois.
        In *French Colonial Archaeology: The Illinois Country and the Western
        Great Lakes,* edited by John A. Walthall, pp. 85–122. Urbana and Chi-
        cago: University of Illinois Press.

Gundaker, Grey
    2000   Discussion: Creolization, Complexity, and Time. In Creolization, edited
            by Shannon Dawdy. *Historical Archaeology* 34(3): 124–33.
Hagy, James W.
    1993   *This Happy Land: The Jews of Colonial and Antebellum Charleston.*
            Tuscaloosa: University of Alabama Press.
Hann, John H.
    1988   *Apalachee: The Land between the Rivers.* Gainesville: University Presses
            of Florida.
    1989   St. Augustine's Fallout from the Yamasee War. *Florida Historical Quar-
            terly* 68:180–200.
    1990   Summary Guide to Spanish Florida Missions and Visitas with Churches
            in the Sixteenth and Seventeenth Centuries. *The Americas* 46(4): 417–
            513.
    1991   *Missions to the Calusa.* Gainesville: University of Florida Press.
    1996   *A History of the Timucua Indians and Missions.* Gainesville: University
            Press of Florida.
Hann, John, and Bonnie McEwan
    1998   *The Apalachee Indians and Mission San Luis.* Gainesville: University
            Press of Florida.
Hann, Richard L.
    1982   The "Trade Do's Not Flourish as Formerly": The Ecological Origins of
            the Yamasee War of 1715. *Ethnohistory* 28:341–58.
Harrington, M. R.
    1908   Catawba Potters and Their Work. *American Anthropologist* 10:399–
            407.
Hartley, Michael O.
    1987   *Wachovia in Forsyth.* Salem, North Carolina: Old Salem, Inc.
    1993   *The Bethania Town Lot Archaeological Survey.* North Carolina Depart-
            ment of Cultural Resources, Division of Archives and History, Raleigh.
Hartley, Michael O., and Martha Brown Boxley
    1989   *Bethania in Wachovia: A Preservation Plan.* North Carolina Depart-
            ment of Cultural Resources, Division of Archives and History, Raleigh.
    1990   Bethania Historic District Amendment and Boundary Increase. Na-
            tional Register of Historic Places Nomination Form, National Park Ser-
            vice, Washington, D.C. Copy on file at North Carolina Department of
            Cultural Resources, Division of Archives and History, Raleigh.
    1997   *Salem Survey.* Salem, North Carolina: Old Salem, Inc.
Haviland, William A.
    1999   *Anthropology.* New York: Harcourt College Publishers.
Headlam, Cecil (editor)
    1928   *Calendar of State Papers, Colonial Series, America and West Indies, Au-
            gust 1714–December 1715.* His Majesty's Stationery Office, London.
    1930   *Calendar of State Papers, Colonial Series, America and West Indies, Au-
            gust 1717–December 1718.* Her Majesty's Stationery Office, London.

Henry, James

   1859   *Sketches of Moravian Life and Character*. Philadelphia: J. B. Lippincott.

Henry, Susan

   1980   Physical, Spatial, and Temporal Dimensions of Colono Ware in the
          Chesapeake, 1600–1800. Master's thesis, Department of Anthropology,
          Catholic University of America, Washington, D.C.

Herd, E. Don

   1981   *The South Carolina Upcountry, 1540–1980*. Greenwood, South Caro-
          lina: Attic.

Herman, Bernard L.

   1997a The Embedded Landscapes of the Charleston Single House, 1780–1820.
          In *Exploring Everyday Landscapes: Perspectives in Vernacular Architec-
          ture VII*, edited by Annmarie Adams and Sally McMurry, pp. 41–57.
          Knoxville: University of Tennessee Press.

   1997b The Charleston Single House. In *The Buildings of Charleston: A Guide
          to the City's Architecture*, by Jonathan H. Poston, pp. 37–41. Columbia:
          University of South Carolina Press.

   1999   Urban Hinterlands: The Backcountry and the Town. Paper presented at
          the Eighteenth Century Frontiers in North America conference, Win-
          chester, Virginia.

Herskovits, Melville

   1941   *The Myth of the Negro Past*. Boston: Beacon.

Hicks, Theresa, and Wes Taukchiray

   1998   *South Carolina Indians and Indian Traders*. Spartanburg, South Caro-
          lina: Reprint Press.

Hirsch, Arthur H.

   1928   *The Huguenots of Colonial South Carolina*. Durham, North Carolina:
          Duke University Press (reprinted 1999 by the University of South Caro-
          lina Press, Columbia).

Hofstra, Warren R.

   1990   Land, Ethnicity, and Community at the Opequon Settlement, Virginia,
          1730–1800. *Virginia Magazine of History and Biography* 98:423–48.

Hofstra, Warren R., and Robert D. Mitchell

   1993   Town and Country in Backcountry Virginia: Winchester and the
          Shenandoah Valley, 1730–1800. *Journal of Southern History*
          59:619–46.

Holmes, William H.

   1903   *Aboriginal Pottery of the Eastern United States*. Bureau of American
          Ethnology Annual Report for 1898–99. Washington, D.C.

Horn, James

   1994   *Adapting to a New World: English Society in the Seventeenth Century
          Chesapeake*. Chapel Hill: Institute of Early American History and Cul-
          ture, University of North Carolina Press.

Horning, Audrey J.

   1995   "A Verie fit place to Erect a Great Cittie": Comparative Contextual

Analysis of Archaeological Jamestown. Ph.D. dissertation, University of Pennsylvania, University Microfilms, Ann Arbor, Michigan.

Huddleston, Connie M.
1998   Plates and Scalloped Rims: Indications of Temporal Change in Low Country Colonoware Production. Paper presented at the annual meeting of the Southeastern Archaeological Conference, Greenville, South Carolina.

Hudson, Charles M.
1971   *Red, White and Black: Symposium on Indians in the Old South.* Southern Anthropological Society Proceedings 5, University of Georgia Press, Athens.

Hudson, Charles M., Marvin Smith, and Chester DePratter
1984   The Hernando De Soto Expedition: From Apalachee to Chiaha. *Southeastern Archaeology* 3:65–77.

Huffman, John Croft
1997   Preliminary Investigation of New Windsor Township from the Perspective of the Insular-Cosmopolitan Paradigm. Master's thesis, Anthropology Department, University of Idaho, Moscow.

Huger, Daniel
n.d.   The Dan Huger letter. Manuscript Collection, South Carolina Historical Society, Charleston.

Idol, Bruce S., Stephen T. Trage, and Roger W. Kirchen
1996   *Report on Excavation at the Bethabara 1754 Sleeping Hall Site, Forsyth County, North Carolina.* Wake Forest University Laboratories, Winston-Salem, North Carolina.

Ivers, Larry E.
1972   Scouting the Inland Passage, 1685–1737. *South Carolina Historical Magazine* 73:117–29.

Jackson, James Brinckerhof
1984   *Discovering the Vernacular Landscape.* New Haven: Yale University Press.

Johnston, Hugh B. (editor)
1959   The Journal of Ebenezer Hazard in North Carolina, 1777 and 1778. *North Carolina Historical Review* 36(3): 358–81.

Jones, George F.
1967   *Colonial Georgia's Second Language.* Rincon, Georgia: The Georgia Salzburger Society (reprinted from *Georgia Review* 21[1, Spring 1967]).
1968   *Detailed Reports of the Salzburger Emigrants Who Settled in America,* vol. 1 (1733–1734), edited by Samuel Urlsperger. Athens: University of Georgia Press.
1969   The Secret Diary of Pastor Johann Martin Boltzius. *Georgia Historical Quarterly* (Savannah) 53(1): 78–110.
1992   *The Georgia Dutch: From the Rhine and Danube to the Savannah, 1733–1783.* Athens: University of Georgia Press.

1996   *The Germans of Frederica.* National Park Service, Fort Frederica Association, St. Simons Island, Georgia.

Jones, Grant D.

1978   The Ethnohistory of the Guale Coast through 1684. In *The Anthropology of St. Catherine's Island: Natural and Cultural History,* edited by D. H. Thomas, G. D. Jones, R. S. Durham, and C. S. Larsen, pp. 178–210. Anthropological Papers of the American Museum of Natural History, vol. 55(2), New York.

Jones, Lewis P.

1971   *South Carolina: A Synoptic History for Laymen.* Columbia, South Carolina: Sandlapper.

Jones, Steven L.

1985   The African-American Tradition in Vernacular Architecture. In *The Archaeology of Slavery and Plantation Life,* edited by Theresa A. Singleton, pp. 195–213. New York: Academic.

Jordan, Terry G.

1985   *American Log Buildings: An Old World Heritage.* Chapel Hill: University of North Carolina Press.

Jordan, William R., Whitney Smith, Joe Sanders, and Bobby Southerlin

1999   *Archaeological Survey of the Cedar Point Tract, Beaufort County, South Carolina.* Report prepared for Chechessee Land and Timber Company by Brockington and Associates, Inc., Atlanta.

Jordan, Winthrop D.

1974   *The Whiteman's Burden: Historical Origins of Racism in the United States.* New York: Oxford University Press.

Joseph, J. W.

1989   Pattern and Process in the Plantation Archaeology of the Lowcountry of Georgia and South Carolina. *Historical Archaeology* 23(1): 55–68.

1993a *"And They Went Down Both Into The Water": Archaeological Data Recovery of the Riverfront Augusta Site (9Ri165).* New South Associates, Stone Mountain, Georgia.

1993b White Columns and Black Hands: Class and Classification in the Plantation Archaeology of the Lowcountry of Georgia and South Carolina. *Historical Archaeology* 27(3): 57–73.

1997   Unwritten History of the Free African American Village of Springfield, Georgia. *Common Ground: Archaeology and Ethnography in the Public Interest* 2(1): 40–47.

2000   Archaeology and the African-American Experience in the Urban South. In *Archaeology of Southern Urban Landscapes,* edited by Amy L. Young, pp. 109–26. Tuscaloosa and London: University of Alabama Press.

Joseph, J. W., and Judith A. Bense

1995   Many People, One Land: An Overview of Historical Archaeology in the Southeast. Paper presented at the 1995 American Association for the Advancement of Science Conference, Atlanta.

Joseph, J. W., and Rita F. Elliott

1994   *Restoration Archeology at the Charleston County Courthouse, Charleston, South Carolina.* Report submitted to Charleston County by New South Associates, Stone Mountain, Georgia.

Joseph, J. W., and Theresa M. Hamby

1998   *Archaeological Survey of the Charleston Judicial Center Site (38CH1708).* Report submitted to Charleston County Capital Projects by New South Associates, Stone Mountain, Georgia.

Joyner, Charles

1984   *Down by the Riverside.* Urbana: University of Illinois Press.

1999   *Shared Traditions: Southern History and Folk Culture.* Urbana: University of Illinois Press.

Kay, Marvin L., and Lorin L. Cary

1995   *Slavery in North Carolina, 1748–1775.* Chapel Hill: University of North Carolina Press.

Kelso, William

1979   *Captain Jones's Wormslow: An Historical, Archaeological and Architectural Study of an Eighteenth Century Plantation near Savannah, Georgia.* Athens: University of Georgia Press.

1984   *Kingsmill Plantations, 1619–1800: Archaeology of Country Life in Colonial Virginia.* Orlando, Florida: Academic.

Kennedy, Linda, and Christopher T. Espenshade

2001   Recognizing Individual Potters in Nineteenth Century Colonoware. Paper presented at the Thirty-fourth Meeting, the Society for Historical Archaeology, Long Beach, California.

Kennedy, Linda, Marian Roberts, and Christopher T. Espenshade

1994   *Archaeological Data Recovery at Colleton River Plantation (38BU647), Beaufort County, South Carolina: A Study of an Early Nineteenth Century Slave Settlement.* Brockington and Associates, Atlanta.

Klein, Rachel

1990   *Unification of a Slave State: The Rise of the Planter Class in the South Carolina Backcountry, 1760–1808.* Institute for Early American History and Culture, University of North Carolina Press, Chapel Hill.

Klingberg, Frank J.

1956   [Editor] *The Carolina Chronicle of Dr. Francis Le Jau, 1706–1717.* Berkeley: University of California Press.

1960   Early Attempts at Indian Education in South Carolina, A Documentary. *South Carolina Historical Magazine* 41:1–10.

1962   The Mystery of the Lost Yamasee Prince. *South Carolina Historical Magazine* 63:18–32.

Kniffen, Fred, and Henry Glassie

1986   Building in Wood in the Eastern United States: A Time-Place Perspective. In *Common Places: Readings in American Vernacular Architecture,* edited by Dell Upton and John Vlach. Athens: University of Georgia Press.

Kuehne, Dale S.

  1996 *Massachusetts Congregationalist Political Thought 1760–1790.* Colum-
        bia: University of Missouri Press.

Kupperman, Karen Ordahl

  2000 *Indians and English: Facing Off in Early America.* Ithaca, New York:
        Cornell University Press.

Lanning, John T.

  1935 *The Spanish Missions of Georgia.* Chapel Hill: University of North
        Carolina Press.

Lapham, Samuel

  1925 Notes on the Granville Bastion, 1704. *South Carolina Historical and
        Genealogical Magazine* 26:224.

  1970 *Our Walled City: Charlestown, Province of Carolina, 1678–1718, Con-
        struction, Cannons and Conflicts.* Society of Colonial Wars in the State
        of South Carolina, Mt. Pleasant, South Carolina.

Larson, John C.

  2000 Moravian Architecture and Its North Carolina Piedmont Environment.
        Museum of Early Southern Decorative Arts, Summer Institute Lecture,
        Old Salem, Winston-Salem, North Carolina.

Lautzenheiser, Loretta E., Thomas Hargrove, Jane Eastman, Patricia Samford, Jody
Carter, and Mary Holm

  1997 *Archaeological Testing, Neils Eddy Tract, International Paper, Riegel-
        wood Operations, Riegelwood, Columbus County, North Carolina.*
        Coastal Carolina Research, Tarboro, North Carolina.

Lautzenheiser, Loretta E., Mary Holm, Jane Eastman, and D. O'Brien

  1995 *Archaeological Survey, Proposed Treated Wastewater Holding Ponds,
        Federal Paper Board, Riegelwood Operations, Columbus County, North
        Carolina.* Coastal Carolina Research, Tarboro, North Carolina.

Lee, Lawrence

  1965 *Lower Cape Fear in Colonial Days.* Chapel Hill: University of North
        Carolina Press.

Lees, William B.

  1980 *Old and in the Way: Archaeological Investigations at Limerick Planta-
        tion, Berkeley County, South Carolina.* Anthropological Studies 5, Insti-
        tute of Archaeology and Anthropology, University of South Carolina,
        Columbia.

Lefler, Hugh Talmadge (editor)

  1967 *A New Voyage to Carolina,* by John Lawson. Chapel Hill: University of
        North Carolina Press.

Lesesne, J. M.

  1972 The French Huguenots of New Bordeaux. *Transactions of the Huguenot
        Society of South Carolina* 77:1–8.

Lesser, Charles H.

  1995 *South Carolina Begins: The Records of a Proprietary Colony, 1663–
        1721.* South Carolina Department of Archives and History, Columbia.

Lewis, G.
1845   *Impressions of America.* Edinburg, Scotland.
Lewis, Kenneth
1979   *The Guillebeau House: An Eighteenth Century Huguenot Structure in McCormick County.* Research Manuscript Series 143, Institute of Archaeology, University of South Carolina, Columbia.
1984   *The American Frontier: An Archaeological Study of Settlement Pattern and Process.* New York: Academic.
Lewis, Kenneth E., and Helen Haskell
1980   *Middleton Place: Initial Archaeological Investigations at an Ashley River Rice Plantation.* Research Manuscript Series 148, Institute of Archaeology and Anthropology, University of South Carolina, Columbia.
Linder, Suzanne
1996   Willtown: Colonial Village on the Edisto. Ms. on file, The Charleston Museum, Charleston, South Carolina.
Loewald, Klaus G., Beverly Starika, and Paul S. Taylor
1957   Johann Martin Bolzius Answers a Questionnaire on Carolina and Georgia. *William and Mary Quarterly,* 3d ser., 14(2): 1–67.
Loftfield, Thomas C., and Michael Stoner
1997   Brunswick Town Colono Wares Re-examined. *North Carolina Archaeology* 46:6–15.
Long, Bobby M.
1980   *Soil Survey of Berkeley County, South Carolina.* USDA Soil Conservation Service, Washington, D.C.
McCleskey, Turk
1998   Shadow Land: Provisional Real Estate Claims and Anglo-American Settlement in Southwestern Virginia. In *The Southern Colonial Backcountry: Interdisciplinary Perspectives on Frontier Communities,* edited by David Colin Crass, Steven Smith, Martha Zierden, and Richard David Brooks, pp. 56–69. Knoxville: University of Tennessee Press.
McCrady, Edward R.
1897   *The History of South Carolina under the Proprietary Government.* New York: Russell & Russell.
McDaniel, George C.
1982   *Hearth and Home: Preserving a People's Culture.* Philadelphia: Temple University Press.
McDowell, William L. (editor)
1955   *Journals of the Commissioners of the Indian Trade, September 20, 1710–August 29, 1718.* South Carolina Department of Archives and History, Columbia.
McInnis, Maurie, and Angela Mack (editors)
1999   *In Pursuit of Refinement: Charlestonians Abroad, 1740–1860.* Columbia: University of South Carolina Press.
McKivergan, David A., Jr.
1991   Migration and Settlement among the Yamasee of South Carolina. Mas-

ter's thesis, Department of Anthropology, University of South Carolina, Columbia.

Mandelbaum, David G.

1964   Social Groupings. In *Cultural and Social Anthropology: Selected Readings,* edited by Peter B. Hammond, pp. 146–62. New York: Macmillan.

Maness, Harold S.

1986   *Forgotten Outpost: Fort Moore and Savannah Town, 1685–1765.* Privately printed, Beech Island, South Carolina.

Marshall, Frederic William

1769   Document of January 1769. In *Selected Documents Concerning Bethania Land Matters, 1759–1769.* Unpublished translation of documents held by the Moravian Archives, Winston-Salem. Bethania Historical Association, Bethania, North Carolina.

Martin, Joel

1994   Southeastern Indians and the English Trade in Skins and Slaves. In *The Forgotten Centuries,* edited by Charles Hudson and Carmen Tesser, pp. 304–24. Athens: University of Georgia Press.

Mathewson, R. Duncan

1973   Archaeological Analysis of Material Culture as a Reflection of Sub-Cultural Differentiation in Eighteenth Century Jamaica. *Jamaica Journal* 7(1-2): 25–29, 6:54–56.

Mayer, O. B.

1982   *The Dutch Fork.* Reprint. Columbia, South Carolina: Dutch Fork Press.

Memorials

n.d.   Plat for 390-acre tract, in vol. 6, p. 19. South Carolina Department of Archives and History, Columbia.

Menard, Russell

1995   Slave Demography in the Lowcountry, 1670–1740: From Frontier Society to Plantation Regime. *South Carolina Historical Magazine* 96(4): 280–303.

Meriwether, Robert L.

1940   *The Expansion of South Carolina, 1729–1765.* Kingsport, Tennessee: Southern Publishers.

Merrell, James H.

1984   The Indians' New World: The Catawba Experience. *William and Mary Quarterly* 91:538–65.

1989   "Our Bond of Peace": Patterns of Intercultural Exchange in the Carolina Piedmont, 1650–1750. In *Powhatan's Mantle,* edited by Peter Wood, Gregory Waselkov, and Thomas Hatley, pp. 196–222. Lincoln: University of Nebraska Press.

1992   *The Indians' New World: The Catawba and Their Neighbors.* Lincoln: University of Nebraska Press.

Miller, E. N., Jr.

1971   *Soil Survey of Charleston County, South Carolina.* USDA Soil Conservation Service, Washington, D.C.

Miller, George
  1980   Classification and Economic Scaling of Nineteenth Century Ceramics. *Historical Archaeology* 14:1–40.
  1991   A Revised Set of CC Index Values for Classification and Economic Scaling of English Ceramics from 1787 to 1880. *Historical Archaeology* 25(1): 1–26.
Milling, Chapman
  1940   *Red Carolinians.* Chapel Hill: University of North Carolina Press.
Mintz, Sidney
  1974   *Caribbean Transformations.* Baltimore: Johns Hopkins University Press.
Mitchell, Robert D.
  1991   *Appalachian Frontiers: Settlement, Society, and Development in the Pre-industrial Era.* Lexington: University Press of Kentucky.
  1998   The Southern Colonial Backcountry: A Geographical House Divided. In *The Southern Colonial Backcountry: Interdisciplinary Perspectives on Frontier Communities,* edited by David Colin Crass, Steven Smith, Martha Zierden, and Richard David Brooks, pp. 1–36. Knoxville: University of Tennessee Press.
Mobley, Joe A.
  1981   *James City: A Black Community in North Carolina, 1863–1900.* Research Reports No. 1, Division of Archives and History, Raleigh, North Carolina.
Moltmann, Günter (editor)
  1982   Three Hundred Years of German Emigration to North America. In *Germans to America: Three Hundred Years of Immigration 1683–1983,* pp. 8–15. Institute for Foreign Cultural Relations, Stuttgart, Federal Republic of Germany.
Montagu, Ashley
  1964   *Man's Most Dangerous Myth: The Fallacy of Race.* 4th ed. New York: World.
Moragne, William C.
  1854   An Address Delivered at New Bordeaux, November 15, 1854, on the Ninetieth Anniversary of the Arrival of the French Protestants at That Place. Reprinted in 1972 by the McCormick County Historical Society, McCormick, South Carolina.
Moravian Museum of Bethlehem
  1999   Historic Sites. October 21, 1999, http://www.moravianmuseum.org/histori.htm.
Morgan, Phillip D.
  1983   Black Society in the Lowcountry, 1760–1810. In *Slavery and Freedom in the Age of the American Revolution,* edited by Ira Berlin and Ronald Hoffman, pp. 83–142. Urbana and Chicago: University of Illinois Press.
  1988   Work and Culture: The Task System and the World of Lowcountry Blacks, 1700–1880. In *Material Life in America, 1600–1860,* edited by

Robert Blair St. George, pp. 203–32. Boston: Northeastern University Press.

Morrison, Alfred J. (editor)

1911 *Travels in the Confederation (1783–1784): From the German of Johann David Schoepf.* New York: Bergman.

Mouer, L. Daniel, Mary Ellen N. Hodges, Stephen R. Potter, Susan L. Henry Renaud, Ivor Noel Hume, Dennis J. Pogue, Martha W. McCartney, and Thomas E. Davidson

1999 Colonoware Pottery, Chesapeake Pipes, and "Uncritical Assumptions." In *"I, Too, Am America": Archaeological Studies of African-American Life,* edited by Theresa A. Singleton, pp. 82–115. Charlottesville: University Press of Virginia.

Mrozowski, Stephen A., and Mary C. Beaudry

1990 Archaeology and the Landscape of Corporate Ideology. In *Earth Patterns: Essays in Landscape Archaeology,* edited by William M. Kelso and Rachel Most, pp. 189–210. Charlottesville: University Press of Virginia.

Neiman, Fraser

1999 Dimensions of Ethnicity. In *Historical Archaeology, Identity Formation, and the Interpretation of Ethnicity,* edited by Maria Franklin and Garrett Fesler, pp. 139–49. Williamsburg, Virginia: Colonial Williamsburg Research Publications.

Nobles, Gregory H.

1989 Breaking into the Backcountry: New Approaches to the Early American Frontier. *William and Mary Quarterly* 3(46): 641–70.

Noel Hume, Ivor

1962 An Indian Ware of the Colonial Period. *Quarterly Bulletin of the Archaeological Society of Virginia* 17(1).

Oldmixon, John

1969 *The British Empire in America, Containing the History of Discovery, Settlement, Progress and State of the British Colonies on the Continent and Islands of America.* 2 vols. Reprint; originally published in 1741. New York: August M. Kelley.

Olmstead, Fredrick L.

1968 *A Journey in the Seaboard Slave States, with Remarks on Their Economies.* Originally published in 1856. New York: Negro Universities Press.

Orser, Charles E., Jr.

1988 Toward a Theory of Power for Historical Archaeology: Plantations and Space. In *The Recovery of Meaning,* edited by Mark P. Leone and Parker B. Potter, Jr., pp. 313–43. Washington, D.C.: Smithsonian Institution Press.

Orser, Charles E., Annette M. Nekola, and James L. Roark

1982 *Exploring the Rustic Life: Multidisciplinary Research at Millwood Plantation, a Large Piedmont Plantation in Abbeville County, South Caro-*

lina and Elbert County, Geogia. Mid American Research Center, Loyola
University, Chicago.

Otto, John Solomon

1975 Status Differences and the Archaeological Record: A Comparison of
Planter, Overseer and Slave Sites from Cannon's Point Plantation (1794–
1861), St. Simons Island, Georgia. Ph.D. dissertation, Anthropology Department, University of Florida, Gainesville.

Outland, Robert B., III

1996 Slavery, Work, and Geography of the North Carolina Naval Stores Industry, 1835–1860. *Journal of Southern History* 62(1): 27–56.

Palerm, Angel

1952 San Carlos de Chachalacas: Una Fundacion de los Indios de Florida en
Veracruz. *Indices de Cuadernos Americanos* 11:165–84.

Poplin, Eric C.

1989 *True Blue Plantation: Archaeological Data Recovery at a Waccamaw
Neck Rice Plantation*. Brockington and Associates, Atlanta.

Posnansky, Merrick

1999 West Africanist Reflections on African-American Archaeology. In *"I,
Too, Am America": Archaeological Studies of African-American Life*,
edited by Theresa A. Singleton, pp. 21–37. Charlottesville: University
Press of Virginia.

Poston, Jonathan H.

1997 *The Buildings of Charleston: A Guide to the City's Architecture*. Columbia: University of South Carolina Press.

Pury, Jean Pierre

1731 A Description of the Province of South Carolina. October 29, 1999,
http://www.netside.com/~genealogy/purry.htm.

Ravenel, Beatrice St. Juliaen

1964 *Architects of Charleston*. Charleston: Carolina Art Association.

Reese, Trevor R.

1974 *Our First Visit in America: Early Reports from the Colony of Georgia
1732–1740*. Savannah, Georgia: Beehive.

Riemensperger, Hans Jacob

1740 *True and Fully Dependable Good News From the English Royal Province Carolina*. October 29, 1999, http://www.netside.com/~genealogy/
remsb.htm.

Reuter, Philip Christian Gottlieb

1758 "The Great Map of Wachovia." Begun August 1758 and continued
throughout Reuter's life (d. 1777) and beyond. Moravian Archives,
Winston-Salem, North Carolina.

1760 Document dated February 22, 1760. In *Selected Documents Concerning
Bethania Land Matters, 1759–1769*. Unpublished translation of documents held by the Moravian Archives, Winston-Salem. Bethania Historical Association, Bethania, North Carolina.

Richards, Jeffrey H.
  2000   The Literary Archaeology of Dorchester, South Carolina, 1700–1800. Paper presented at the Society for the Study of Southern Literature National Conference, Orlando, Florida.

Robinson, G. C., B. F. Buie, and H. S. Johnson
  1961   *Common Clays of the Coastal Plain of South Carolina and Their Use in Structural Clay Products.* Research Bulletin 25, Division of Geology, South Carolina State Development Board, Columbia.

Robinson, Kenneth W.
  1997   Port Brunswick and the Colonial Naval Stores Industry: Historical and Archaeological Observations. *North Carolina Archaeology* 46:51–68.

Rogers, George C.
  1989   *Charleston in the Age of the Pinckneys.* Columbia: University of South Carolina Press.

Rowland, Lawrence S., Alexander Moore, and George C. Rogers, Jr.
  1996   *The History of Beaufort County, South Carolina.* Vol. 1, *1514–1861.* Columbia: University of South Carolina Press.

Royal Grants
  n.d.   Plat for 239-acre grant to Michael Meyer, in vol. 10, p. 359. South Carolina Department of Archives and History, Columbia.

Russell, Aaron E.
  1997   Material Culture and African American Spirituality at the Hermitage. *Historical Archaeology* 31(2): 63–80.

Rust, Tina M., Elsie I. Eubanks, and Eric C. Poplin
  1995   *Archaeological Testing of Five Sites on the Bull Point Development Tract, Beaufort County, South Carolina.* Report prepared for Metropolitan Properties, Inc., by Brockington and Associates, Inc., Mt. Pleasant, South Carolina.

Rutman, Darrett
  1985   Assessing the Little Communities of Early America. *William and Mary Quarterly* 3(43): 163–78.

Sainsbury, W. Noel
  1928–1947   *Records in the British Public Record Office Relating to South Carolina: 1663–1710.* Atlanta: Foote and Davis.

Salley, Alexander S., Jr. (editor)
  1907a   *Journals of the Commons House of Assembly of South Carolina for the Four Sessions of 1693.* Historical Commission of South Carolina, Columbia.
  1907b   *Journal of the Grand Council of South Carolina, April 11, 1692–September 26, 1692.* Historical Commission of South Carolina, Columbia.
  1911   *Narratives of Early Carolina.* New York: Charles Scribner's Sons.
  1912   Stock Marks Recorded in South Carolina, 1695–1721. *South Carolina Historical and Genealogical Magazine* 13:224–28.
  1916   *Commissions and Instructions from the Lords Proprietors of Carolina*

to the Public Officials of South Carolina, 1685–1715. Historical Commission of South Carolina, Columbia.

1924   *Journals of the Commons House of Assembly of South Carolina for 1700*. Historical Commission of South Carolina, Columbia.

1932   *Journals of the Commons House of Assembly of South Carolina for 1702*. Historical Commission of South Carolina, Columbia.

1934   *Journals of the Commons House of Assembly of South Carolina for 1703*. Historical Commission of South Carolina, Columbia.

1967   *Narratives of Early Carolina, 1650–1708*. Reprint. New York: Barnes and Noble.

1973   *Warrants for Land in South Carolina, 1672–1711*. South Carolina Department of Archives and History, Columbia.

Saunders, Rebecca

2000   *Stability and Change in Guale Indian Pottery, A.D. 1300–1702*. Tuscaloosa: University of Alabama Press.

Savage, Elizabeth J.

1986   *Andre and Francois Andre Michaux*. Charlottesville: University Press of Virginia.

Schuyler, Robert L. (editor)

1980   *Archaeological Perspectives on Ethnicity in America: Afro-American and Asian American Culture History*. Farmingdale, New York: Baywood.

Shields, David S.

n.d.   The Streets of Charleston. Ms. in possession of the author.

Shlasko, Ellen

1997   Carolina Gold: Economic and Social Change on a South Carolina Rice Plantation, 1760–1820. Ph.D. dissertation, Department of Anthropology, Yale University, New Haven.

Sickels-Taves, Lauren B., and Michael S. Sheehan

1999   *The Lost Art of Tabby Redefined: Preserving Oglethorpe's Architectural Legacy*. Southfield, Michigan: Architectural Conservation Press.

Sigmon, D. Ray

1992   Dorchester, St. George's Parish, South Carolina: The Rise and Decline of a Colonial Frontier Village. Master's thesis, Department of History, University of South Carolina, Columbia.

Silver, Timothy

1990   *A New Face on the Countryside: Indians, Colonists, and Slaves in South Atlantic Forests, 1500–1800*. New York: Cambridge University Press.

Simmons, Slann Legare Clement

1962   Records of Willtown Presbyterian Church, 1747–1841. *South Carolina Historical Magazine* 61:150–51.

Simms, William Gilmore

1841   Loves of the Driver. *The Magnolia: or Southern Monthly* (Savannah, Georgia) 3:222–23.

Singleton, Theresa A.

1980   The Archaeology of Afro-American Slavery in Coastal Georgia: A Regional Perception of Slave Household and Community Patterns. Ph.D. dissertation, Department of Anthropology, University of Florida, University Microfilms, Ann Arbor, Michigan.

1985   [Editor] *The Archaeology of Slavery and Plantation Life.* New York: Academic.

1999   An Introduction to African-American Archaeology. In *"I, Too, Am America": Archaeological Studies of African-American Life,* edited by Theresa A. Singleton, pp. 1–17. Charlottesville: University Press of Virginia.

Smith, Henry A. M.

1988   *The Historical Writings of Henry A. M. Smith: Articles from the South Carolina Historical and Genealogical Magazine.* Spartanburg, South Carolina: Reprint Company.

Smith, Marvin T. (compiler)

1986   *Archaeological Testing of Sixteen Sites in the Fort Howard Development Tract.* Garrow and Associates, Atlanta, for Law Environmental, Kennesaw, Georgia.

Smith, Steven D.

1993   Landscapes and Historic Contexts: Research and Management on a Regional Level. In *Historic Landscapes in South Carolina: Historical Archaeological Perspectives of the Land and Its People,* edited by Linda F. Stine, Lesley M. Drucker, Martha Zierden, and Christopher Judge, pp. 17–19. Council of South Carolina Professional Archaeologists, USC, SCIAA, and Savannah River Archaeological Research Program, Columbia.

Smith, William R.

1903   *South Carolina as a Royal Province, 1719–1776.* New York: MacMillan.

Snell, William R.

1973   Indian Slavery in Colonial South Carolina, 1671–1795. Ph.D. dissertation, Department of History, University of Alabama, Tuscaloosa.

Society for the Propagation of the Gospel

n.d.   Letter Books. Reel 6, vol. 18, pp. 69–75. The South Carolina Room, Charleston County Public Library, Charleston, South Carolina.

n.d.   Letter Books. Reel 6, vol. 19, pp. 104–8. The South Carolina Room, Charleston County Public Library, Charleston, South Carolina.

South, Stanley

1959   *Description of the Ceramic Types from Brunswick Town at Brunswick Town State Historic Site.* State Department of Archives and History, Brunswick Town State Historic Site, Brunswick, North Carolina.

1977   *Method and Theory in Historical Archeology.* New York: Academic.

1999   *Historical Archaeology in Wachovia: Excavating Eighteenth-Century Bethabara and Moravian Pottery.* New York: Kluwer Academic/Plenum Publishers.

2000   Archaeological Pathways to Historic Site Development. Ms. in possession of the author.

South, Stanley, Russell K. Skowronek, and Richard E. Johnson
  1988   *Spanish Artifacts from Santa Elena.* Anthropological Studies 7, South
         Carolina Institute of Archaeology and Anthropology, University of
         South Carolina, Columbia.

Southerlin, Bobby
  2000   *Archaeological Testing at the Cedar Point Development Tract, Beaufort
         County, South Carolina.* Report prepared for Chechessee Land and Tim-
         ber Company by Brockington and Associates, Inc., Atlanta.

Southerlin, Bobby, Dawn Reid, Connie Huddleston, Alana Lynch, and Dea Mozingo
  2000   *Return of the Yamasee: Archaeological Data Recovery at Chechesy Old
         Field, Beaufort County, South Carolina.* Draft report prepared for
         Chechessee Land and Timber Company by Brockington and Associates,
         Inc., Raleigh.

Stacy, James
  1987   *History and Published Records of the Midway Congregational Church,
         Liberty County, Georgia; with addenda by Elizabeth Walker Quarter-
         man; and new index by Margaret H. Cannon.* Spartanburg, South Caro-
         lina: Reprint Company.

Starobin, Robert
  1970   *Industrial Slavery in the Old South.* New York: Oxford University Press.

Staski, Edward
  1982   Advances in Urban Archaeology. In *Advances in Archaeological Method
         and Theory,* vol. 5, edited by Michael Schiffer, pp. 97–150. New York:
         Academic.

State of North Carolina
  1886–1890 The Colonial Records of North Carolina, vol. 4, p. 612. P. M.
         Hale, state printer, Raleigh.

Steen, Carl
  1993   Archaeology of the British Colonial Period in South Carolina. *South
         Carolina Antiquities* 25(1-2): 56–62.
  1999   Stirring the Ethnic Stew in the South Carolina Backcountry: John de la
         Howe and Lethe Farm. In *Historical Archaeology, Identity Formation,
         and the Interpretation of Ethnicity,* edited by Maria Franklin and Gar-
         rett Fesler, pp. 93–120. Williamsburg, Virginia: Colonial Williamsburg
         Research Publications.

Steen, Carl, Dan Elliott, Rita Folse-Elliott, and Anthony N. Warren
  1996   *Further Excavations at John de la Howe's Lethe Farm.* Report submit-
         ted to the South Carolina Department of Archives and History, Colum-
         bia, South Carolina, by Diachronic Research Foundation, Columbia,
         South Carolina.

Steen, Carl, Christopher Judge, and Tariq Ghaffar
  1998   *The Search for the Pee Dee Indian Town in Marion County, SC.* South
         Carolina Department of Natural Resources, Columbia.

Stewart, Mart A.

1996 "*What Nature Suffers to Groe*": *Life, Labor and Landscape on the Georgia Coast, 1680–1920*. Athens: University of Georgia Press.

Stewart-Abernathy, Leslie C.

1986 Urban Farmsteads: Household Responsibilities in the City. *Historical Archaeology* 20(2): 5–16.

Stilgoe, John R.

1982 *Common Landscape of America, 1580–1845*. New Haven: Yale University Press.

Stine, Linda, Melanie Cabak, and Mark Groover

1996 Blue Beads as African American Cultural Symbols. *Historical Archaeology* 30(3): 49–75.

Stuck, William M.

1980 *Soil Survey of Beaufort and Jasper Counties, South Carolina*. USDA Soil Conservation Service, Washington, D.C.

Stuckey, Benjamin N.

1982 *Soil Survey of Georgetown County, South Carolina*. USDA Soil Conservation Service, Washington, D.C.

Swanton, John R.

1946 *The Indians of the Southeastern United States*. Bulletin 137, Smithsonian Institution, Bureau of American Ethnology, Washington, D.C.

Taylor, Gwynne S.

1981 *From Frontier to Factory*. North Carolina Department of Cultural Resources, Division of Archives and History, Raleigh.

Terry, George

1981 "The Champagne Country Lies Chiefly on the River": A Social History of an Eighteenth-Century Lowcountry Parish in South Carolina. Ph.D. dissertation, University of South Carolina, Columbia.

Thomas, David H.

1990 The Spanish Missions of La Florida: An Overview. In *Columbian Consequences: Archaeological and Historical Perspectives on the Spanish Borderlands East*, vol. 2, D. H. Thomas, editor, pp. 357–98. Washington, D.C.: Smithsonian Institution Press.

Thornton, John

1991 African Dimensions of the Stono Rebellion. *American Historical Review* 96(4): 1101–13.

Tobler, Johannes

1753 A Description of Carolina. *Alter und verbesserter Schreib-Calender*, October 29, 1999, http://www.netside.com/~genealogy/toblr.htm.

1756 *The South Carolina Almanack*. South Carolina Historical Society, Charleston.

Tresp, Lothar

1963 Pastor Bolzius Reports. *American-German Review* 29(4, April-May): 20–23, National Carl Schurz Association, Philadelphia, Pennsylvania.

Trinkley, Michael

   1995 *Archaeological Data Recovery Excavations at 38CH1107, Kiawah Island, South Carolina.* Research Contribution 178, Chicora Foundation, Columbia, South Carolina.

Trinkley, Michael (editor)

   1990 *Archaeological Excavations at 38BU96: A Portion of Cotton Hope Plantation, Hilton Head Island, Beaufort County, South Carolina.* Research Series 21, Chicora Foundation, Columbia, South Carolina.

   1991 *Further Investigations of Prehistoric and Historic Lifeways on Callawassie and Spring Islands, Beaufort County, South Carolina.* Research Series 23, Chicora Foundation, Columbia, South Carolina.

  1993a *The History and Archaeology of Kiawah Island, Charleston County, South Carolina.* Research Series 30, Chicora Foundation, Columbia, South Carolina.

  1993b *Archaeological and Historical Examinations of Three Eighteenth and Nineteenth Century Rice Plantations on Waccamaw Neck.* Research Series 31, Chicora Foundation, Columbia, South Carolina.

Trinkley, Michael, Debi Hacker, and Natalie Adams

   1995 *Broom Hall Plantation: "A Good One and In a Pleasant Neighborhood."* Research Series 44, Chicora Foundation, Columbia, South Carolina.

Turner, Frederick Jackson

   1894 *The Frontier in American History.* American Historical Association, Annual Report for 1893, pp. 199–227.

Upper Town Brethren

   1768 Documents of April 2 and 11, 1768. In *Selected Documents Concerning Bethania Land Matters, 1759–1769.* Unpublished translation of documents held by the Moravian Archives, Winston-Salem. Bethania Historical Association, Bethania, North Carolina.

Van Ravenswaay, Charles

   1977 *The Arts and Architecture of German Settlement in Missouri.* Columbia: University of Missouri Press.

Varner, John G., and Jeanette J. Varner (translators)

   1988 *The Florida of the Inca.* Austin: University of Texas Press.

Vlach, John Michael

   1975 Sources of the Shotgun House: African and Caribbean Antecedents to Afro-American Architecture. Ph.D. dissertation, Indiana University, Bloomington.

   1978 *The Afro-American Tradition in the Decorative Arts.* Cleveland Museum of Arts, Cleveland, Ohio.

Voigt, Gilbert P.

   1921 The German and German-Swiss Element in South Carolina, 1732–1752. *Bulletin of the University of South Carolina* (Columbia) 113:12–14.

Waddell, Eugene
　1974　*Indians of the South Carolina Lowcountry, 1562–1751.* Spartanburg,
　　South Carolina: Reprint Company.
Wallace, David D.
　1951　*South Carolina: A Short History.* Columbia: University of South Caro-
　　lina Press.
Walker, Iain C.
　1975　The American Stub-Stemmed Clay Tobacco-Pipe: A Survey of Its Ori-
　　gins, Manufacture, and Distribution. In *The Conference on Historic
　　Sites Archaeology Papers 1974,* vol. 9, pp. 97–128. Institute of Archae-
　　ology and Anthropology, Columbia, South Carolina.
Walthall, John A.
　1991　French Colonial Fort Massac: Architecture and Ceramic Patterning. In
　　*French Colonial Archaeology: The Illinois Country and the Western
　　Great Lakes,* edited by John A. Walthall, pp. 42–64. Urbana and Chi-
　　cago: University of Illinois Press.
Wayne, Lucy B., and Martin F. Dickinson
　1990　*Four Mens' Ramble: Archaeology in the Wando Neck.* Gainesville,
　　Florida: Southarc.
Webber, Jennifer Z., and Elizabeth Reitz
　1999　Animal Use on the Eighteenth Century Frontier. In *Willtown: An Ar-
　　chaeological and Historical Perspective,* by Martha Zierden, Suzanne
　　Linder, and Ronald Anthony, pp. 283–98. South Carolina Department
　　of Archives and History, Columbia.
Weinand, Daniel C., and Elizabeth J. Reitz
　1996　Further Studies of Vertebrate Fauna from the Nathaniel Russell House,
　　Charleston, South Carolina. In *Big House/Back Lot: An Archaeological
　　Study of the Nathaniel Russell House,* pp. 232–89. Archaeological
　　Contributions 25, The Charleston Museum, Charleston, South
　　Carolina.
Weir, Robert M.
　1983　*Colonial South Carolina: A History.* Millwood, New York: KTO Press.
Westmacott, Richard
　1992　*African-American Gardens and Yards in the Rural South.* Knoxville:
　　University of Tennessee Press.
Wheaton, Thomas R.
　1999　Culture Change and Continuity at Curriboo and Yaughan Plantations.
　　Paper presented at the World Archaeological Conference IV, Cape
　　Town, South Africa.
　2000　Colonial African American Villages. Paper presented at the annual meet-
　　ing of the Society for Historical Archaeology, Quebec City, Canada.
Wheaton, Thomas R., Amy Friedlander, and Patrick Garrow
　1983　*Yaughan and Curriboo Plantations: Studies in Afro-American Archae-
　　ology.* Soil Systems, Marietta, Georgia.

Wheaton, Thomas R., and Patrick H. Garrow

   1985   Acculturation and the Archaeological Record in the Carolina Low-country. In *The Archaeology of Slavery and Plantation Life,* edited by Theresa A. Singleton, pp. 239–59. New York: Academic.

Wheaton, Thomas R., Mary Beth Reed, Rita Folse Elliott, Marc Frank, and Leslie Raymer

   1990   *James City: A Nineteenth-Century, African-American Urban Village.* Report on file at New South Associates, Inc., Stone Mountain, Georgia.

White, M.

   1852   Letter from M. White to M. White, Jr., March 17, 1852. White Papers, Southern Historical Collection, University of North Carolina, Chapel Hill.

Wilder, Effie L.

   n.d.   Henry Woodward: Forgotten Man of American History. Ms. on file at the South Carolina Department of Archives and History, Columbia.

Williams, Mark

   1990   *Archaeological Excavations at Shinholser.* Watkinsville, Georgia: LAMAR Institute.

Wood, Joseph S.

   1988   Village and Community in Early Colonial New England. In *Material Life in America, 1600–1860,* edited by Robert Blair St. George, pp. 159–67. Boston: Northeastern University Press.

Wood, Peter H.

   1974   *Black Majority: Negroes in Colonial South Carolina from 1670 through the Stono Rebellion.* New York: W. W. Norton.

Woolverton, John F.

   1984   *Colonial Anglicanism in North America.* Detroit: Wayne State University Press.

Worth, John E.

   1995   *The Struggle for the Georgia Coast: An Eighteenth-Century Spanish Retrospective on Guale and Mocama.* Anthropological Papers of the American Museum of Natural History No. 75, University of Georgia Press, Athens.

   1998   *The Timucuan Chiefdoms of Spanish Florida.* Vol. 2, *Resistance and Destruction.* Gainesville: University of Florida Press.

Zierden, Martha A.

   1993   The Urban Landscape, the Work Yard, and Archaeological Site Formation Processes in Charleston, South Carolina. In *Historical Archaeology and the Study of American Culture,* edited by Lu Ann De Cunzo and Bernard L. Herman, pp. 285–318. The Henry Francis du Pont Winterthur Museum, Winterthur, Delaware.

   1997a The Urban Landscape in South Carolina. In *Carolina's Historical Landscapes: Archaeological Perspectives,* edited by Linda F. Stine, Martha Zierden, Lesley M. Drucker, and Christopher Judge, pp. 161–74. Knoxville: University of Tennessee Press.

1997b   *Archaeology at the Powder Magazine: A Charleston Site through Three Centuries.* Archaeological Contributions 26, The Charleston Museum, Charleston, South Carolina.

1999   A Trans-Atlantic Merchant's House in Charleston: Archaeological Exploration of Refinement and Subsistence in an Urban Setting. *Historical Archaeology* 33(3): 73–87.

Zierden, Martha, and Jeanne Calhoun

1983   *An Archaeological Investigation of the Greenfield Borrow Pit, Georgetown County.* Archaeological Contributions 4, The Charleston Museum, Charleston, South Carolina.

1986   Urban Adaptation in Charleston, South Carolina, 1730–1820. *Historical Archaeology* 20(1): 29–43.

Zierden, Martha A., L. M. Drucker, and J. Calhoun

1986   *Home Upriver: Rural Life on Daniel's Island, Berkeley County, South Carolina.* Carolina Archaeological Services/Charleston Museum, Charleston.

Zierden, Martha, and Bernard L. Herman

1996   Charleston Townhouses: Archaeology, Architecture, and the Urban Landscape, 1750–1850. In *Landscape Archaeology: Reading and Interpreting the American Historical Landscape,* edited by Rebecca Yamin and Karen Besherer Metheny, pp. 193–227. Knoxville: University of Tennessee Press.

Zierden, Martha, Suzanne Linder, and Ronald Anthony

1999   *Willtown: An Archaeological and Historical Perspective.* The Charleston Museum Archaeological Contributions 27, South Carolina Department of Archives and History, Columbia.

Zierden, Martha, and Linda Stine

1997   Introduction: Historical Landscapes through the Prism of Archaeology. In *Carolina's Historical Landscapes: Archaeological Perspectives,* edited by Linda F. Stine, Martha Zierden, Lesley M. Drucker, and Christopher Judge, pp. xi–xvi. Knoxville: University of Tennessee Press.

Contributors

Natalie Adams received her master's degree in the Public Service Archaeology program at the University of South Carolina. She has been extremely active in the plantation archaeology of the Carolinas, having worked on a number of excavations at plantation sites, primarily in the South Carolina Lowcountry. Ms. Adams serves as the branch manager of the New South Associates office in Columbia, South Carolina.

Ronald W. Anthony received his master's degree in anthropology through the University of South Carolina in 1989. Originally trained in southeastern prehistoric archaeology, his research interests since the late 1970s have focused on plantation archaeology, particularly that of slave communities. He has been a staff archaeologist at The Charleston Museum since 1989 and an adjunct professor at the College of Charleston since 1990, previous to which he worked for twelve years in cultural resource management archaeology.

Monica L. Beck received her master's degree in anthropology with a graduate certificate in museum management from the University of South Carolina. She is the director of research and interpretation for the Sea Island Historical Society, where she focuses on excavation and interpreting the colonial and antebellum sea island cotton plantations near Charleston, South Carolina. Her research interests include landscape and spatial studies and African American culture.

David Colin Crass is the State Archaeologist for Georgia. He received his doctorate in anthropology from Southern Methodist University. He has contributed articles to *Historical Archaeology* and other journals and is the co-editor of *The Southern Colonial Backcountry: Interdisciplinary Perspectives on Frontier Communities* (with Martha Zierden, Steven D. Smith, and Richard D. Brooks, University of Tennessee Press, 1998).

Chester B. DePratter received his master's and doctoral degrees in anthropology from the University of Georgia and is a research professor at the South Carolina Institute of Archaeology and Anthropology and the Institute for Southern Studies, University of South Carolina. He has conducted extensive ethnohistorical and archaeological research on the contact period in the southeastern United States. He is co-director of the Santa Elena Project.

Daniel T. Elliott is a native Georgian, who graduated in 1980 with a master's degree in anthropology from the University of Georgia and has been employed as a professional archaeologist by federal and state agencies, private universities, and numerous cultural resource management companies. His twenty-three years of experience in archaeological fieldwork, primarily in the southeastern United States, and reports on the same, give him a unique perspective on multiethnic enclaves that dotted the southern landscape in historical times. His colonial-era research began in 1983 with the recognition of the Huguenot settlers in the "French Santee" and has culminated with his (and Rita Elliott's) dedicated study of Ebenezer on the Savannah River.

Rita Folse Elliott received her master's degree in maritime history and underwater research from East Carolina University in 1988. She has conducted archaeological research and public archaeological programming in the public and private sector for the past sixteen years. Ms. Elliott is education coordinator for the nonprofit LAMAR Institute, immediate past president of The Society for Georgia Archaeology, and Georgia education coordinator for the Society for American Archaeology.

Tammy Forehand is a research archaeologist and curator at the South Carolina Institute of Archaeology and Anthropology. She received her bachelor's degree in anthropology from Georgia Southern University. She is the author and co-author of numerous articles and monographs on the southern colonial backcountry.

William Green has a master's degree from the University of South Carolina and is currently a doctoral candidate (ABD) at the State University of New York at Albany. He has over thirteen years' experience in the archaeology and ethnohistory of the eastern United States, with specialties in protohistoric and early historic Native American archaeology, cultural resource management, and Geographic Information Systems (GIS). Mr. Green is currently employed as a program manager for TRC-Garrow in Columbia, South Carolina.

Michael O. Hartley is the director of archaeology at Old Salem, Inc., in Winston-Salem, North Carolina. He has long experience in colonial and postcolonial historic archaeology of the Carolinas, ranging from earliest European contact to the present. He has worked extensively with the archaeology and history of the Moravian communities in the Winston-Salem area.

J. W. (Joe) Joseph received his master's degree in American civilization and a doctorate in historical archaeology from the University of Pennsylvania. He has worked on colonial and antebellum historic sites throughout the southeastern United States as well as the Caribbean, including work on a number of urban sites in cities such as Mobile, Savannah, Augusta, and Charleston, and he has published the results of his research in *Historical Archaeology, South Carolina Antiquities, Early Georgia,* and several edited volumes. He is currently the president of New South Associates.

Julia A. King received her master's degree from Florida State University and her doctorate from the University of Pennsylvania. Most of her work has been done in the Chesapeake Tidewater region, although she has also done work in South Carolina and in Florida. Currently she serves as director of the Maryland Historical Trust's Maryland Archaeological Conservation Laboratory and as an adjunct associate professor of anthropology at St. Mary's College of Maryland.

Bruce Penner received his master's degree in applied anthropology from the University of Maryland and is a historical archaeologist at URS/BRW, Inc. He is the author and co-author of numerous articles on the southern colonial backcountry in various regional, national, and international journals, including *Historical Archaeology* and the *International Journal of Historical Archaeology.*

Katherine Saunders received her bachelor's degree in historic preservation from Mary Washington College in Virginia. She worked as an archaeologist at Thomas Jefferson's Poplar Forest in Bedford, Virginia, before settling in Charleston, South Carolina, in 1992. In Charleston, she has been extremely active in the research and documentation of the appearance of the city's colonial fortifications. Ms. Saunders is currently the manager of preservation initiatives for Historic Charleston Foundation.

Ellen Shlasko is an assistant professor of anthropology at the University of Memphis. She earned a master's degree from the College of William and Mary in Virginia and a doctorate from Yale University, both in anthropology. Her dissertation, entitled "Carolina Gold: Economic and Social Change on a South Carolina Rice Plantation," focused on agriculture, economics, and ethnicity in the South Carolina Lowcountry. She is particularly interested in the formation of ethnic and cultural identity, examining the role that competition plays in this process.

Bobby Southerlin (MA, University of Georgia) has almost twenty years of experience in southeastern archaeology, gained through both cultural resource management projects conducted by various private companies and research projects initiated by the University of Georgia and the University of South Carolina. Mr. Southerlin's skills include analyses of prehistoric technologies and subsistence patterns, with specialities in faunal analyses and ceramic and lithic replication. Mr. Southerlin currently serves as vice president of Brockington and Associates, Inc., and as program manager of the Raleigh office.

Carl Steen was born in Charleston, South Carolina, and grew up in the Lowcountry. He received a master's degree from the College of William and Mary in historical archaeology/anthropology in 1989. Mr. Steen worked for Colonial Williamsburg and the University of South Carolina and several cultural resource management firms before forming the nonprofit Diachronic Research Foundation in 1992.

Thomas R. Wheaton received his master's degree in anthropology from the University of the Americas in Mexico City. He is one of the pioneers in African American archaeology in the southeast, having directed the landmark excavations at Yaughan and Curriboo plantations as well as excavations at numerous other African American sites. He is a past editor of *African American Archaeology* and has published numerous articles on the topic. He is currently the vice president of New South Associates as well as the executive director of the American Cultural Resources Association (ACRA), a national trade association of CRM firms.

Martha Zierden is curator of historical archaeology at The Charleston Museum. She received her master's degree in anthropology from Florida State University. Her research focuses on the social fabric of urban life and the relations between urban, plantation, and frontier residents of the eighteenth- to nineteenth-century Carolina Lowcountry. She is co-editor of *The Southern Colonial Backcountry: Interdisciplinary Perspectives on Frontier Communities* (with David Colin Crass, Steven D. Smith, and Richard D. Brooks, University of Tennessee Press, 1998) and editor of "Charleston in the Context of Trans-Atlantic Culture" (*Historical Archaeology* 33[3], 1999).

Index

Abercorn, 82

Acculturation, 2, 6; among Africans, 40–41, 46, 140–41; among Germans, 86–90; among French, 153–59

acorn (*Quercus* sp.), 19

Africanism, xiv, 33, 37, 134

Africans, African Americans, xiii, xvi, xvii, 1; and rice agriculture, 3; and colonoware, 34, 39, 217–19; and cultural change, 30; and naval stores industry, 65–78; and power on the plantation, 37, 140; and the Stono Rebellion, 185–86; archaeology, 47; architecture, 37, 222–23; as a unifying southern culture, 2; as immigrants, 37; cultural interactions with the French, xv, 142–44; cultural interactions with Native Americans, 9, 58, 63, 182, 185, 194, 220–22; demographics, 34, 71, 139, 146–47, 185, 218–20; ethnic identities, 10–11; foodways, 40–41; landscapes, 30–33, 41–43, 226–28. *See also* Bakongo

Albemarle Point, 199

Alpine-Alemannic architecture, 89

Alpine Region of Switzerland, 147

Alsace, 79

Altamaha: archaeological site (38BU1206), 13; cacique, 21, 27; ceramic series, 56; chiefdom,

17; Yemasee town, 14–16, 18, 19, 21, 27–28

Amelia, South Carolina, 1, 5, 82

Amelia Island, Georgia, 20–22

Anacape (mission), 16

Anglican: Anglicans and Anglican religion, 161–80; churches, xvi, 171–72, 177; communities, 161; free school, 176; minister, 151, 162, 163; political party, 163

Apalachee: Native American group, 18; province, 23, 194

Appalachicola town, 147

Appenzell-Ausserhoden, Switzerland, 108

Archdale, Governor, 21

Artifact Pattern, Carolina, xiv

Asao, 17, 18

Ashepoo River, 18, 21–23

Ashley, ceramic series, 56

Ashley River, 166, 172, 176, 199

Aspalaga, 18

Augusta, Georgia, 83, 84, 96, 109

Aust, Gottfried, 89

Austria, 79

Avirett, James, 67, 73

Bakongo: people, religion of, 193, 195; cosmogram, 48, 193. *See also* colonoware

Barbados, 139

Barnwell, John, 14